ASK MOM!

ASPEN WEST

From the Publishers of

"WHERE'S DAD NOW THAT I NEED HIM?"
SURVIVING AWAY FROM HOME

11th printing

Aspen West Publishing Co., Inc.
8535 South 700 West Unit C
Sandy, Utah 84070
801-565-1370
www.aspenwest.com

Library of Congress TX145F721992
Vinyl three-ring binder ISBN: 1-885348-14-2
Paperback ISBN: 1-885348-16-9

Editor: Kristi Glissmeyer
Contributing Editor: Cheryl Acton
Cover Design: Ann Wolfer
Inside Layout Design: Shellie Lott
National Marketing Director: Sheri Nielson

For information on volume orders, contact our office or email us at info@aspenwest.com.

*Someone once said, "A father is a man who picks you up
and holds you tight when you're little and afraid."
We dedicate this book to all Dads . . . because no matter how old we are,
we still feel little and afraid sometimes.*

———

Thanks Dad, for teaching me to work,
to be honest and not to swear in front of Mom.

Love, Kent

Introduction

Where's Dad? Ask Mom!

It's not that a father can't whiten whites or cook a meal on the stove, it's just that most Dads for decades have been the ones to change a flat tire or fire up the grill instead. That's why we first published *Where's Dad Now That I Need Him? Surviving Away From Home* in 1987 as a companion guide to the best-selling *Where's Mom Now That I Need Her? Surviving Away From Home.* We realized that not all the necessary tips on how to survive away from home come from Mom. Dad, too, has some tricks up his sleeve.

In general, Moms are great generalists and Dads are super specialists. Moms do just about anything well in a pinch, while Dads know how to do a few specific things almost to inspection ready.

So, now you live away from Mom and Dad. You may be on your own, but you're not alone. Whether you realize it or not, your parents likely taught you the essentials of daily living and the basics of surviving away from home, even if simply by example. Just in case you weren't taking notes or didn't catch the finer points, *Where's Dad Now That I Need Him?* offers important father-specific tips and advice. While times have changed, expectations of what a man should know and what a father should teach his sons and daughters have pretty much remained the same as decades gone by, such as how to:

- Rent your first apartment and furnish it,
- Buy your first car and barter like a pro,
- Deal with contracts, guarantees and warranties,
- Grill a steak, make a meal and carve a turkey,
- Prepare a resume, find a job and work smart,
- Budget and save your money wisely,
- Fix a leaky faucet, plugged toilet or squeaky door,
- Keep a house clean and make a comfortable home,
- Do almost anything like set a table, wrap a gift,
  fillet a fish, hold a baby, shine your shoes and tie a tie.

You will find places in *Where's Dad?* that say: "Ask Mom!" These boxes will give you a reference page in *Where's Mom Now That I Need Her?* to provide you with even more information. The books work together to help you navigate life away from home. Enjoy!

Kent P. Frandsen, author

Contents

Bustin' Loose
Renting Your First Apartment

The time has come to break out on your own, cut the apron strings, fly the coop, bust loose and make your own way in the world.

Most likely your parents made it look easy. By the time you came along, they had figured a lot of things out. Once you understand a few important details, you'll be a responsible, independent adult before you know it. Okay, responsibility doesn't sound like fun, but adulthood isn't something to be dreaded either. *Just remember to look before you leap, think before you sign and gather all of the facts before making important decisions.*

Your signature on paper has value. When you sign your name to any contract it means you've evaluated all of the information you need to make a wise decision and you've committed yourself to making things work on your end. Your first legally binding contract as an independent adult will likely be a rental agreement or lease for a place to live.

Of course, some of you may have already purchased a vehicle and signed on the bottom line, with help from Dad or Mom. But a roof over your head is more important than wheels, so follow these worthwhile tips on finding your own apartment, home, room or dormitory—preferably a place where you can invite Mom and Dad for a visit someday.

Finding Your Own Space

There are many reasons for moving out of your parents' house. You may have just graduated from high school or college and want to experience more independence. Some people move away to get married or to take a job in another city. Others move away to live independently in a different state, country or culture. Or Dad just said, "Get off my couch and get a job—you're on your own!"

Renting a room, apartment or home is not cheap. Put some serious thought and preparation into it. Don't waste money on rental companies that charge a fee ($50 to $100) for a list of apartments or homes available for rent. You can do better yourself with a little effort and legwork. Follow these simple suggestions to find a great place to live, saving at least $50 in the process. And don't pay an application fee, which is usually only a ploy to make money. You do not want to be a tenant to a landlord or rental agency that would charge an application fee anyway.

Step 1: Decide what you need first, then what you want. Start the process at least a month, if not three months, before you plan to move. Decide what type of housing you'll need, what you can afford, if you want a roommate or roommates and how long you want to live there. Any real estate broker will tell you that the three most important factors in choosing a place to live are location, location, and location. Do you need a place within walking distance of work or school? How far are you willing to commute? Do you want to live in a complex packed with amenities like a dishwasher, central air, laundry, covered parking, swimming pool, exercise room and social activities? Or would you prefer to live alone in a quiet basement of an older home? Maybe you need a place that allows pets or smoking. If you share the apartment with others, is it important to you to have a private room? Sharing a room may radically reduce your living expenses.

Step 2: Decide what you can afford. Monthly housing costs should not exceed 30 percent of your total monthly income. Housing costs include rent, electricity, heat, telephone, water, and garbage pickup. If you rent an apartment or a house, most landlords take care of water and garbage bills – in some cities they are required by law to do so. But you (and your roommates, if you have them) will be responsible for electricity, heat and telephone.

If you work full-time making $8 an hour and bring home $1,280 per month before taxes, you should spend only $384 a month on rent and utilities combined. (Your income before the government deducts taxes is called your *gross* income. The money you actually get when you cash your check is called your *net* income.) Your best bet here is to find a working friend to share a 1- or 2-bedroom apartment. Or gather some buddies to share a larger apartment or home. Rent will be cheaper if you share a room, but make sure any place you choose is big enough to fit all the adults you cram into it.

Dad says: *Always protect your good name. You are building a credit history, which will be very important throughout life. If utilities are in your name, make sure bills are paid on time. Utility companies won't care about arrangements you've made with roommates—they will hold you responsible. Being responsible will pay off for you in the not-too-distant future.*

Student Housing Costs

If you attend college and plan to live in a pre-paid dormitory or residence hall, know what type of housing bargain you are getting before you pay. If you are a full-time student who doesn't work and someone else is footing the bill for your housing (like Dad, Mom, a student loan or a scholarship) these financial tips still apply. A dormitory or on-campus apartment should be a good deal, but run the numbers. On-campus living may not be your ideal independent living situation, but it will often get you through school without plunging you or your parents into major debt.

*D*ad says:
Ask the telephone company to <u>*block long distance access on your line*</u> *and use pre-paid calling cards instead. People out of local range will be able to call you without a problem, but you and your roommates will have more control over your phone bill. Many people who are away from home run up outrageous long distance bills. Don't risk losing local phone service, running up a major debt or squabbling with roommates over who placed what calls.*

Step 3: Know the real cost of utilities. You might want to look for an apartment that includes electricity, heat and cable television in the rent. However, these types of apartments are scarce. You will likely have to open accounts in your name (or a roommate's name) with the electric company for lights and central air, the fuel company for heat and gas appliances, a phone company and cable or broadband provider for television and Internet access. Ask the landlord for copies of electric and fuel bills, or at least an estimate, for high-use months. If the landlord is not sure, utility companies will often verify high, low, and average monthly usage at a specific address. You need to know what it costs to heat the place in the winter and cool it in summer. Include these costs in your estimated total rental expenses.

Electric heat costs more, so choose natural gas. If you live in a hot climate, make sure the house has central air conditioning. If your new home, apartment or room does not have central air, you'll need ceiling fans, table, upright, or window fans or an evaporative cooler. Remember that all of these options use electricity and they won't keep you as cool as air conditioning.

Beware of high telephone, cable and Internet rates. Remember, these are optional housing expenses. You may want to budget for them separately. Decide if you really need them and can afford them. Many people decide to use a cell phone exclusively and do not have a landline at home. If you do choose to have a residential telephone, consider getting only basic telephone service without long distance, especially if you have roommates. Long distance bills are unpredictable and difficult to budget for. Use a pre-paid calling card or a cell phone with free long distance to place long distance calls.

In this information age, you may consider an Internet connection a necessity, especially if your classes require computer research and email access. Look into plans that include telephone, cable and Internet in one package, but keep in mind that most college campuses have computer labs you can use (in fact, the fee is usually included in your tuition). If your university, college or city offers Internet service for free, use it. For email, many websites offer free accounts you can access from any computer. Look into all of your options before purchasing a computer and signing up for an Internet service. Frequenting the campus computer lab to do your homework may also cut down on the time you waste playing computer games, chatting online and pursuing other distractions.

Step 4: Save enough money. You will need a lot of cash to get started—enough to cover a deposit plus first and last months' rent. Depending on the quality of the apartment, you may have to fork over $1,000 or more before you put your suitcase on the bed. If you think you can move in just by giving the landlord a $50 holding fee, you likely won't see that $50 or the apartment again. In most cities, affordable housing is tight. The landlord can demand more because of low vacancy rates.

When demand for good housing exceeds supply, it's a landlord's market. As such, landlords usually ask for first and last months' rent and a deposit before you move in. For example, if you find a one-bedroom apartment for $350 rent, you will need at least $1,050 to move in. (This is rent only. It does not include utility deposits.) Some landlords will negotiate, so ask before you give up that perfect dwelling. (They will sometimes allow you to pay more month by month to pay for the deposit until the total is paid in full.) Otherwise, be ready with cash, money order, cashier's check or credit card in hand if you want to sign a rental agreement on the spot.

It's best to shop around. Start looking early. If you put money down and decide on a move-in date with a landlord, get a receipt signed by the landlord. Also get a copy of the rental agreement and, of course, a key once you have paid money and signed the paperwork. You cannot trust every property manager you meet. Cover your assets and always get a receipt.

Dad says:
If you don't have a savings account, start one now. The longer you have an account in good standing, the better your credit.

Ask Mom

To learn more about how to save money on utility expenses, see *Where's Mom Now That I Need Her?*, pages 62-64 "Cutting Costs."

The deposit usually equals one month's rent and should cover any damage done to the apartment while you're living there, beyond reasonable wear and tear. Most, if not all, of the deposit will be refunded to you at the end of your lease as long as you have abided by all of the requirements stated in the rental agreement. Make sure the rental contract states the deposit amount and how it will be returned to you before you sign.

Step 5: Get information about vacancies that meet your needs. Check out bulletin boards at your school or work, even bulletin boards at grocery stores in the neighborhoods you're interested in. Visit the college campus student union building, dormitories, residence halls and sorority or fraternity houses. Check the college and city newspapers for "roommate-wanted" and "for-rent" ads. Get an apartment advertisement book free in stands at supermarkets. Look in the yellow pages for apartment complexes. Search the Internet for rentals in your area. Drive around or walk through neighborhoods where you would like to live and write down the phone numbers on "for-rent" signs.

When you have a list of a few possibilities, start calling landlords. Politely ask if the apartment or home is still available. Make sure you have a notepad and pen available because you will want to ask some important questions and record the information for comparison purposes.

Meeting a landlord is like interviewing for a job.

Questions to Ask a Landlord

- When is the space available for move-in?
- What information will you need with you to complete a tenant application?
- Does the manager or landlord fill roommate vacancies in the apartment or will you be responsible to find roommates?
- How much money do you need to put down to hold the apartment until you move in?
- Does the landlord want a check, money order, credit card or cash?
- How long will it take the landlord to make a decision?
- When can you meet to check out the place? (Get the exact address and directions. Make an appointment and don't be late.)

You want to leave the landlord or apartment manager with the impression that you are a trustworthy, responsible individual who can and will pay rent on time and who won't trash the place. As with any relationship, social, professional or contractual, first impressions count! Impressing a landlord or apartment manager, of course, is just one step in the process of getting a new place to live. The room, dormitory, apartment or house must meet your expectations as well.

Making a Rental Application

Identification: In-state driver's license and an original social security card. If you have only an out-of-state driver's license, bring instead: a photo student identification card, a photo work identification card or a photo state identification card. (You can obtain one at the motor vehicle department for a small fee, but you'll need a copy of your birth certificate to get the state ID.)

References: The names, addresses and phone numbers of four people not related to you who live in the city or state where you plan to reside. These can be employers, coworkers, school advisers, clergy, church members or friends. Never burn your bridges with good prospective references if you can avoid it, especially previous employers and landlords. You never know when you'll need a good word from them. You will also need to provide the names, addresses and phone numbers of four of your nearest relatives. Call all of your references before hand to ask if you can list them as references. You'll want to be sure they can and will say something positive about you.

Previous Addresses: The landlord will need to know something about your rental history—where you lived and for how long. If you have had negative experiences with landlords in the past, you may choose to give your parents' names and address instead. Or you can explain to your prospective landlord the

Dad's says:
Sometimes it's best to take small steps toward independent living, moving from smaller to larger digs in increments.
For example, if you are a student, start with a room in an on-campus dormitory, then move to an apartment shared with other students. After graduation, you might be ready to rent an apartment or house with one or two dependable friends.
After some time on a job, consider saving money for a down payment to buy a home of your own.

7

Checklist

Apartment Move-in

Make sure these items are in good working order before signing a rental agreement. If they are not, indicate on the rental agreement that they need to be repaired/installed before you move in.

☐ Smoke detector
☐ Carbon monoxide detector
☐ All sinks draining smoothly
☐ Garbage disposal
☐ Dishwasher
☐ All stove burners
☐ Oven and broiler
☐ Fan and light above stove
☐ Refrigerator light
☐ Freezer and defroster
☐ Air conditioner
☐ Furnace
☐ Water heater
☐ Water pressure in all taps
☐ All lights fixtures
☐ Toilets flush and do not run
☐ Drapes/blinds/carpets in good condition
☐ Sliding closet doors

Have these in place:

☐ Stoppers for all drains
☐ Shower curtain
☐ Window locks
☐ Screens
☐ Deadbolt on all exterior doors
☐ Locks on bedroom and bathroom doors

nature of the disagreement with the previous landlord before you offer this reference information.

Employment Information: The landlord will want reassurance that you have employment income or some other means of paying your monthly rent. He or she may need a brief work history including company names, addresses, phone numbers, supervisors' names and duration of employment, including starting and ending dates. If your work history or financial credit is poor or non-existent, tell your prospective landlord up front. Explain the circumstances then and how things have changed for the better for you now.

Check for Home Safety

Step 1: Insist upon safety features. Before you sign a rental agreement for any property, check that the apartment, dormitory or home has a working smoke detector, carbon-monoxide detector, fire extinguisher, outdoor lighting, deadbolt locks on front and back doors and window locks and screens. If any of these are missing, ask the landlord to provide them or get permission to buy them out of your own pocket and be reimbursed. Keep receipts to give the landlord for reimbursement or deduction from your rent, but be sure to save a copy for your own files. It is always easier and better simply to ask the landlord to provide these before you move in.

Step 2: Look for structural damage. If there are cracks in walls or ceilings, misaligned doors, water marks or paint bulges in ceilings, holes in floors, sloping floors, or mold on walls or under floor boards, carpet or linoleum, or you can smell mold or pet odors – *don't rent the apartment*. It will take more effort and money than the landlord has to make the place livable.

Step 3: Get a "check-in" list. Make notes concerning anything damaged or in disrepair in the dwelling *before you move in*. Then you won't be paying for something someone else did. If your landlord holds onto all or part of your deposit when you move out, get a list of damages and costs claimed against you. If they allow pets, most landlords require a pet deposit. You likely won't get this back because the landlord will use the money to clean the apartment or house thoroughly of pet odors after you leave. (Regarding pets, it can be extremely difficult to find a decent rental that allows them. If at all possible, wait until you own a residence before acquiring a pet.)

Step 4: Read before you sign. The contract you sign as a tenant (the person renting the home, apartment or room) is a legal agreement with the landlord. You agree that certain rules will be followed in order for you to live there. The landlord agrees to provide services, such as maintenance, landscaping and repairs. Make sure the landlord's duties are spelled out as clearly as the tenant's. You will likely be asked to sign a lease that lasts six months to a year. This protects you so that the landlord does not raise rent during that time or rent the apartment to someone else while you are still living there. The agreement also guarantees that you will pay timely rent and won't take off without notice or payment.

Pack & Move Right

Step 1: Get moving boxes that one person can handle. After all, though friends and family may volunteer, on moving day you might be completely on your own. Good moving boxes include heavy cardboard file boxes with lids and carry holes on each side, or boxes with flaps that can be taped closed. (You can cut out carry holes with a utility knife if none exist.) Invest a few bucks in some sturdy moving boxes available at home building supply stores and moving van rental places. These can save you from breaking something valuable—especially your back.

Step 2: Pack in enough time to have a yard sale. Sort through your rooms and pack two or three boxes

*D*ad's says:
Never sneak a dog or cat or ferret or snake into a "no-pets" apartment—if you do, it always turns out very badly for you and your pet. Even if you only want a bird or a fish, ask the landlord first.

Ask Mom

For more home safety tips, see Dad's companion guide *Where's Mom Now That I Need Her?*, page 303.

a day—at that rate you'll be finished in a few weeks. Go through everything, separating items into three piles: things you'll *need* to take, things to *throw away* and things to *give away,* donate or sell. You'll be surprised how much you'll be able to toss out.

Step 3: Separate the items you *need* into three piles.

• *Important items you'll need at a moment's notice.*

Campus Housing

If you attend college or a trade school and your parents pay for your housing, you will likely live in a dormitory where you share a room with another student or in a campus apartment complex where you may share a three-bedroom apartment with five other students. This provides more independence than living at home, but you still have to get along with those living with you. Other housing options include sorority or fraternity houses near campus.

Off-Campus Housing

If you go to college and work full-time or part-time, you might be able to afford to rent a room in an off-campus house or rent a one-bedroom basement apartment in a home near campus. If you are a newlywed, find a one-bedroom apartment or rental home. Be money conscious and start small. You don't want to be strapped every month to pay rent, unable to pursue any other activities. Rent a modest place for a few years while saving money to buy a home. Owning a home is always a wise investment, whether you are single or married. Remember, too, that many colleges and trade schools offer married student housing on campus at very reasonable rates.

These are the items you will take with you as you travel to your new home, such as important documents, maps, day planner, wallet, medicines, eyeglasses, keys and moving clothes. Pack these in easy-to-open carry along bags with a good zipper (such as a sports bag, large tote bag or duffel). Put important tickets, travel checks, credit cards and small, but expensive or irreplaceable items in a secure fanny pack, backpack, briefcase, money belt or purse.

• *Stuff to unpack first.* Sheets, blankets, pillows, towels, clothing, food, toiletries, cleaning items, kitchen and bathroom supplies, including dishes and utensils, extra light bulbs and toilet paper and basic home repair tools such as a hammer and nails, screws and screwdriver. Pack these things in marked boxes to be placed into the truck last and unpacked first.

• *Things by room.* Items you might not need for a few weeks or months including seasonal clothing and shoes, home decorations, books, small appliances, DVDs, games, etc. Pack these items according to where they will be used or stored in your new apartment, then label them: livingroom, bedroom, den, bathroom or storage. (In your exuberance, don't overstuff a box until it is dangerously heavy. It's better to have air in the box than to have a box no one can lift.)

These boxes also might include items such as yearbooks, photo albums, important documents and other memorabilia that you want to keep stored long-term in sturdy, safe boxes. Use a heavy-duty permanent marker to label boxes on all four sides so that you can easily see what the box contains. Also label the top or cover of the box. (Though they cost more, clear plastic boxes might be preferable for long-term storage, ensuring that your mementos are not damaged by flood, rodents, etc.)

Host a Yard Sale

If you have an attic, a garage, a spare bedroom or even an apartment loaded with items you no longer want or need, turn your unwanted belongings into cash—you might even have fun doing it. A good yard sale or moving sale isn't very difficult and will often bring in a tidy sum of money for a few days' work.

Step 1: Plan ahead. Hold the sale on a weekend. You can even start on a Friday afternoon and end on a Sunday evening. You want to avoid dragging all of your items out onto the yard and having to pull them all back in again if you don't get a big crowd. Selling items from your garage or even right from the house might be a good idea, especially if you have a lot you want to sell in just a few days. Set up the sale in the yard if you don't have a lot of heavy, expensive items and if you can trust the weather in your area.

*D*ad says:
Label all boxes with the name of the room where those particular items belong.
No exceptions.
There's nothing more frustrating than having to empty a dozen boxes to find one item.
And remember, this is no time to be a pack rat.
Sort, discard, and store items carefully.
Every item you decide to pack will have to be boxed, labeled, hauled and unpacked – then packed again at some future date.
Make sure you really, really want to take it with you.

Step 2: Get the word out. Take out a classified advertisement in the local newspaper, especially if you live in a secluded neighborhood or suburb. If, however, you live near a busy street, a few strategically placed signs might bring in enough shoppers. Staple or tape signs on corner telephone poles. Check to see if any regulations prevent advertising a yard sale this way.

A Word of Caution

You may include your phone number and/or address on advertisements or fliers to spread the word about your yard sale. However, do not put yourself in danger when dealing with strangers. Have friends or family present to help you. Only conduct the sale during daylight hours.

If litter laws in your town prevent posting signs on public property, ask some neighbors if you can put a yard sale sign (with your address, of course) on their fence or in their yard to lead people to your storefront. Grocery store and coffee shop bulletin boards also attract weekend bargain shoppers. Ask if you can tack up your announcement a week or two before the big sale. You may even want to list some items and prices on the flyer to peek interest.

Step 3: Run it like a small business. On the day of the sale, have about $20 in coins and dollar bills to make change. *Deal only in cash—do not accept personal checks*. Price items at what you would pay for them at a yard sale. For unused items in original containers, you should ask for about two-thirds of the price for an equivalent item in a store. For antiques, request 60 percent of the price for an equivalent item in an antique store. If you need cash and just want to get rid of the things you don't want or need, give your shoppers a real bargain and price everything to sell. Invest in some masking tape and a permanent marker to put a price on every item. This will save you a lot of time answering the question, "How much do you want for this?" Let people know you will consider any reasonable offer. You may even want to post a sign saying so.

Use bookshelves, boxes, outdoor tables and chairs to display items. String a clothesline to hang up used clothing for sale. Don't make the display too elaborate, because you'll have to lug back into the house or garage anything that doesn't sell. Involve friends and family in the event to make a fun weekend out of what might otherwise be a chore.

Furnishing Your Place

If your dorm or apartment isn't furnished, you may need to acquire a few basic pieces of your own. Remember to keep it simple. No one expects your first apartment to look as elegant as your parents' living room. This is a time to have fun with furnishings. Ingenuity pays off. Put your own personality into it.

Step 1: Make a list of what you need. You will need a comfortable bed to sleep in, a lamp, a place to study and a place to eat. You might want some book shelves, a computer desk, a dresser, a television stand and a couple of additional chairs for company. *Always buy what you need before buying what you want.*

Step 2: Look for good deals on furniture. Check advertisements, college newspapers and weekly circulars. New furniture sales are most common in the spring, but retail furniture is famous for having huge mark-ups. College students moving back home or graduating might be persuaded to part with their furniture in exchange for some quick cash. Shop yard sales and thrift stores in your new area to find good deals. Buy sturdy pieces that are scratched or need a new coat of paint, but nothing that needs a major overhaul. You won't have time or tools to re-upholster, for example, despite your good intentions.

If you like something, ask the seller how much they want for it, then offer $20 less. You might come away getting it for $10 off the asking price. If you think the price is already rock bottom, don't feel obligated to

*Dad's says:
Don't rent-to-own furniture! By the time you've finished making weekly payments at elevated interest rates, you could have saved for a down payment on a new home!*

Ask Mom

To learn how to furnish your new kitchen with basic necessities, see *Where's Mom Now That I Need Her?*, page 48 "Kitchen Essentials," page 50 "Cooking Essentials" and page 60 "Spices."

try to get an even better deal. And remember to take cash to yard sales—they rarely accept checks.

Step 3: Furnish within your means. If your furniture budget is very limited, look for a couch that doubles as a bed or a day-bed that doubles as a couch. A good table might work for eating and studying. Don't go into debt to buy furniture. Live as simply as possible.

Step 4: Consider making or assembling your own furniture. Discount retailers and home building supply stores often sell furniture in boxes, ready for home assembly. You can also build your own shelves for books and canned goods, etc., using wood planks and cinder blocks. Wooden or plastic crates can be used for a variety of purposes, too. Be creative and have fun with it.

Do Almost Anything
Special Tips from Dad

At the end of each chapter, you will find some extra helpful Dad tips; how to set a table, wrap a gift, fold an American flag, carve a turkey, fillet a fish, hold a baby, tip like a pro, pack for a trip, shine your shoes and tie a tie—tasks Dad discovered are quite essential for both sons and daughters to know as independent adults.

Do Almost Anything

Set a Table

Whether you're planning a dinner for two or 12, properly setting the table will make your meal more inviting. You'll also be able to utilize table space and provide your guests everything they'll need to consume what you've prepared in comfort. How you set the table depends on whether you plan a casual or a formal meal.

Step 1: Decide casual or formal. For a casual meal, you may use placemats and paper napkins. For a formal dinner, however, bring out the table cloth and cloth napkins. If you use placemats, the bottom edge should be an inch away from the edge of the table.

Step 2: Set the plate and the napkin. The dinner plate should go right in the middle of the placemat or place setting. For casual dining, place the folded napkin on the left side with the crease facing the plate. For formal dining, place the folded napkin on top of the plate in the center.

Step 3: Position silverware and drinking glass. For casual dining, place the dinner fork on top of the napkin to the left 1/2 inch from the plate. Place the knife 1/2 inch from the right of the plate with the cutting edge facing the plate. The spoon goes 1/2 inch right of the knife. Place the drinking glass about 2 inches from the top of the knife. Done! *(see Illustration A on page 16.)* That's a place setting for casual dining.

Step 4: Place additional items for formal dining. You will serve more food and different courses at a formal dinner, so you'll need more dinnerware and silverware. Start with the casual place setting, then set the additional utensils you plan to use. If you serve bread, soup and salad, this is how the place setting should go: Place the salad fork on the left side of the dinner fork, 1/2 inch away. Place the soupspoon on the right side of the dinner spoon, 1/2 inch away. Place the salad plate 1 inch from the top of the dinner plate, and the soup bowl on top of the salad plate. (You will serve the soup before the salad.) Place the smaller bread plate to the left side, 1 inch away from the salad fork. Place the butter knife on the right edge of the bread plate with the cutting edge facing the bread plate. You are now ready to present your meal to your guests. *(see Illustration B on page 16.)*.

A. Casual Setting

B. Formal Setting

Notes

CHAPTER

2

Making Tracks
All Things Auto

he average American's love affair with the automobile begins soon after passing a driving test and lasts well into retirement. Use of a parent's car or public transportation may delay the inevitable, but sooner or later almost every American decides to buy a car.

The prospect of negotiating the purchase of a new or used car can intimidate even the savviest consumers. Products and services usually come with price tags, but the sticker price on a car window is only the starting point for negotiations. The more you know about the process, the better prepared you will be to handle the tactics of expert salespeople and the responsibilities of car ownership.

Not so fast. Before making the decision to buy a car, tally up all of the ongoing expenses involved: car payments, insurance, maintenance, registration fees, property taxes, roadside service plans and fuel costs. If you are ready to make the financial commitment, proceed with cautious optimism. By following these suggestions, you will soon be sitting in the driver's seat, literally and figuratively.

Choosing a New Car

Step 1: Decide what kind of car you need, want, and can afford. Ultimately a car is a means of transporting people and goods as safely as possible from place A to place B. How many people? How many goods? How far is place A from place B and what are the roads like between them? If you really only need to drive a short distance each day on city roads, you probably do not absolutely have to have an all-wheel drive sport utility vehicle, though you may really want one. Do you need that new car smell, which is really only the lingering aroma of glues used in the assembly process, or would a used car without glue aroma be just as useful to you? (If so, skip ahead to *Choosing a Used Car* on page 25.) You have to balance all three factors at once: what you need, what you want and what you can afford. Make these decisions before you step onto a new car sales lot.

Step 2: Gather information about makes and models that meet your criteria. Consumer magazines, available by subscription, online and at public libraries, are indispensable for this purpose. To maintain neutrality, their publishers do not accept advertising and buy cars anonymously at regular dealerships, then evaluate comparable models across a spectrum of categories. Careful reading of a consumer magazine could help you avoid a costly mistake. The Internet can also be a valuable tool in narrowing the field of possible purchases down to a few manufacturers and models. You'll save time, shoe leather and cash by eliminating unworthy contenders before stepping onto a car lot, where you are more vulnerable to high-pressure salespeople who will capitalize on any lack of information on your part. It pays to know exactly what you do and do not want before you visit your first dealership. Ideally, you should try to make yourself as knowledgeable as the salesperson you are dealing with so that you'll be operating on an even playing field.

Step 3: Get pre-approved for a car loan (unless you are paying cash). How much do you earn each month and how much of your income goes toward debt? Have you saved for a down payment? What is your credit history? These are questions any potential lender will ask, and they'll want hard numbers. You'll need to provide them with a list of all of your debts (original balances, current balances, monthly payment amounts and account numbers). They will calculate your debt-to-income ratio then pull a credit report to see if they think you are an "acceptable risk"—in other words, whether or not they believe you will be able to make car payments consistently until the loan has been paid in full.

A loan officer will look over the numbers with you and tell you how much money their institution would be willing to finance and at what interest rate. It's a good idea to "shop the interest rate around" among competing credit unions, banks and dealerships to see which one will give you the best deal. (In most states credit unions can be more competitive because of advantageous tax laws.) Once you know exactly how much money you can borrow, you won't be at the mercy of the dealership to finance the car, though you may later decide to finance the car through them after all. Soon you'll be able to step onto a car lot and talk turkey. (For a more thorough discussion of financing your car, see *Getting the Best Loan* on page 24)

Step 4: Compile a list of reputable car dealers. Anyone who has had a very good or very bad experience with a particular car dealership will be happy to tell you about it, in detail. Ask around. Whenever possible, buy your car close to home where it can be serviced conveniently.

Step 5: Shop 'til you drop. A car is a major purchase—don't swoon over the first one you see. Stay with the game plan and look at cars that meet, but do not exceed, your original criteria. It can be difficult to find a base model car with nothing but standard

*D*ad says:
Don't give into high-pressure salespeople. Stay in control. If they offer you a special "deal" that is only good for today, walk out. They should be willing do a "deal" for you on any day.

equipment because dealers want to sell upgrades and packages to increase profit. Ask the dealer to pull a list of cars at regional dealerships with specific features — he can usually get the right one into his inventory to make the sale. Always remember that the dealer is more interested in selling a car than you are in buying one.

When you shop can be as important as *where* you shop. If you want to look at the dealer's inventory without being pressured by salespeople, walk through the lot when the business is closed. You can call back during business hours to inquire about a specific car and arrange for a test drive. Some have suggested buying a car on the last day of the month when the dealer is motivated to meet sales projections. Others swear by shopping midweek during the day when salespeople have more time to spend with you. As a dependable rule of thumb, you can get a better deal on a new car at the end of the model year when dealerships need to clear remaining inventory to make room for next year's offering.

Step 6: Test drive several models. You may think you know which car you want, but until you've driven it, you can't be sure you'll like how it feels to sit in it and how it handles on the road. Even little things like cup holders and dashboard lights can irritate you after the purchase if you didn't take the time to acquaint yourself with the car before buying it. Drive the car for at least 20 minutes down neighborhood streets, major thoroughfares and the highway. Check acceleration and passing power. Climb hills, take some turns and do some stop-and-go driving. You might even want to try parking it just to see how nimbly it maneuvers. Notice the ride, the ventilation system, the ease of handling . . . don't overlook anything that troubles you. You haven't bought the car yet. You can afford to be critical. On the other hand, if you really like what you're driving, you might be ready to talk about making a purchase.

The Art of the Deal

Step 1: From the outset, remember that YOU are in control of the deal. The dealership has to sell cars to stay in business, but you do not have to buy one—you can take your business elsewhere. For best results, project the image of being somewhat aloof, vaguely interested and completely in control of your emotions. Dealerships are highly motivated to sell you a car for several reasons. Their inventory next year depends on how many cars they sell this year and they know that if they don't sell a car to you, one of their a competitors will. The dealer would rather turn over inventory at a modest profit than make no profit at all and lose potential service bay business.

Step 2: Call around to get price quotes. Some dealerships capitalize on consumers' reluctance to haggle over prices and offer a "no-dicker" price sticker. Great! Just be sure to check with other dealers to ensure that you are getting the best price. Ideally you should have three dealers' price quotes on the same car when you enter into negotiations. Prices may vary widely based on a variety of factors that do not affect you—you are only interested in buying the right car at the best price possible. You have to represent your own interests in this negotiation.

Step 3: Find out the dealer's asking price. Most salespeople want to get you talking about monthly payment instead of total purchase price. Tell them that you want to talk about a price, one that is reasonable and fair to both parties.

Step 4: Negotiate the price. Now that you know what you can afford to spend and what other dealers will charge, you are prepared to talk to this dealer from an informed position.

Never automatically give the dealer the asking price. Always ask for a lower price. If the price does not come down enough, ask him to "sweeten the deal" by

Dad says: Interest rates can range from zero to 21% depending on several factors. It pays to "shop the interest rate around." If your loan amount is $5,000 at 10% interest, you'll pay an additional $500 yearly for the car above the purchase price. Save as much as you can toward a larger down payment and borrow less.

throwing in some extras—an extended warranty, tinted windows, rust-proofing, a sun roof, a spoiler, etc. The dealer fully expects you to ask. Remember that the asking price is almost always artificially elevated as a buffer in the event of intense negotiations. Be calm, casual and friendly, but don't hesitate to leave the dealership if you cannot agree to terms. If you do agree on a price, and eventually you will somewhere, a sales agreement will be drawn up to finalize the purchase.

Step 5. Carefully review the sales agreement. It should list the exact price of the car, including options, sales tax, dealer prep, shipping charges and other fees. These should be itemized clearly so that you understand each one. Nothing should be unclear. Don't be afraid to ask questions and check the numbers yourself. Sometimes mistakes are found. If anyone or anything makes you feel uneasy, do not sign. Take a copy of the proposed contract with you to review at home where you can make a rational decision. A good dealership or salesperson will allow you to do this.

Step 6. If everything is in order and feels right, sign and drive. Enjoy your new car and follow the manufacturer's maintenance schedule so that it runs like new for years to come.

Getting the Best Loan

Step 1: Check on a credit union loan first. Credit union loans usually charge lower interest rates. To avoid last-minute hassles, check with your credit union about a pre-approved loan. The car dealership wants to sell you the car. It's the bank that you need to convince you will make payments on time. Some banks or credit unions will process your loan for a specified amount and hold the loan for 60 to 90 days until you find the right automobile in that price range.

Step 2: Look into a manufacturer's pre-approved loan. Some new-car dealerships will offer loans on certain models. In these cases, your credit will be pre-approved as long as you have proof of income and you don't have a poor credit history. Just make sure you get the best loan deal. Some dealerships won't even require a down payment, but they might have an interest rate so high that you can't afford that convenience. Always check to find out if the manufacturer offers any incentives. Many of them run specials that offer a lower interest rate to first-time car buyers.

Step 3: Borrow for as short a time as possible. You will always pay less in total financing charges if you take out a three-year loan rather than a four- or five-year loan. Don't drive beyond your pocketbook. Choose a vehicle you can comfortably afford, then save for something better. You will always get a better deal if you have a large down payment. Insist on a good deal so that your down payment does make a difference and you aren't throwing away the trade-in value of your old car.

Buying a Used Car

If you decide to buy a used car, take a few extra precautions. Used cars can be quite reliable, but they are usually sold as is, without warranty, so you'll need to rely on the assessment of a good mechanic. You can buy a used car from a dealership or from a private individual.

Step 1: Decide whether to buy from a dealer or an individual. It is usually less expensive to buy a used car from an individual than from a dealer. Dealerships mark up their cars to cover overhead, but a previous owner may only be interested in making a quick deal with someone like you who has cash in hand.

Dealerships do offer some risk protection, especially if they have limited warranties on their vehicles. With a limited warranty you have some recourse in the event the car breaks down within days, weeks or months of purchase. Dealerships depend on repeat business for their success—they want satisfied customers. A reputable used car dealer won't take the chance of selling you a lemon.

Financing Costs

If you finance the car through the dealer, the sales agreement should also list the financing costs. If you find your own financing, make sure the sales agreement allows you to cancel without losing your down payment in the event that you do not get a loan. If you trade in another car, make sure the agreement lists the exact price the sales person quoted you. If it doesn't, speak up.

*D*ad says:
Buy a car with your head not your heart. Young people tend to purchase their first car based upon an emotional reaction to it. Don't be driven by how you look in the car, how attractive the car or truck is to others, what the particular car might say about your financial status, intelligence or attraction to the opposite sex. A car is a car. Make sure it works.

With a private party, however, you assume all of the risk that the automobile will work as expected and promised.

Step 2: Find out the "high and low" *Blue Book* price. The used-car buyer's Bible, the *Blue Book*, lists the price for the make and model of vehicles, with or without extras, taking into consideration mileage and age of the car. Most banks or credit unions will give you this information on the telephone (you need to get the mileage of the particular vehicle you want first). The Internet also has information about *Blue Book* prices, and public libraries always have the *Blue Book* in their reference sections.

If you decide to buy from an individual, try to buy from a relative or friend. This will give you some assurance of the car's history. Was it well maintained? Did the previous owner spend a fortune in costly repairs? You will have a much better idea of how much wear the car has had, what maintenance has been done and whether the car has been in an accident or has become a chronic repair headache.

If you go to a dealer, look for an "off-brand" car. For example, at a Chevrolet used-car dealership, look for a Chrysler or a Toyota. A dealer may be more willing to work a better deal on an off-brand. Steer clear of exotic models and foreign luxury cars because they will cost more to repair. Sports cars and recreational vehicles usually have had more abuse. Luxury cars, loaded with options, have more things that can go wrong with them.

Step 3: Do some in-person research. When you visit used car lots, take pen and notebook with you and write down the year, make, model and mileage on particular vehicles that meet your needs and wants. Test drive those that spark your interest. Look for a car with the lowest mileage. An average driver racks up about 10,000 miles per year. So, multiply the age of the car by 10,000 miles and stick as close to that number as possible. Then research fair asking prices for those specific makes, models and years on the Internet or by calling banks or credit unions for *Blue Book* quotes.

If you buy from an individual, ask a few questions about the vehicle over the phone before you check it out in person (make, model, year, mileage, extras, accidents?), then check the *Blue Book* so you will have a good idea of it's worth before you take it for a test drive.

Step 4: Check the car out yourself! You should reject a used car if you find rust spots anywhere on the body, uneven tread wear on the tires, uneven engine idling, noisy brakes, gears that stick, squeal or grind or a jerking, uneven clutch. Also look for too much free play in the steering wheel or smoke pouring out of the exhaust pipe. You don't need to know exactly how a car works to realize when one doesn't work right. If you feel uncomfortable with how the car or truck handles in stop-and-go traffic or at faster speeds on the freeway, don't buy it. *Your love for this car will not grow with time.*

Step 5: Recruit extra help to check out the vehicle. Check the recent issue of *Consumer Reports* magazine dedicated to automobiles. You can also access this information in several forms from a computer. Look up the "frequency of repair" records for the make and model of car or truck you want to buy. Modify your choices, if necessary, aiming for a car with a low rate of repairs.

Insist that a reputable mechanic, preferably one you personally know, inspect the car before you make a final decision. If you buy from a used automobile dealer, take the car to an independent mechanic. (You may need to leave a small deposit with the seller to do this.) *If the owner or dealer won't allow an inspection, close off negotiations right then.* There's obviously something to hide if they aren't willing to let you check out the car before you buy it.

If you don't know a mechanic who will do a check for you at no cost, find one who will do it for a fair

*D*ad says:
Plan ahead and save. Set aside $1,500 to $3,000 to pay outright for a used car or arrange for your financing ahead of time. First of all, you need to find out how much your bank or credit union will loan on the car you want to buy. Financial institutions have strict guidelines, and you will need to fall within these to borrow money on the vehicle. Be sure to figure in interest charges, finance fees and other hidden costs so you can make sure you get a good deal.

price. It's worth the investment. If the mechanic says your car needs repairs, get an estimate on costs. Add these costs to the sales price of the car to find out whether you will still be getting a good deal.

Step 6: Confirm inspection, registration and title. If you decide to buy a car through the classified ads on the Internet or in a newspaper, consider only those cars with current registration. This means the license plates have current stickers or "tags" registered with the Department of Motor Vehicles in the owner's name. Most importantly, the car should be owned free and clear to the seller, who must have the car title (proof of ownership) and sign it over to you. *When you hand over the money for the car, you should get the keys and the title.* You'll have financial entanglements you do not want if you buy a car that someone still owes money on or that can't be registered easily.

At used-car dealerships, the car likely will have up-to-date inspection and emissions tests. When you buy from an individual, you take the risk that your new purchase may not pass inspection and emissions. You might get stuck with repair costs just to get it legally registered in your name. The more information you gather about the car before you buy, the better off you will be.

Finding a Good Mechanic

When should you look for a good mechanic? Before your car breaks down! Standing on the side of the road, wiping your brow as your car gets hitched to a tow truck, would not be the best time. Look for a good mechanic before or right after you buy your car.

Step 1: Find a shop that has been approved by its profession. Start by looking at independent garages, service stations, auto dealerships, specialty shops or nationwide department or specialty stores such as Sears. Find a shop approved by the *American Automobile Association* that employs at least one mechanic certified by the *National Institute for Automotive Service Excellence.* These mechanics have to pass tough tests to prove their competence in a variety of areas before they get certified. If you own a diesel car, look for a shop bearing the *Association of Diesel Specialists* logo. These shops have mechanics well versed on the latest diesel techniques.

Step 2: Ask for recommendations. Ask friends, neighbors and family members which shops or mechanics they like and use. Also ask for the ones they didn't like or had a negative experience with. Check with the Better Business Bureau to find out if any complaints have been registered against the shop you think you'll go with. Because of the nature of the business, most car repair shops will have an occasional complaint, but steer clear of those who seem to have a lot of unsatisfied customers.

Step 3: Visit the shop yourself. Is it reasonably clean? That's a good indication that the owners take professional pride in their work. Is it busy? That's good, too. If you can, talk to a few people waiting for service. If they're repeat customers, find out whether they like the work, prices and reliability. Talk directly to the owner, the manager, or the mechanic who does the work. You'll notice attitude right away. Look for someone who seems interested, knowledgeable, friendly and willing to listen to your concerns. Ask what services the shop provides, then price a few basic services (such as a front-end alignment or an electronic tune-up). Do some comparison shopping, even though you should choose quality over price.

Step 4: Ask about any extra services. Some repair shops offer loaners while they work on your car, while others run extra diagnostic and road tests to pinpoint potential problems. To be on the safe side, try out a new mechanic for the first time on a small, inexpensive job. If you're satisfied, you will feel more secure when the big one repairs come along.

Checklist

Mechanic's Priorities

- ❏ Odometer accuracy
- ❏ Accident damage
- ❏ Engine
- ❏ Spark plugs
- ❏ Emissions
- ❏ Exhaust system
- ❏ Suspension
- ❏ Shock absorbers
- ❏ Tires
- ❏ Alignment
- ❏ Brakes
- ❏ Fuel lines/Brake lines
- ❏ Electrical system
- ❏ Charging system
- ❏ Rust
- ❏ Cooling system

Avoiding Repair Rip-Offs

Step 1: Steer clear of specials. Some shops attempt to lure customers by offering specials, then once you get there, they persuade you to do something that costs significantly more. If you have questions about what your warranty covers, clear them up before you take your car in for repairs. When you take your car in, insist on talking to the mechanic who will be doing the work. Some shops hire people who write up service orders and pass them on to the mechanic—but these people rarely know what repairs you will need. Instead of asking for a specific repair, describe to the mechanic the symptoms of the problem. Then let the mechanic make the diagnosis and determine necessary repairs. Find out which repairs must be done immediately and which ones can wait.

Step 2: Get a second opinion on any major job. Take the car to a different mechanic, describe the problem and ask for a diagnosis as well as a price estimate. You should also seek a second opinion on smaller jobs if you feel uncomfortable with the first mechanic's assessment. Always get a written estimate for repair work, and do not authorize the shop to exceed the estimate without your approval.

If a repair shop charges you more than 10 percent above their written estimate, you can initiate legal action. Read the repair order carefully to find out what you authorize the shop to do. Find out what will happen if the repair fails. Will it be corrected at no cost to you? Never authorize a shop to do "any necessary" repairs. You might end up paying a small fortune for work that didn't have to be done.

Step 3: Inspect your repair bill before you pay. Be wary of a mechanic who calls later and says additional work must be done. If you feel uncomfortable, tell the mechanic to fix only what you agreed on until you can get some more information. When you get the bill, read it carefully. If you don't understand something, ask for an explanation. Refuse to pay for repairs that have not been itemized. Each individual repair, part and labor or service expense should be listed with the corresponding price.

Changing a Flat Tire

Before you leave on any trip, make sure you have a good spare tire in your car, a tire jack and lug nut wrench that fits your tires. (New cars are sold with all of the tools needed to change a tire, and used cars are usually equipped as well.) It is better to carry a full-sized, new or slightly used tire instead of the smaller, weaker factory spare that is really only a stop-gap measure to get you to the nearest tire repair place.

Step 1: Pull as far off the road as you can. Activate your flasher lights to alert other drivers. If you have a manual transmission, put your car in first gear. If you have an automatic transmission, put your car in park. Turn off your car. Set the emergency brake. If you can, anchor the car by placing a large rock or some kind of block on both sides of the wheel that is diagonally opposite the flat tire.

Step 2: Loosen lug nuts before you jack up the car. Use a screwdriver or the end of the lug wrench to remove the hubcap or wheel cover of the flat tire. Loosen, but don't remove, each lug nut with the wrench. If the lug nut is marked L, turn it clockwise. If it's marked R, turn it counterclockwise.

Step 3: Jack up the car in the area nearest the flat tire. Get the spare tire and the jack out of the trunk. Refer to your owner's manual for specific instructions on how to operate your jack. The jack should be perpendicular to the ground and placed firmly under the car. Jack up the car until the flat tire is as least three inches above the ground.

Step 4: Completely remove the lug nuts. Put them in the hubcap or wheel cover that you already removed so they won't get lost. Remove the flat tire from the wheel axle.

Step 5: Put on the spare tire. Make sure all bolt holes are aligned. Replace all lug nuts, tightening them first by hand. Then lower the car using the jack until the tire touches the ground firmly. Now, use the lug wrench to tighten the lug nuts completely.

Step 6: Finish lowering the car. Remove the jack and check the lug nuts again to make sure they are completely tightened. Replace the hubcap or wheel cover. Put all your equipment including the flat tire back in the trunk. Turn off your flasher lights before you get back on the highway. Be careful as you re-enter the flow of traffic.

Checking Your Oil

An engine without oil will freeze up right in the middle of driving. You'll hear some huge clunking noises, a horrible death roar, then—nothing. If your engine seizes up, that's the end of it. You will be forced to buy new guts for your car. A new engine, even a rebuilt one, is not cheap. You could be looking at thousands of dollars for a new engine that could have been saved if only you had regularly checked and changed the oil. *It's a good idea to check your oil every time you stop for gas, especially if your car is older and has a tendency to burn oil.*

Step 1: Stop your car and turn off your engine. Lift the hood. Find the dip stick. Make sure you have an old rag with you or use a paper towel provided outside at most gas stations. Pull out the dip stick, wipe off the oil, push it all the way back into the oil reservoir, wait a moment and pull it slowly back out.

Step 2: Check that the oil is at the fill line, not above or below. If you over fill your oil, your car will burn the excess and smell horrible. If your oil shows 1/4 inch or more below the fill line, buy a quart of oil and pour half of it in. Check the oil level again. Put in enough oil that it reaches the fill line.

Step 3: Never ignore your oil light or skip oil changes. In fact, you should change your oil every 3 months or 3,000 miles. An oil change, with new oil and filter, will cost about $28. A quart of oil, just to bring your oil level up costs $1 to $5, depending on the brand. Both are cheaper than replacing an entire engine.

Step 4: Know what oil to use. Buying oil for your car can suddenly become pretty complicated when you look at the label. You're likely to find a whole smattering of letters and numbers. The numbers you're looking at indicate viscosity, the oil's relative thickness and its ability to flow at outside temperatures.

If it gets too thick in cold weather, your car will be hard to start. If it gets too thin in hot weather, your engine parts won't be lubricated enough. Here's a general guide to the ones you should pick: 5W-30 for four-cylinder engines, 10W-30 for six and eight cylinder engines and diesel engines, and 10W-40 for everything else (this is the most widely used engine oil.) Check the owner's manual to see which grade of oil is recommended for your vehicle.

Maintaining Your Battery

Your car's battery converts chemical action into the electrical energy that makes your automobile run. If it's kept clean and filled with water, a car battery will continue to hold a charge—and keep things running smoothly.

Step 1: Keep it filled with water. To properly hold a charge, your battery needs water. Many batteries now are self-contained and you do not need to check the water levels. If yours is not, however, check the water level in your battery once a month. Pull the covers off the top of each cell and look inside. The water should cover the metal plates inside and come to within one-fourth of an inch of the top. If the fluid level is low, add enough distilled water to fill it to the proper level. Replace the covers and wipe the top of the battery dry.

Ask Mom
For additional quick tips on basic automobile maintenance, refer to *Where's Mom Now That I Need Her?*, pages 301- 302.

Note: If the weather is cold, don't add water to the battery unless you will drive the car for at least five miles immediately afterward.

Step 2: Keep the battery clean. To clean dirt from the top of your battery, cover the vent holes with masking tape. Mix one part baking soda with two parts water. Use a scrub brush to clean the top of the battery with the baking soda mixture. Rinse the battery with clear water and wipe it dry. Make sure you remove the tape that's covering the vent holes afterward.

Step 3: Remove corrosion. Battery posts and clamps can become corroded, making it difficult to start your engine. To remove corrosion, use a wire brush. Scrub posts and clamps until they shine and all signs of corrosion are gone. To prevent more corrosion, coat the clamps lightly with petroleum jelly.

Step 4: Keep it warm. If the weather is really cold, try to park your car in a garage—or at least in a sheltered area. If temperatures dip low, your battery might need some help to stay warm. Fold up an old blanket and tuck it around the battery or run a low-wattage light bulb on an extension cord and put in under the hood near the battery.

Driving Defensively

Say you pull around a corner one December morning and find yourself skidding across a sheet of black ice . . . or you are heading for an appointment in rush-hour traffic when your radiator hose splits open . . . or another vehicle slams into yours as you race down the road.

Step 1: Be prepared. Driving a car is a hazardous and frustrating business these days. The National Highway Traffic Safety Administration reports that one in eight people is involved in some kind of collision every year. Exactly half of us will be injured in a car accident during our lifetime. Driving is no joke. And it's not for show offs or goof offs. If you want to reduce the odds that you will be one of those injured in an accident, learn some basic defensive driving techniques and become familiar with how to drive safely in specific climates.

Step 2: Fasten your seat belt. For some reason this obvious safety rule, which is now a law across most of the United States, has become some kind of political or philosophical issue with young people. It's not a matter of your boring parents or an intrusive government trying to get you to conform to their ways. Using your seat belt is simply a smart thing to do. People buckled into their seats can walk away from an accident that may kill someone who doesn't wear a seat belt.

Step 3: Be aware of traffic around you. Check out what's going on around you and in front of you. Most specifically, be keenly aware of the vehicle directly in front of you, behind you and beside you. You need to consciously practice defensive driving from the minute you pull out of your driveway. Most serious accidents happen to drivers who are within 25 miles of their homes. You are three times as likely to be involved in a serious accident on a rural road as on the interstate.

Step 4: Keep your eyes on the road and devote your attention to driving. You are more likely to be involved in an accident when your mind is on something else besides driving, when you purposely don't follow traffic rules or when you let yourself be distracted from the road . . . to turn up the radio, change a tape, munch a hamburger or be the center of attention with your passengers. Really, they just want you to get them wherever they're going in one piece.

Even if you are talking to a passenger or listening to the radio, keep your thoughts on driving. Trying to figure out your relationship, put on make-up, make a phone call or inhale your lunch while you drive puts you and others at great risk.

35

*D*ad says:
Don't let anyone convince you that your knee, elbow, pinky finger or even your foot can steer hundreds of pounds of speeding steel safely down any road for even a second. This type of driving isn't cute, hip or happening. It's just stupid.

Step 5: Cut down on distractions before you get on the road. If you need the heater or the air conditioner, adjust them while you're idling in the driveway, not after you are headed down a highway at 40 miles per hour. Find a radio station you want before you leave the driveway, too. If you need sunglasses, take them out of the glove compartment and put them on your head before you start out. In the few seconds you are fiddling with the radio, glove compartment, fast food, purse or wallet while you are driving, your car can travel a hundred yards and you can miss your chance to avoid an accident. Be alert. Take a breath and put on the hat of driver before you pull into traffic.

Step 6: Sit up straight and make sure your view is clear. Your mother told you to stop slouching and she was right, especially when you are driving. Sit squarely in the driver's seat with your back against the seat. Place both feet firmly on the floor, and adjust the seat so you can easily reach the pedals. In this position, you should be able to see clearly out the windshield. Adjust your rearview and side mirrors to give you full vision of vehicles around you.

Step 7: Wash the windshield. Keep all of the windows and mirrors clean. Don't rush off on a winter morning with just a small clear hole on the front windshield. Take time to clear the entire car. This simple step could save your life or that of some unfortunate soul who might end up in your blind spot. Make it a habit to wash your windows when you fill up with gas. Carry a spray bottle of window cleaner and a roll of paper towels in your car in case your washer fluid runs out. Also carry a pair of warm gloves and an ice scraper.

Step 8: Keep your hands on the wheel. The steering wheel is the face of a clock and your hands should be at the positions of 9 and 3, or 10 and 2, depending on the driver's education teacher you had. The point is, both hands need to be squarely on the steering wheel. Keeping this grip at all times allows you to react with split-second speed if you begin to lose control of your vehicle or find yourself near someone who has lost control of theirs.

Step 9: Focus on the big picture. Pay attention to the 360-degree circle around your car. While you are driving, keep your eyes moving. Resist the temptation to read billboards or something else that grabs your interest. Your eyes should be in constant motion. You should check your rearview and side mirrors every five seconds. The rest of the time, look ahead, far ahead. You should be watching the scene you will be into 15 seconds from now, a practice that gives you plenty of warning if there are impending dangers.

Step 10: Let other drivers know what you are doing. If you are going to change lanes or turn, signal. Sounds basic, but it's amazing how many people neglect this. When you need to slow down because of an obstacle in the roadway ahead of you, start slowing as soon as possible and use your brake lights to your advantage. Lightly step on your brakes as a warning to cars behind you. This is common courtesy and common sense. If you can see that another driver hasn't noticed you and isn't slowing, tap the horn to let them know where you are.

Road Trip!

Step 1: Avoid all drugs. If you need to drive, especially a long distance, don't use drugs, coffee, caffeinated drinks or tobacco. The caffeine in no-doze drugs, coffee and carbonated drinks has a greater let-down than the temporary up it provides. The activity of smoking may keep you awake, but it will also distract you from driving. You may be too relaxed after finishing the cigarette. Of course, don't drink alcohol or use any illegal drugs while driving.

Step 2: Eat light foods. Avoid heavy meals and snacks that are oily, greasy or difficult to digest. Choose instead fresh fruits (already cut up to eat on the road), crackers, nuts and fruit drinks or water.

Checklist

Emergency Kit

- ❑ Fire extinguisher
- ❑ Jumper cables
- ❑ Tow rope
- ❑ Spare tire
- ❑ Jack
- ❑ Lug wrench
- ❑ Screwdrivers
- ❑ Pliers
- ❑ Flares or reflectors
- ❑ First-aid kit
- ❑ Empty gas can
- ❑ Jug of water
- ❑ Non-perishable food
- ❑ Old blanket
- ❑ White rags
- ❑ Flashlight and batteries
- ❑ Pocketknife
- ❑ Cell phone or four quarters
- ❑ Window cleaner
- ❑ Paper towels

Winter Extras:
- ❑ Sand, road salt or non-clumping cat litter
- ❑ Ice scraper
- ❑ Small shovel
- ❑ Gloves, boots, hat, etc.

*Did you know?
The worst time to
drive is between
midnight and 3 am,
when you are 13
times more likely to
have an accident than
between 6 am and 6 pm.*

Source: University of California
at Davis.

Step 3: Keep plenty of fresh air flowing through the car. You'll stay more alert if your car is slightly on the cool side. Turn your vent to fresh to draw air into the car from outside, and open a window occasionally. Even in the winter, crack a window now and then.

Step 4: Stop often to get a break and stretch. Get out and walk briskly at rest stops, gas stations or parking lots. If you are traveling with others, challenge them to a foot race. The exercise will refresh you.

Step 5: Wear sunglasses to cut down on glare. Sunlight will make you squint and eventually you'll want to close your eyes. Wear polarized sunglasses during the day.

Step 6: Change your posture or position. Move your seat closer to or farther from the pedals. Adjust the back. If you get used to one position, you can become too comfortable and fall asleep.

Step 7: Turn on the radio or cassette player. Find something interesting. You might like a stimulating talk show or some fast-paced jazz. You might even choose something you personally find irritating such as loud heavy metal music or country music. If you try all these tricks and still find yourself feeling drowsy, *pull off the highway immediately.*

Step 8: Pull over and get some sleep. If you can, find a protected area in which to park your car, lock the doors and take a short nap. Busy rest stops and police station parking lots are usually safe. But if you still have hours to go to arrive at your destination, play it safe—find a motel for the night.

Ask Mom

For more on traveling
and auto safety, see
*Where's Mom Now That I
Need Her?,*
pages 303-304.

Do Almost Anything

Wrap a Gift

Anyone who is important enough for you to purchase a gift is important enough for you to take the time to wrap the gift also. Expensive small gifts, such as jewelry, usually come in attractive boxes that may not need to be wrapped. Tying a ribbon around the box might suffice. Many stores will provide gift wrapping if you ask, sometimes for free. If you decide to wrap the gift on your own, follow these steps:

Step 1: Decide on a box or bag. Boxes are easier to wrap than free-standing gifts. If the gift doesn't come in its own box, purchase a box that fits. With large or free-standing gifts, your best bet is to buy a decorative bag and coordinating tissue paper. Get a bag that is larger than the gift. Wrap tissue paper around gift to cover, place inside the bag, then place two or three large sheets of tissue paper in the bag with corners sticking out of the top at random. Bring the handles of bag together and tie.

Step 2: Buy coordinating paper, ribbon and bow. If you plan to wrap gifts for several different people, mark each recipient's name on a nametag and adhere the tag to the wrapped package *before you wrap the next one.* This way you won't lose track of what goes to whom. If you only have one package to wrap, you may want to purchase a pre-cut amount of wrapping paper, usually folded into a square, that often comes with a bow and tag. Just make sure pre-cut paper is big enough to fit your box. If you want to make the gift extra special, buy a cloth ribbon that matches the wrapping paper and tie your own bow.

Step 3: Cut the paper to the correct size. It's better to cut too big a piece of wrapping paper than too small. The length of the wrapping paper should equal all four sides of the box lengthwise (or vertically) plus 2 inches. The width of the wrapping paper should be double the width of the box. You can measure with a measuring tape or simply use the box to measure how much paper you'll need.

Step 4: Cut length first. It's best to wrap gifts on a sturdy table, but the floor will do. Pull wrapping paper out lengthwise with the decorative side facing down on the table or floor. For length, set the gift box down on the paper, making one wide side of the box even with the bottom edge of the wrapping paper. (See Illustration A on page 40.) Push the box over onto paper to measure length. Push box onto side again, then over again to get double the length. Measure two inches more, and mark. Cut horizontally at mark.

Step 5: Measure and cut width. For width, set the box on the paper with left side of box even with left side of paper, make a light pencil mark on the paper at right edge of box. (See Illustration B on page 40.) Pick up the box, set the left edge of box at mark, and make a mark on paper at the right edge of the box. Cut vertically at second mark.

Step 6: Center box and wrap length. Place box in center of wrapping paper, face down, with equal amounts of wrapping paper on sides, and at top and bottom. First wrap paper around length of box. Pull top edge of wrapping paper over onto box and secure edge with a clear piece of tape. (See Illustration C on page 41.) Pull bottom edge of wrapping over onto box and secure edge with tape also. This edge should overlap the top edge so that no part of the box shows through. (See Illustration D on page 41.)

Step 7: Wrap width. Starting at one side, push short edges of wrapping paper in against box. This will make the long edges fold into a V-shape. Crease V-shape on top and bottom using fingers. Now, fold over top V-shaped flap and secure with a piece of tape. Fold up bottom V-shaped flap and secure with tape. Repeat with other side of package. (See Illustrations E and F on page 41.)

Step 8: Finish with ribbon and bow. To make things easy, you can top a gift with a self-adhesive bow. If you want to use cloth ribbon to tie a bow, measure the width, plus the length of the package and double that. Cut one length of ribbon to these measurements. Lay ribbon vertically. Center package face down on ribbon so that the length of the package lies top to bottom. Bring loose ends of ribbon up and tie it in middle bottom of package as you would the first step in tying your shoe. (See Illustration G on page 41.) Now the ribbon ends should be horizontal. Wrap ribbon ends around width of package, turning the gift over to reveal top. Tie again and finish bow as you would the final step in tying your shoe. Clip ends at angle to fit package size. (See Illustration H on page 41.)

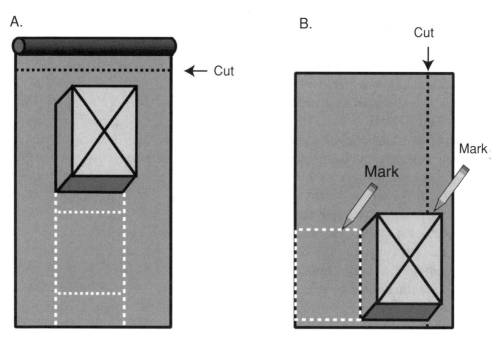

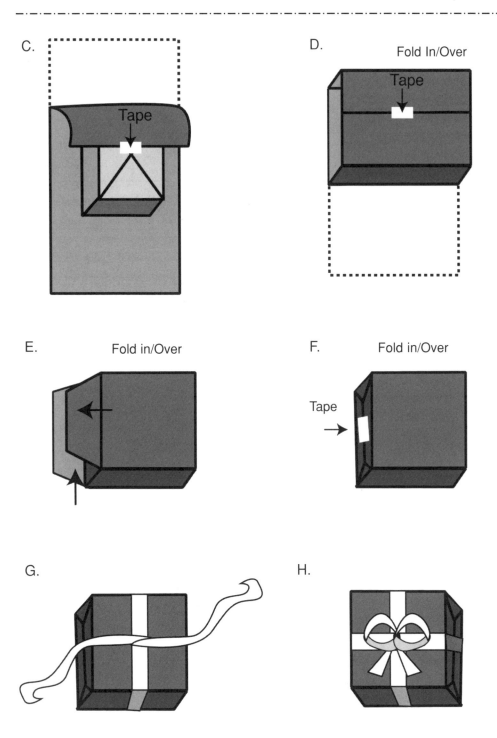

C.

Tape

D.

Fold In/Over

Tape

E.

Fold in/Over

F.

Fold in/Over

Tape

G.

H.

CHAPTER 3

The Fine Print
Contracts and Warranties

D ealing with contracts, agreements, warranties, and guarantees is one of the premier tests of adulthood. Legal paperwork, contracts and agreements are an unavoidable part of modern life. A few good pointers will keep you out of trouble.

In the business and excitement of moving into your first apartment, for example, don't forget that a rental agreement is a legal document. If you break the lease, the landlord can take you to small claims court to recoup any unpaid rent for the contract period. If the landlord breaks the lease or does not give your deposit back after you complete your stay, you can take the landlord to small claims court to retrieve your deposit.

If you have ever bought anything or done business with any kind of establishment, you have probably signed hundreds of contracts without even knowing it. Many businesses now include mini versions of their sales contracts in microscopic print on sales or credit card receipts. They are even printed on theater ticket stubs and on lift tickets at ski resorts.

Dealing with Contracts

Step 1: Read it. A contract is a legal agreement between two people or a business and a person. One party agrees to provide a product or service, and the other agrees to pay for it. A contract can be written or verbal. A verbal contract is sometimes called "a gentlemen's agreement" (no matter your gender), sealed with a handshake. A verbal agreement can be binding by law. A contract doesn't have to be signed. If you accept the product or service, you have, basically, signed the contract.

Understand the contract thoroughly before you sign. If you don't understand something, ask for clarification. If you want something in the contract changed or deleted, make the change on the document and have the other party initial the changes. If you cannot reach an agreement, don't sign. Know what you are agreeing to before you sign.

Step 2: Understand the payment terms of the contract. Federal law requires that any contract list four different figures—sale price, annual percentage rate, finance charges and total monthly payment. Look those over carefully. Know the exact extent of the commitment you are making before you sign. Having figures listed also enables you to comparison shop. You might find a lower interest rate or arrange lower monthly payments somewhere else for the same item.

Step 3: Decide the amount of your down payment. If the contract specifies that you will forfeit your down payment if you cancel, put down as little money as possible. Then, if the product turns out to be defective, the seller has more to lose by not satisfying you immediately. In any case, you are only out a small amount. If, however, you don't want to make payments over a long period of time, a larger down payment may better meet your needs.

Step 4: Beware of balloon payments. Read the contract carefully to make sure you will not have to pay one large payment at the end of the loan, often called a balloon payment. You don't want to risk repossession of the item if you can't make the last payment.

Step 5: Check the full description of the merchandise. The contract should contain a detailed description of the item, including the color, size, serial or model number and any other identifying characteristics. This protects you from having someone deliver inferior merchandise.

Step 6: Don't allow blank spaces. Do not sign any contract that has a blank space—an unscrupulous seller may add information to the document after you've signed. Insist that every blank line is either filled in or X'd out before you sign.

Step 7: Reject terms you don't agree with. If you don't agree with a term or clause in the contract, draw a line through it and sign your initials next to the line. Then ask the seller to initial the changes, too. Some will and some won't, but it's worth a try. If you can't come to terms, don't sign. Take your business elsewhere.

Step 8: Document verbal promises. If a seller makes a verbal promise to you, make sure it's included in the written contract. If it isn't, write the terms of the verbal promise in ink, initial the addition and have the seller initial it, too. Make sure that the addition is written on both your copy and seller's copy of the contract.

Step 9: Get a copy of the final agreement. Once you've agreed to everything and signed the contract, make sure you get a copy for your files. Your copy should have both your signature and the seller's signature, as well as any additions or changes made.

Step 10: Get a receipt for money paid. The receipt should say how you paid—cash, check, or credit card. Sometimes business-to-business people trade services in lieu of cash. This is called an "in-kind" transaction. Goods and services can be given and accepted as fair trade and full payment for the merchandise.

*D*ad says:
Keep receipts for major purchases and copies of all contracts and written agreements, including warranties and guarantees, in a designated place, such as a fire-proof safe. Some day you'll be glad you know just where you placed a vitally important document.

Dad says:
If you regularly pay by money order, label the money order receipt with the specific bill or service the amount went toward. You may have to track the money order by its tracking number if the receiver claims he or she never received the payment.

Shopping for a Bargain

Step 1: Shop at thrift stores for furniture. You've heard the saying, *"They just don't make 'em like they used to."* In many cases, especially with furniture, that's true. Look for used or second-hand items that hold their value. Become an observant shopper at thrift stores, yard sales, flea markets and auctions. Keep an eye out for antiques—items more than 50 years old—that have investment value as well as used merchandise durable enough to serve you well for a good price. These items may include hand-made wood furniture, books printed on heavier paper with higher-quality bindings, cooking utensils and appliances, costume jewelry, silver flatware, rose-colored "Depression" glass, Swiss watches and tools made before 1940.

Step 2: Look for gently used clothes at vintage or thrift shops. In recent years thrift stores have become trendy. Some of the newer thrift stores buy and sell slightly used clothing. A smart shopper can find $35 jeans for $6. Establish a style of your own and build your wardrobe with unique pieces by purchasing clothes at a substantial discount. Thrift stores usually have great deals on coats, sweaters, dresses and sport jackets. You can find gently used brand names that will cost only a fraction of the price charged at regular retail stores. A trip to the area thrift stores can be a fun activity for friends, or even a cheap date. Many thrift stores also carry sturdy furniture that might even make it into your permanent collection. Look for strong wooden tables, chairs, desks, dressers, bookshelves, and couches.

Step 3: Learn to tell a real bargain from a rip-off. It will help you to know and recognize some of the oldest tricks in the book.

The Old Bait 'N' Switch. Some businesses will lure you into the store by making an offer that sounds too good to be true. They will then lead you to a different purchase once they get you through the door. Even though this practice is illegal in many states, it still occurs far too often. Here's how it works: A merchant takes out an advertisement for a sale item available for an incredibly low price, so you rush to the store. The salesperson tells you that the store has run out of that item but offers a similar one at a higher price, of course. Since you had your heart set on making the purchase, you go ahead and buy it. That's not smart shopping. Stand firm. Make the salesperson honor the advertised price.

Did the store really run out? Most likely not. The business may never have intended to sell the item at that price at all. It used the item (the bait) and the price to get you into the store with money in hand. Once you were inside, ready to make a bargain buy, the merchant thought he could persuade you to buy something else and let go of more of your cash. Unfortunately, this old trick often works.

Avoid falling into the bait 'n' switch trap by politely but firmly insisting on the advertised item. If the sales clerk tries to lead you to a similar item at a higher price, refuse to make the purchase. If the item is out of stock, ask for a rain-check, a coupon that will allow you to buy the item at the advertised price when it comes in. Make sure it does not have an expiration date and ask when they expect to get another one in. If they don't have a similar item at the advertised price, you may end up getting a better deal on a more expensive and higher quality item. Insist on it.

A Going-Out-Of-Business Sale Every Week? Don't be surprised when some merchants advertise a sale that really isn't a sale at all. They inflate prices on the merchandise the week before the sale and then mark it down for the sale. Obviously, the marked down price doesn't reflect a true savings; it is the usual price. Before you shop, call or look around different stores for similar items and decide what is a fair price for the merchandise and what would make it a bargain buy. Frequent different stores that you like to shop so you are familiar with prices.

To protect yourself against this false mark-down tactic, become a wise shopper. Window shop occasionally just to acquaint yourself with prices, especially if you plan to buy a certain item, say, when you get our next paycheck. If an item you are interested in is advertised as on sale, do some comparison shopping. Call several other stores in the area and ask for their price on the same item. Take advantage of the sale only if it reflects a true savings over the originally marked price.

You might be offered a certain incentive for acting quickly and purchasing a certain product before you leave the store. A merchant might offer you a free gift if you make an expensive purchase, but the cost of the gift has been built in to the price of the expensive item. In essence, you've paid for the free gift. This is meant to entice you into making a major purchase.

You must buy now! To avoid costly mistakes, never purchase an expensive item without taking time to think it over and do some comparison shopping. A salesperson is naturally eager to make a quick sale and collect commission, but if he or she starts applying undue pressure, back up. You have to think about your own pocketbook and satisfaction.

If you give into pressure tactics, you might lose some of your own hard-earned money. As a customer, the control is yours if you take it—no one can force you to buy. "Thanks, I'll think about it." Then politely leave the store and walk or drive around the block for a few minutes, enjoy a meal or sleep on the decision overnight. While you're thinking about it, call around to compare prices on the same item at two or three other stores. A salesperson will very rarely deny you an incentive for taking your time to decide. In fact, a savvy salesperson will often sweeten the deal to make the sell. If you decide that you still want the item, return to the store and buy it. As a courtesy, ask for the salesperson who worked with you earlier so that he or she can receive the commission.

Step 4: Don't let your guard down at home. You

don't even have to leave your house to shop, but even though you're at home you are not necessarily safe from consumer rip-offs. Items sold over the Internet, on television, in mail-order catalogs and by door-to-door sales people can be especially difficult to resist. By law, you have an out if you succumb and regret your purchase immediately, or even a few days afterward.

Under federal law, you have a cooling off period that allows you to cancel any sales contract within *three days* as long as you bought the merchandise anywhere other than the seller's place of business. That includes your home, office, a flea market, a swap meet and so on. On large purchases, the cooling off period may be as long as *ten days* from the date of purchase. Some states protect used car buyers with "lemon laws." Check with your local Better Business Bureau to see if these laws apply in your area. You don't want to wait too long to cancel a sales contract. Remember the old adage: *Buyer Beware!*

The Internet is trickier. Internet companies come and go; they often disappear without a cosmic trace. The problem is if they go, they still have your credit card number, and you may have no recourse. Deal with reputable companies that give you a phone number on their website, preferably toll-free, so that you can discuss potential problems with a real person. Having a physical address for the company also provides a measure of safety. However, the only way to buy most Internet merchandise is by using a credit card. If you do not know the company, you may have just given your credit card number to someone who will use it or sell it. Be cautious. Find out about the return and refund policy, shipping costs, guarantees and warranties.

If you decide to buy through the mail, deal only with reputable, established companies. If you have a question about the business, call the Better Business Bureau or Department of Business Regulations in their area. These watchdog groups often have sites on the Internet to help consumers make wise decisions. See if

*D*id you know? *Impulse buys made from door-to-door salespeople or telemarketers need not be binding. Under Federal Trade Commission rules, you have three days to reconsider at-home purchases and cancel the transaction without penalty.*

there have been any complaints filed against the company. The Department of Business Regulations can give information about how long they have been in business and how often they have changed addresses. They can also tell you of there have been complaints lodged against the business you are considering dealing with.

Step 5: If you're not satisfied, return the item. You don't have to give a reason for a return—you simply need to give the seller written notice that you want to cancel the contract for a large purchase and return the item intact. The salesperson should give you a printed cancellation of the contract. If you don't get one, write a note stating that you want to cancel the purchase. Mail it to the seller by registered or certified mail. Be sure to cancel the contract within 72 hours after the purchase.

What happens next? You're entitled to your money back. You can also get back anything you used as a trade-in. Of course, you must return the item. The company should pay for return postage and handling or send an agent to pick it up. If the salesperson doesn't come to get the merchandise within 30 days (you'll have the date from the certified mail receipt), you get to keep it in addition to your refund. In most cases, you can insist on receiving your refund and paid return mail certificate before sending the merchandise back.

Step 6: *Never* send cash through the mail. If you send cash, you have no proof you ever made the purchase. Likewise, do not send a personal check to a mail-order company that you haven't checked out. *Checking account numbers can be used like credit card numbers.* You can ask that the merchandise be delivered COD (cash on delivery), but few companies offer such a service because in most cases the customer doesn't have the money at the time of delivery or has reconsidered the purchase.

Many companies won't do business COD because the merchandise is often rejected at the door. Don't let yourself be "guilted" into buying something you never asked for. If you did ask for it, however, and fail to pay for it, the company can and will make a negative report about you to at least one credit bureau.

Warranties & Guarantees

Simply stated, a warranty or guarantee tells you by law the degree to which a manufacturer, distributor or retailer must stand behind the products he or she sells. Historically, warranties and guarantees have been difficult to understand. While laws vary from state to state, the basics regarding warranties and guarantees are much the same. First, you need to understand the difference between the two kinds of warranties.

Warranty Type 1: An 'implied warranty' is just that—implied. It's not written down, but it does provide protection when you are purchasing merchandise. An implied warranty basically says that you are entitled to a refund or replacement of the merchandise if the item doesn't work properly when used as intended.

Let's say you buy two molded plastic chairs. You take them home, plunk them down at your kitchen table and start sitting on them during meals. After three weeks, the chairs start buckling and cracking. Are you entitled to a refund or replacement? Yes, you are, because it is logical to assume that chairs are meant to be sat on and should last for more than three weeks unless the label expressly stated some use restrictions that you violated. Since you were using the chairs in a reasonable manner, your implied warranty should provide a refund.

Now, let's say you buy the same two molded plastic chairs. You take them home, but instead of plunking them down at your table, you use them to stand on so you can reach the high shelves in your closet. After

Dad says:
If you receive something through the mail that you did not order, do not pay for it. By federal law, you are entitled to consider unordered merchandise as a gift. You can use it, give it away or throw it away, but you are under no obligation to pay for it or pay the mailing costs to have it returned to the company.

three weeks, they start buckling and cracking. Are you entitled to a refund or replacement? No. Chairs aren't made to stand on. You shouldn't assume that a chair will hold up if you stand on it. Since you used the chairs to stand on (a use other than the one they were intended for) you are out of luck.

An implied warranty also protects you in some other situations. If you ask a salesperson for an item that will meet a specific need or use, but you get something else, an implied warranty allows you to return the item for a refund or exchange. If you specifically ask a clerk for a food processor that will also grind meat and you find that the food processor he sells you won't do the job, you're entitled to your money back—or a replacement with a food processor that will grind meat.

Warranty Type 2: An 'expressed' or 'formal written warranty' spells it out. This should tell you exactly what your rights are. Written warranties accompany many different kinds of manufactured items, from computers and washing machines to pocket calculators and television sets. Warranties offer you certain rights, but they also spell out certain limitations and conditions. For example, many warranties specify that the item is no longer covered if you have tried to repair it yourself or if you have taken it to an unauthorized repair agent or dealer.

Written warranties may be limited or full and are generally in effect for a specified amount of time. A limited warranty is one that covers only certain things, such as parts but not labor, in case something goes wrong with the merchandise. A full warranty, on the other hand, covers all costs associated with repair or replacement. You should know that warranties can be invalidated if you have abused an item or clearly used it in a way other than the way intended by the manufacturer. As a consumer, you have an obligation to use products in a reasonable way.

Did you know? Practically everything you buy in a store is covered by an implied warranty. It's understood the item will hold up for a reasonable length of time.

Understanding Warranties

Step 1: To be legal, warranties have to meet certain standards. The warranty must be written in clear language that is understandable to any person who reads it—it can't be garbled with legal or unfamiliar terms. The length of a full warranty has to be written at the top of the warranty, and the length of a limited warranty must be spelled out in the text.

The warranty must be made available to you as a prospective buyer before you agree to purchase the item. It must clearly spell out what you should do if problems arise, and it must contain clear directions on how to register a complaint about the product. Warranties should also tell you where to go for repairs and service. Look for an anti-lemon clause that entitles you to replacement or refund, if you have tried to have it repaired a reasonable number of times.

Finally, you can transfer a full warranty to someone else if you sell or give the product away while still protected under warranty. The new owner retains all rights as though he or she bought the item originally. A limited warranty may or may not be transferable, but that distinction must be clearly made in the warranty itself so that there will be no confusion.

Step 2: If there's a problem, send a written complaint. If you have a problem with a product that is covered by warranty, start by sending a written complaint to the seller or manufacturer. The address will likely be on the warranty itself. The warranty should contain information on how to settle a dispute. Follow that procedure. If you still don't get satisfaction, you are entitled to sue. If the product falls within dollar limitations, you can take the case to small claims court. You can file a registered complaint against the manufacturer or seller with the Federal Trade Commission, Sixth and Pennsylvania Avenues N.W., Washington, D.C. 20580.

Dad says:
File warranties in an accessible place. Don't throw them away. If you do chuck a warranty, fate will have it that the merchandise is sure to break down.

Getting Your Money Back

Do you feel cheated as a consumer? You only need two things, a telephone and a pen, to make your voice heard and get the satisfaction you deserve. As a consumer, you have rights (usually under implied warranty), and the law will protect you. But it only happens if you make it happen by working some strategies in your favor.

Before you do anything at all, carefully review the problem. Make certain that you are not at fault. If you are satisfied that the fault lies with the seller or manufacturer, decide what you would like them to do about it. Do you want the item repaired at no charge? Do you want the item replaced with a similar model? Or do you just want your money back? Would you accept a merchandise credit at the store where you bought the item, or would you rather not deal with that store or salesperson again?

Step 1: Start with a personal contact. If the business is local, visit in person. If it's some distance away, call. Ask for the customer service representative or the manager. Write down the name of the person you speak with. Tell what you purchased, the date you purchased it, what's wrong and what you would like done. Make sure all your facts are straight. Be courteous, unemotional, brief and to the point. Be firm, but don't get angry or confrontational, and don't use profanity.

Step 2: Get a promise. If the customer service representative or manager agrees to your demands, restate what has been agreed to, such as, "Then I can expect a store representative here on Wednesday morning to pick up the television set for repairs at your expense?" Be sure to make a notation of the call, recording the date, time, person's name and the outcome or agreement. If the person you speak with refuses to help you, inform him that you want to speak with someone who has more authority.

Step 3: If things aren't resolved, make one more call. Call the store again and ask to speak to the person you dealt with before. Find out the status of your complaint. What is being done? Why didn't someone arrive as promised or follow through with the agreement? Set up another appointment for the matter to be resolved. Give the store a deadline such as seven or ten days in which to get the problem fixed. State firmly but politely that you will need to take further action if this commitment falls through.

Step 4: Write to the manufacturer. If you are still not satisfied and the store has failed to resolve the situation, write to the manufacturer. They need to know which retailers are not customer friendly. The manufacturer's address is usually printed on the product label. If you can't find it, call the store and ask for it. Again, make sure you have all the facts straight before you call or write the manufacturer.

Your letter needs to look neat, and if possible, professionally typed. Type it single spaced on plain white paper or letterhead. Don't lose you temper or make threats. Keep the letter business-like and to the point. Make it short – one page or less. Remember: You get more bees with honey than with vinegar. If you're polite, you'll get some cooperation. Begin the letter or conversation with a compliment, if possible. For example, express why you were attracted to the product to begin with. Describe what you purchased, including model or serial number. Tell what the problem is, then describe precisely what you have done to try to get the problem resolved to this point. Use names and dates, if possible.

Step 5: Tell them how you want the problem resolved. Again, give a time limit, such as two weeks. Let the manufacturer know what you will do if the problem is not resolved to your satisfaction. Close the letter with a pleasant hope that the matter will be remedied quickly. Always ask for exactly what you want—you may get what you ask for. Mail the letter by

Did you know? Unsatisfied customers do have an outlet for public complaint. Many television stations, radio stations and newspapers have consumer-action reporters who expose unsavory business practices in the community. If there is one where you live, take advantage of it. You'll be doing fellow consumers a favor.

registered or certified mail so that you have proof that it was mailed to and received by the manufacturer. Keep photocopies of all correspondence relating to the situation.

Step 6: Try one last time. Wait four to six weeks after mailing the first letter to the manufacturer before doing anything further. If six weeks have passed and you haven't heard anything, call or write again. This time, use a firmer tone. Send a copy of the first letter you sent along with this follow-up letter. Give a specific deadline and clearly outline what you intend to do if the problem continues, such as issuing a formal complaint to the Better Business Bureau, writing letters to newspapers and magazines, encouraging a consumer boycott or suing in court.

Step 7: As a last resort, sue. Take it to court, especially if this is a high-cost item or if the defect is a safety hazard. If you have tried all the above approaches and the matter is not resolved, sue the store and the manufacturer. This is where your receipts, notes, dates, times, names and copies of letters will serve you well. For small investments, you can take the matter to small claims court. You may also report the store and manufacturer to the State Business Licensing Division and the Federal Trade Commission with details of your transaction. These agencies will not give you relief, but your complaint will serve as a red flag to other consumers who are contemplating a similar purchase involving the same store or manufacturer.

Finally, contact the consumer protection agency and register a complaint. The agency may be able to get some relief for you and will monitor the business for future violations. When your hard-earned money is involved, don't hesitate to stand up for your rights.

If the problem involved mail-order merchandise, register your complaint with the Chief Postal Inspector, U.S. Postal Inspection Service, Washington, D.C., 20260-2100. If postal fraud is proven, you could get some or all of your money back.

Small Claims Court

Minor legal problems and those involving a limited amount of money, usually a few hundred dollars, can be settled in small claims court. It's a way for you to get legal relief without the expense of any attorney. Basically, small claims court is an arbitrator. It allows two parities who disagree to come together, present their evidence, have it heard by a qualified judge and have a judgment rendered. Small claims courts award money only. They do not have the authority to require a specific action. If the wrongful party refuses to pay, most small claims courts will assist you by assigning law enforcement to collect.

Step 1: Make sure you have the right court. You'll find the courts listed in the yellow pages of your telephone directory. Call the clerk and find out where you should file your complaint. Generally, you will need to sue in the city or county where the person you are suing lives or does business. The clerk can verify any local laws for you. You'll need to pay a nominal fee, usually about $10, and fill out a complaint. Detail your problem on the complaint form, and be specific. You will be assigned a court date. The court will notify the person you are suing by mail.

Step 2: Gather all possible witnesses and evidence. Friends, colleagues or others who have been involved in or who witnessed the situation are qualified to testify in your behalf. Collect all of the documents you can, such as photocopies of letters, cancelled checks, contracts, photographs and related bills. You won't have an attorney to represent you. At small claims court, you represent yourself. In the week or two before your hearing, organize your thoughts and evidence to present to the judge. Create a written outline to help you remember details.

Step 3: Show up on time. Dress conservative and comfortable in casual business attire. Because you are the one suing, you'll be asked to present and explain

any documents you brought to back you up. Introduce witnesses and ask that the judge give them a chance to speak. When you've finished, the judge may ask you questions about the case.

After you've finished presenting your case, the judge will cross-examine that person as well. Then depending on time and the judge's opinion, your witnesses may be given a chance to speak and may be cross-examined.

In some courts, judgment will be rendered at the end of the hearing. Many courts mail you a decision within a week. If you obtain a judgment but the person you sued refuses to pay, try writing him or her a letter. If that doesn't work, contact the court clerk and ask for help from law enforcement.

A person who does not show to a court proceeding may have a bench warrant written against them, meaning they can be picked up by police to show at another court proceeding, or pay bail. There are no debtors' prisons, but having a few bench warrants out on you for civil court proceedings can land you in jail.

If You Sue, Follow These Guidelines:

• Don't joke around. Listen carefully to each question and answer it as well as you can. If you're not sure what the judge is asking, politely ask for clarification. Answer questions briefly and clearly.
• Don't lose your temper.
• Don't volunteer information you are not being asked.
• Don't get distracted and talk about unrelated matters.
• Don't lie or exaggerate. Never make up information to make your case stronger—an experienced judge will see through it. If you do not know the answer to a question, be truthful and say, "I don't know."

Handling Bill Collectors

If you regularly receive bills from credit card companies, loan companies, doctors' offices, etc., you know by now that you're dealing with a computer, not a human being. You also know that computers, like human beings, can make mistakes. They are only as good as the information put into them. What if a mistake turns up on your utility bill? You're protected by federal law and you have the right to be heard—by a person.

Step 1: Let the company know there's a mistake on your bill. You need to inform the company by voice and in writing, if possible. Explain exactly why you think the bill is wrong. Some experts suggest that you make purchases and payments by credit card, because credit card companies usually offer extra protection against misrepresentation. For example, if you made the purchase in your home state or within 100 miles of your home, or you were responding to an advertisement from the credit card company and the merchandise cost more than $50, you can simply inform the credit card company of the problem and that you will not pay the bill. If you have tried unsuccessfully to settle the problem with the merchant, you are generally not required to pay the bill.

Step 2: Stand up for yourself, and get the bill adjusted. If the company finds that you are right, it must adjust the bill. When your next bill arrives, make sure the disputed amount and any associated charges have been taken off. If the company still thinks you are wrong, the company needs to give you a reason why.

What if you remain convinced that you are right? You have ten days in which to send the company another letter stating that you still dispute the bill. *That's a critical deadline you shouldn't miss.* It keeps negotiations open, and the company is required by law to report to all credit agencies that the matter is being disputed. As a result, you won't be reported as just casually making a late payment. At that point, you need to produce documentation to prove your case. Keep copies of receipts and all correspondence with the company. Stand up for your rights and keep fighting until you are satisfied with the decision.

Do Almost Anything

Fold An American Flag

"I pledge allegiance to the Flag
of the United States of America,
and to the Republic for which it stands:
One Nation under God, indivisible,
with Liberty and Justice for all."

When folding an American flag, special care should be taken to ensure that no part of the flag touches the ground. The flag is carefully folded into the shape of a tri-cornered hat, symbolic of the hats worn by colonial soldiers during the country's fight for independence in the American Revolutionary War.

Step 1: You will need a partner to fold the flag properly. Begin by holding the flag waist-high between the two of you so that its surface is parallel to the ground. The person at the top of the flag (the blue end) should grasp the corner of the blue field in his left hand and the striped corner in his right hand. The other person takes the two striped corners so that the flag is laid out lengthwise between you. *(See Illustration A on page 61.)* The second person does most of the folding. For these instructions, you will be the person doing the folding.

Step 2: Fold the flag twice lengthwise. Do this by folding the striped section lengthwise to your right so that the stripes fold over the blue field of stars. *(See Illustrations B and C on page 61.)* The fold will be at your left and the open edges at your right. Make sure the edges meet evenly. Repeat *(see C)*. Now the blue field should be on top, and the open edges still at your right.

Step 3: Make a triangular fold. Bring the striped corner of the folded edge at your left across to meet the open edge of the flag at your right. *(See Illustration D on page 62.)* Now a point should be in your right hand. Fold the outer point up and parallel to the open edge. *(See Illustration E on page 62).* Now fold from right to left so the point is in your left hand. *(See Illustration F on page 62).* Then fold point up, parallel to the folded edge.

Step 4: Repeat triangular folding. When the flag is completely folded, only a triangular blue field of stars should be visible. *(See Illustration G on page 62).*

If you weren't in Scouts, you may not know proper flag etiquette. The handling, display and storage of the American flag is spelled out in the U.S. Flag Code. Some points taken from that code include:

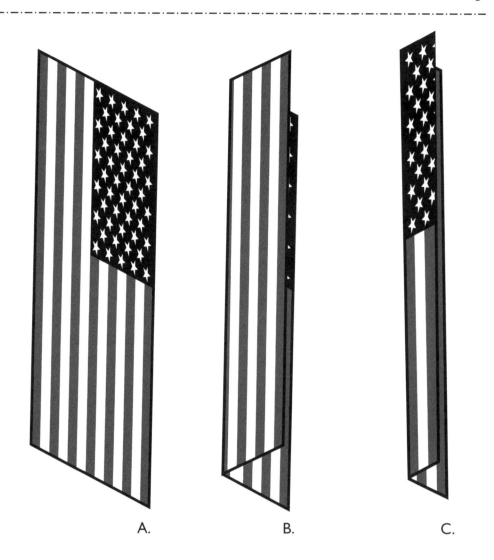

A.   B.   C.

• The flag should never be displayed with the union (blue field) down, except as a signal of dire distress in instances of extreme danger to life or property.

• The flag should never touch anything beneath it, such as the ground, the floor, water, or merchandise.

• The flag should not be used as wearing apparel, bedding, or drapery. It should never be used as a covering for a ceiling.

• The flag should not be used for advertising purposes. It should not be embroidered on such articles as cushions or handkerchiefs, printed or otherwise impressed on paper napkins or boxes or anything that is designed for temporary use.

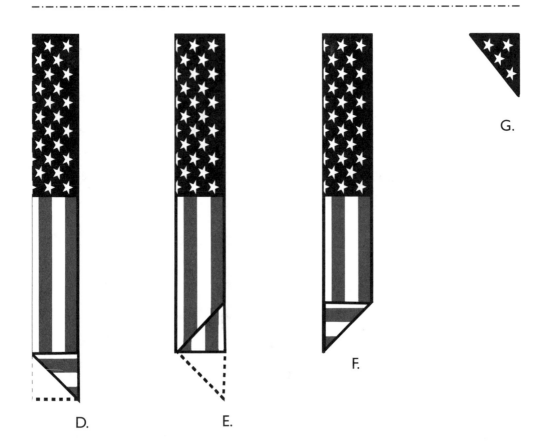

D. E. F. G.

• No part of the flag should be used as a costume or athletic uniform. However, a flag patch may be affixed to the uniform of military personnel, fire fighters, police officers and members of patriotic organizations.

• The flag represents a living country and is itself considered a living thing. The lapel flag pin, being a replica, should be worn on the left lapel near the heart.

• The flag, when it is in such condition that it is no longer a fitting emblem for display, should be destroyed in a dignified way, preferably by burning.

Notes

4

Fill Your Belly
Dad's Favorite Recipes

Most of the recipes make enough to satisfy four to six people.

Dad seems to gravitate toward extreme cooking. He does things that require a bit of risk and some specific talent such as dutch oven cooking, outdoor grilling and tailgaiting picnics. Fathers also seem to have some food specialties they enjoy cooking, like homemade rootbeer, various types of chili, marinated steak or old-fashioned ice cream. You will find quick, nutritious recipes with a unique Dad-style twist. While the companion book *Where's Mom Now That I Need Her?* provides traditional basic recipes, Dad's recipes reach a bit further into the surprising and exotic. Try great recipes for quick and easy appetizers, beverages, eggs, breakfast favorites and sandwiches. Learn how to select and cook the best meats. You'll find recipes from a good old meat and potatoes to exotic (but simple) tailgating grub and secrets to a fantastic game-day celebration. Dad has a few tricks up his sleeve that make cooking fun. ***Use the blank pages following each section to jot down your Dad's Specialties.***

Never-Fail Appetizers

Bacon Spinach Snacks

8-oz. tub low-fat sour cream
1 bunch fresh spinach
1 red onion, diced well

1/2 cup Swiss cheese, grated
1 lb. bacon, cooked crisp and crumbled

Clean and chop spinach leaves. Mix sour cream, spinach, red onion, Swiss cheese and bacon. Let sit in refrigerator for one hour. Spread on large crackers.

Crab on Avocado

8-oz. pkg. frozen crab meat, thawed
2 tsp. onion, minced
2 Tbsp. ketchup
4 Tbsp. mayonnaise or salad dressing

Salt and pepper
1 large avocado, peeled and sliced
3 slices American cheese, halved
Large round snack crackers

Combine crab meat, onion, ketchup and mayonnaise or salad dressing. Add salt and pepper to taste. Top large, round crackers each with avocado slice. Spoon crab-meat mixture onto avocado. Top with half slice of cheese. Broil 4 to 5 minutes or until cheese melts. Makes 12 appetizers.

Creamy Ham Rollups

6 small flour tortillas
8-oz. tub spreadable cream cheese
6 slices sandwich ham

6 green onions
Wooden toothpicks

Spread thin layer of cream cheese on flour tortillas. Top with one slice ham. Spread ham with thin layer of cheese. Wash and trim green onions to the width of ham slices. Place one green onion at end of each ham slice. Roll tortilla and ham around onion. Cut into bite-sized pieces. Secure with toothpicks, if needed. Makes 24 appetizers.

Designer Dipped Veggies

3 cups fresh cauliflower flowerets
1 1/2 cups fresh snow pea pods
8-oz. pkg. cream cheese, softened
1 cup mayonnaise or salad dressing
2 tsp. lime peel, finely shredded

1/4 cup lime juice
2 Tbsp. Dijon mustard
2 tsp. horseradish
1/4 tsp. salt

In large saucepan, cook cauliflower about 1 minute (or until tender but crisp) in enough boiling water to cover. Drain. Run under cold water. Repeat with fresh pea pods except cook for only 30 seconds. Cover vegetables and chill. In medium bowl, stir together cream cheese and mayonnaise or salad dressing. Stir in lime peel, lime juice, mustard, horseradish and salt. Cover and chill several hours. Arrange cauliflower and snow peas on serving plate with bowl of sauce.

Free-Range Buffalo Wings

24 chicken wings
1/2 cup melted butter
1/4 cup hot sauce

3 Tbsp. apple cider vinegar
2 pkg. dry ranch dressing mix
1/2 tsp. paprika

Clean chicken wings and pat with paper towel to dry. Mix together melted butter, hot sauce and vinegar. Dip chicken into mixture. Place in baking pan. Sprinkle with dry dressing mix. Bake at 350 degrees for 20 to 25 minutes or until browned, turning once. Sprinkle with paprika. Serve with prepared ranch dressing and celery sticks.

Little Italy Pizza Bits

1 prepared pizza shell
1 Tbsp. olive oil
1 tsp. Italian seasoning
1 tsp. onion, minced
1/2 tsp. thyme leaves

1/2 cup mozzarella cheese, shredded
1 cup thinly sliced vegetables such as red
    pepper, zucchini, mushrooms, onions
1 can sliced black olives, drained
1/4 cup Parmesan cheese, shredded

Place pizza shell on cookie sheet. In a medium bowl, toss together olive oil, Italian seasoning, onion, thyme, mozzarella cheese and vegetables. Spread mixture over pizza shell. Top with olives and Parmesan cheese. Bake for eight to ten minutes. Cut into two-inch squares.

Ginger Egg Rolls

4 oz. Chinese cellophane noodles
1/2 lb. ground pork
1/4 lb. frozen shrimp, peeled and deveined
1 cup carrots, shredded
1/4 cup green onions, chopped
2 tsp. fresh ginger, finely chopped

2 cloves garlic, minced
1 Tbsp. soy sauce
1 tsp. sesame oil
10 egg roll skins
1 Tbsp. all-purpose flour
Cooking oil

Soak noodles in cold water for 10 minutes. Drain. In medium pan, cook noodles, pork, shrimp, carrots, onions, ginger and garlic until pork is cooked through. (Add one tablespoon cooking oil if needed.) Drain off fat. Stir in soy sauce and sesame oil. Spoon one rounded tablespoon of mixture along half the width of each egg roll skin. Fold opposite ends to center, then, starting from the long side, roll up envelope-style. Mix together flour and 1 tablespoon of water and brush on edges of each egg roll. Press to seal. Deep fry in hot oil about one minute or until golden brown. Drain well.

Orange-Barbecue Mini Dogs

1/3 cup packed brown sugar
1 Tbsp. cornstarch
1 tsp. chili powder
8-oz. can tomato sauce
1/2 cup white vinegar

1/2 cup ketchup
1/2 cup dark corn syrup
1/4 cup orange liqueur or orange juice
1 pkg. pre-cooked mini-sausages

In medium saucepan, stir together the packed brown sugar, cornstarch and chili powder. Stir the tomato sauce, vinegar, ketchup and dark corn syrup into the brown sugar mixture in the saucepan. Add 1/2 cup water. Bring mixture to boiling. Reduce the heat to low and simmer, uncovered, for 30 minutes, stirring occasionally. Stir orange liqueur or orange juice into the tomato sauce mixture. Return the mixture to boiling. Add mini-sausages. Reduce the heat. Simmer, uncovered, for five minutes more.

Shrimp Cucumber Toast

1 lb. shrimp, peeled and deveined
2 medium cucumbers, peeled and seeded
8-oz. pkg. cream cheese, softened
1/4 cup onion, chopped
1/4 cup mayonnaise or salad dressing

1/4 tsp. garlic salt
Green food coloring
Soft multi-grain bread, lightly toasted
Fresh dill

Steam shrimp. Chill thoroughly and set aside. Peel cucumbers and remove seeds. Chop. In small bowl, combine cucumbers, cream cheese, onion, mayonnaise or salad dressing, garlic salt, and a few drops of food coloring. Toast bread then cut out middle using cookie cutter. Spread toast rounds with cream-cheese mixture. Top with shrimp. Garnish with dill.

Spiced Baked Onions

3 large white onions
3 Tbsp. brown sugar
1 Tbsp. butter
1 tsp. salt

1/4 tsp. nutmeg
Dash pepper
6 whole cloves garlic
2 Tbsp. toasted slivered almonds

Boil onions for five minutes. Drain. Cut in half and place in baking dish. Melt and mix brown sugar, butter, salt, nutmeg and pepper. Drizzle over onions. Place two whole cloves in the center of each onion. Bake at 325 degrees for 45 minutes until tender. Before serving, sprinkle with toasted almonds.

Zippy Zucchini Bites

2 Tbsp. green onion, chopped
1 clove garlic, minced
1 Tbsp. butter or margarine
1 1/2 cups zucchini, shredded
3 eggs, slightly beaten

1 1/2 cups Monterey Jack cheese,
    shredded
3 Tbsp. cornmeal
1/4 tsp. powdered cumin
1/4 tsp. dried oregano

In large pan, cook onion and garlic in butter or margarine until onion is tender but not brown. Add zucchini and stir about two minutes or until tender. Remove from heat. In large bowl, mix eggs, cheese, cornmeal, cumin, oregano and zucchini mixture. Mix until well combined. Spoon mixture into individual mini-muffin tins. Bake at 325 degrees for 15 to 18 minutes or until set. Serve hot. Makes about 24 appetizers.

Dad's Specialties

DAD'S Specialties

Best Beverages

Very Berry Milk

2 cups milk
1 cup fresh strawberries

4 Tbsp. sugar
2 Tbsp. orange juice

Remove green tops of strawberries. Slice strawberries. Pour all ingredients into blender. Blend until smooth. Serve immediately. Makes two servings.

Chocolate Eggnog

1 1/2 quarts chilled eggnog
3/4 cup chocolate syrup
3/4 cup whipping cream

4 tsp. sugar
1 1/2 tsp. cocoa
1/2 oz. semisweet chocolate, grated

In a large punch bowl, combine eggnog and chocolate syrup. Set aside. In a small bowl, combine cream, sugar and cocoa. Whip at high speed until stiff. Spoon cream onto eggnog and sprinkle with grated chocolate. Makes 12 servings.

Easy Eggnog

2 eggs, well beaten
15-oz. can sweetened condensed milk
1 tsp. vanilla
1/4 tsp. salt

1 quart milk
1/2 pint cream, whipped
Nutmeg

Mix eggs, condensed milk, vanilla and salt until well blended. Gradually blend in milk. Fold in whipped cream and sprinkle with nutmeg. Ladle into cups.

Strawberry Nog

2 eggs
3 Tbsp. honey
1 cup apricot nectar
1 cup orange juice

1/2 cup nonfat dry milk
1 Tbsp. lemon juice
1 cup strawberries
Strawberry slices for garnish

In a small bowl, beat eggs until thick. Gradually add honey, beating constantly. Set aside. In a blender combine the apricot nectar, orange juice, milk powder and lemon juice. Cover and blend until well mixed. Add strawberries, egg and honey mixture and blend until smooth. Pour into four glasses. Garnish with strawberry slices. Store covered in refrigerator. Stir before serving.

24-Hour Root Beer

2 cups sugar
2 Tbsp. root beer extract

1 tsp. dry yeast
1 gallon warm water

In plastic or glass gallon jug or bottle, combine sugar, root beer extract and yeast. Fill jug half full with warm water and shake well to dissolve sugar. Continue filling container with warm water to within 1/2 inch of the top. Cap tightly and put in the refrigerator for at least 24 hours. Serve over crushed ice.

Hot Mulled Cider

1 1/2 quarts cranberry juice
2 quarts apple juice
2 cups unsweetened pineapple juice
1/2 cup brown sugar, firmly packed

1/2 tsp. salt
4 cinnamon sticks
6 whole cloves
1/4 cup butter or margarine

Pour cranberry juice, apple juice and pineapple juice into a large kettle. Tie cinnamon sticks and whole cloves in a cheesecloth bag and add to the juice mixture. Stir in brown sugar and salt. Heat to boiling. Reduce heat and simmer 30 minutes. Remove spice bag. Add butter just before serving. Makes enough for 40 guests.

Hot Pineapple Punch

4 cups pineapple juice
2 cups apple cider
1 cup apricot nectar

1 cup orange juice
3/4 cup brown sugar
6 whole cloves

Combine all ingredients in large saucepan. Heat to boiling. Reduce heat and simmer for ten minutes. Strain out cloves. Serve punch hot.

Hot Spiced Tomato Juice

2 1/2 cups tomato juice
3 Tbsp. brown sugar, firmly packed
3 whole cloves

1 cinnamon stick
2 lemon slices

In saucepan, combine all ingredients. Bring to a boil. Reduce heat and simmer five minutes. Remove cloves, cinnamon stick and lemon slices before serving. Serves four.

Spiced Mocha Mix

1 cup non-dairy creamer
1 cup instant chocolate drink mix
2/3 cup instant coffee

1/2 cup sugar
1/2 tsp. cinnamon
1/4 tsp. nutmeg

Mix well and store in covered container. To serve, put three heaping teaspoons of mix in coffee mug. Add six ounces hot water. To add even more spice flavor, stir with a cinnamon stick.

Banana Fruit Punch

2 1/2 cups sugar
2 1/2 cups water
24-oz. can pineapple juice
Juice of 2 oranges

Juice of 2 lemons
3 bananas, mashed with fork
Ginger ale or lemon-lime soda, chilled
Crushed ice

In a saucepan, heat sugar and water together until sugar is completely dissolved. Remove from heat. Stir in pineapple juice, orange juice, lemon juice and bananas. Mix well. Pour into a container, cover and freeze, stirring occasionally during freezing. When ready to serve, fill a glass 1/3 full with fruit slush, 1/3 with chilled soda and 1/3 full with crushed ice. Makes enough to fill 25 glasses.

---

*D*ad *says:*
You don't have to serve wine or alcoholic specialty drinks to dress up a meal. Whip up a unique, tasty fruit drink and pour it into a fancy glass, then garnish the drink with fresh fruit slices or a mint leaf.

Jamaican Citrus Punch

2 oranges
40 whole cloves
46-oz. can orange Hawaiian punch

2 cups grapefruit juice
1/2 cup light corn syrup
1 orange, sliced

Wash oranges well and stud each orange with 20 whole cloves. Bake in 400-degree oven for one hour. Oranges will turn dark brown. Place oranges in bottom of deep bowl. Mix remaining ingredients and pour over oranges. Chill for eight hours. When ready to serve, remove oranges, peel and section. Place peeled sections into punch. Ladle drink into sugar-rimmed glasses and garnish with orange slices.

Lemon -Lime Quencher

2 quarts cold water
6-oz. can frozen orange juice
6-oz. can frozen lemonade

6-oz. can frozen limeade
32-oz. bottle ginger ale, chilled
Fresh mint leaves for garnish

Combine all ingredients until well mixed. Pour over crushed ice and garnish with mint leaves. Serves 12.

Marshmallow-Peach Shake

1 1/2 cups milk
7-oz. jar marshmallow creme

1 cup ice cubes
2 cups peeled peach slices

Put milk and marshmallow creme in blender. Cover and blend until smooth. Add ice cubes and peach slices. Blend until smooth. Pour into two tall glasses. Garnish with additional peach slices if desired.

Minty Lemonade

1 cup sugar
1 1/4 cups water
1/2 cup orange juice or juice of 1 orange

3/4 cup lemon juice or juice of 3 lemons
1/2 cup fresh mint leaves

In a saucepan, combine sugar and water. Bring to boil, reduce heat and cook for five minutes. Cool. Add fruit juices and stir in mint leaves. Cover and let stand for one hour. Strain into a glass jar, screw on lid tightly and store in refrigerator. To serve, pour 1/3 cup mixture into each glass, filling with crushed ice and water to taste. Serves five.

Orange-Mocha Cooler

2 cups orange juice
1 cup milk
3 Tbsp. chocolate syrup

1 cup coffee-flavored ice cream
1 1/2 cups lemon-lime soda, chilled

In large pitcher, combine orange juice, milk and chocolate syrup. Stir to mix well. Pour, dividing evenly, into four tall glasses. Top each with a generous scoop of ice cream. Finish filling with soda. Stir and serve.

Orange-Peach Delight

2 large ripe peaches, peeled and sliced
1 cup orange juice
1/3 cup lemon juice

1/2 cup sugar
1/4 tsp. cinnamon
Crushed ice

Combine all ingredients in blender. Blend until smooth. Serve immediately.

Orange-Pineapple Cooler

6-oz. can frozen orange juice
1 cup pineapple juice

1 1/2 cups water
1 cup lemon sherbet

In a large pitcher, combine frozen orange juice, pineapple juice and water. Stir until orange juice is thawed. Pour orange juice mixture into four glasses, dividing evenly. Top each with one scoop of sherbet. Stir and serve.

Orange-Vanilla Frosty

1 quart orange juice
1 cup vanilla ice cream

12-oz. can cream soda

Pour equal parts of orange juice into four glasses. Top with one scoop ice cream. Drizzle approximately 1/4 cup soda over each. Stir and serve immediately.

Raspberry Slush

2 cups sugar
3 1/2 cups water
1 cup orange juice
16-oz. can crushed pineapple

Two 10-oz. pkg. frozen raspberries,
   thawed and drained
1 bottle ginger ale or lemon-lime soda

In a saucepan, heat sugar and water until sugar is dissolved. Cool. Stir in orange juice, pineapple and raspberries. Stir until well mixed. Freeze in covered container. To serve, place a scoop of slush in a glass. Pour in ginger ale or lemon-lime soda. Makes enough to fill 12 glasses

Sunny Citrus Slush

1 1/4 cups sugar
1 1/2 cups water
6-oz. can frozen orange juice
6-oz. can frozen lemonade
24-oz. can pineapple juice

1 1/2 cups cold water
2 quarts ginger ale or lemon-lime soda,
   chilled
Orange, lemon and lime slices

In a large kettle, combine sugar and 1 1/2 cups water. Bring to a boil and cook until sugar is dissolved. Remove from heat. Stir in juice concentrates, pineapple juice and cold water until well blended. Pour into a 9x13 baking dish, cover and freeze overnight. Cut frozen mixture into 24 squares. Place squares in bottom of a punch bowl, and pour chilled soda over squares. Stir until the mixture is slushy, and serve by ladling into glasses. Garnish each glass with a slice of orange, lemon or lime. Makes about 16 servings.

Three-Citrus Punch

1 quart orange juice
6-oz. can frozen lemonade concentrate
6-oz. can frozen limeade concentrate

2 cups water
1-liter bottle lemon-lime soda
Orange, lemon and lime slices

In a large container or punch bowl, combine orange juice, lemonade, limeade and water. Stir until frozen concentrates are completely thawed and well blended. Chill until ready to serve. When ready to serve, stir in lemon-lime soda and float fruit slices on top. Makes eight servings.

DAD'S Specialties

Exceptional Eggs

Crab-Stuffed Eggs

6 hard-boiled eggs
1 tsp. dry mustard
1/2 tsp. salt
1 cup crab, cooked and flaked

1 cup celery, chopped
2 Tbsp. green pepper, chopped
1/4 cup mayonnaise
Dash paprika

Peel eggs, cut into halves crosswise and remove yolks. In medium bowl, mash yolks. Mix in mustard, salt, crab, celery, green pepper and mayonnaise. Blend well. Fill egg whites with crab mixture. Sprinkle with paprika. Makes 12 egg halves. Serve with buttered toast and juice.

*D*ad says:
A hard-boiled egg shouldn't really be boiled. Boiling makes eggs tough. For a tender hard-boiled egg, place the egg in a saucepan and cover with cold water. Bring the water slowly to a boil. As soon as the water boils, remove the pan from the heat. Cover the pan and let the egg stand in the hot water. For soft eggs, let stand 3 minutes. For medium eggs, 6 minutes. For hard eggs, 20 minutes. Immediately after cooking, plunge eggs into cold water. They will be easier to peel and the yolks won't have a dark coating.

Fluffy Ham & Egg Nests

6 eggs, separated
6 slices hot buttered toast
6 slices cooked ham

Salt and pepper to taste
Dash paprika

Separate egg yolks from egg whites. (Do this with an egg separator or carefully crack egg in half over a bowl and catch yolk with one shell half while letting the egg white fall into the bowl.) Place yolks in separate bowl. Season egg whites with salt and pepper. Beat until stiff enough to form sharp peaks. Place a slice of ham on each piece of toast. In the center of the ham, heap a mound of egg whites. With a spoon, make a hollow in center of each egg white mound. Slip an egg yolk into each hollow. Season with salt and pepper. Bake at 350 degrees until egg whites are browned and yolks are firm. Garnish with paprika. Serves six.

Baked Scrambled Eggs

6 eggs, beaten
1/2 cup heavy cream
Salt and pepper to taste

2 Tbsp. mushrooms, chopped and sautéed
2 tsp. onion, minced
1 cup small shrimp, cooked and broken

In large bowl, beat eggs with heavy cream. Add salt and pepper, sautéed mushrooms, onion and shrimp. Pour egg mixture into four buttered custard cups. Place custard cups in shallow baking dish with about 1/2 inch water into baking dish. Bake at 350 degrees for 15 minutes or until eggs are set. Serves four.

*D*ad says:
Scrambled eggs shouldn't really be scrambled. If you really scramble an egg, you'll get one tough customer. For tender and fluffy scrambled eggs, mix eggs, milk and dash of salt in bowl. Beat lightly with fork only until mixed. Pour into a hot skillet that contains one tablespoon melted butter. Turn the heat to low and let eggs cook, stirring only occasionally.

Italian Egg Casserole

1 1/2 dozen eggs
2 Tbsp. butter
1/4 cup milk
1/4 tsp. salt
1/8 tsp. pepper

1 cup fresh mushrooms, sliced
1/2 can cream of mushroom soup
1/4 cup sherry
1/2 cup fresh Parmesan cheese, grated
Paprika

In large bowl, combine eggs, milk, salt and pepper. Beat lightly. Pour into greased glass baking dish. In small bowl, combine mushrooms, soup and sherry. Stir well and pour over eggs. Sprinkle with Parmesan cheese and paprika. Cover and refrigerate overnight. Bake at 350 degrees for 30 minutes or until bubbly. Serves six to eight.

Oriental Chicken Omelet

2 Tbsp. onion, minced
1 Tbsp. green pepper, chopped
1 Tbsp. butter or margarine
1/2 cup drained bean sprouts

1/2 cup chicken, cooked and chopped
1/2 tsp. soy sauce
1/8 tsp. ginger

Melt butter in skillet. Add onion and green pepper, cooking until tender. Add bean sprouts, chicken, soy sauce and ginger. Heat through. Prepare Basic Omelet on page 85. Spoon mixture into omelet before folding.

> D*ad says:*
> *For great omelet fillings, mix and match favorite ingredients, such as*
> *mushrooms, cooked and crumbled bacon, chopped cooked ham, shredded*
> *cheese, chopped onions, diced tomatoes, bell peppers and avocado.*

Basic Omelet

2 Tbsp. butter or margarine
6 eggs
6 Tbsp. milk

1/2 tsp. salt
Pepper to taste

In large non-stick frying pan, melt butter over medium heat, tilting pan to coat bottom. In medium bowl, beat eggs, milk, salt and pepper until well mixed. Pour mixture into frying pan. Reduce heat to low and cook without stirring. As edges set, lift edges carefully and allow uncooked egg to flow to bottom of pan, tilting as necessary. Cook until mixture is set but top still looks moist. Spoon desired filling onto omelet. With spatula, loosen edge of omelet and fold in half as you slide omelet from pan to plate. Serves four. With a medium pan, split the mixture in half and cook two omelets.

Mexican Spicy Omelet

3/4 cup avocado, chopped
1/4 cup sour cream
2 Tbsp. green chilies, chopped
1 Tbsp. green onion, chopped

1 tsp. lemon juice
1/4 tsp. salt
Dash Tabasco sauce
1 cup Monterey Jack cheese, shredded

In large bowl, combine avocado, sour cream, chilies, green onion, lemon juice, salt and Tabasco sauce. Set aside. Prepare a Basic Omelet (see above). Before folding omelet, sprinkle with cheese. Spread half the avocado mixture on omelet and fold. Dollop remaining avocado mixture on top of omelet and serve

Ham & Cheese Oven Bake

1 cup all-purpose flour
2 Tbsp. sugar
1 Tbsp. baking powder
1/2 tsp. salt

1 egg, beaten
3/4 cup milk
3 slices ham, cooked and cubed
1 cup sharp cheddar cheese, shredded

In medium bowl, stir together flour, sugar, baking powder and salt. Combine egg and milk then add to dry ingredients. Beat until smooth. Stir in ham. Spread batter evenly in greased and floured baking pan. Bake at 425 degrees for 15 minutes. Sprinkle with cheese. Bake two to three minutes more until cheese melts. Cut into squares.

Ham, Swiss & Almonds

1 Tbsp. butter or margarine	1 cup milk
1 Tbsp. flour	1 cup ham, cooked and cubed
1/2 tsp. instant chicken stock base	1/2 cup Swiss cheese, shredded
1/4 tsp. celery salt	1/4 cup sliced toasted almonds

To make a sauce, melt butter in medium saucepan then stir in flour until well blended. Stir in chicken stock and celery salt. With a wire whisk, gradually add milk and beat in. Cook until thickened, whisking constantly. Set aside. Prepare a Basic Omelet (see page 85). Before folding omelet, sprinkle with cheese and ham. Ladle half of sauce over cheese and ham. Fold omelet. Ladle sauce over omelet and garnish with almonds.

Herbed Swiss Quiche

1 unbaked 9-inch pie shell in pan	1 1/3 cups Swiss cheese, shredded
2 eggs	1/2 tsp. basil
1 cup heavy cream	1/4 tsp. marjoram
Salt and Pepper	

In a medium bowl, combine eggs, cream, salt and pepper. Beat until well blended. Sprinkle cheese, basil and marjoram evenly over bottom of pie shell. Pour egg mixture over cheese. Bake at 400 degrees until knife inserted in middle comes out clean. Let stand five minutes before serving.

Bacon Egg Melt

2 English muffins, split	Salt and pepper
2 eggs	2 slices American cheese
1 Tbsp. water	4 slices bacon, cooked crisp
1 Tbsp. butter or margarine	

Lightly toast muffins and spread with two teaspoons of the butter. Whisk eggs in small bowl with water. Melt two teaspoons butter in pan. Add eggs. Cook until set. Place cheese on top of egg and wait until melted. Place egg on muffins. Top with bacon. Cover with remaining muffin top.

DAD'S Specialties

Breakfast Favorites

Blueberry Pancake Wedges

1 cup instant pancake mix	16-oz. can blueberries
1 tsp. lemon peel	1/3 cup sugar
2 Tbsp. butter or margarine	1 Tbsp. cornstarch

Prepare pancake mix according to package directions. Stir in lemon peel. Set aside. In skillet with oven-proof handle, melt butter or margarine. Remove from heat. Drain blueberries, reserving syrup. Spoon berries into skillet. Pour batter over blueberries. Bake at 400 degrees for 15 to 18 minutes. In saucepan, combine sugar, cornstarch and reserved blueberry syrup. Cook and stir until thickened and bubbly. Loosen edges of pancake in skillet. Invert onto serving plate. Cut into wedges.

Cinnamon Sticky Ring

16 white frozen bread rolls	3/4 cup brown sugar
1/2 cup pecan halves	1 tsp. cinnamon
1 pkg. butterscotch non-instant pudding mix	1/2 cup butter, melted

Spread some butter on the bottom and sides of a large cake pan. Place pecan halves in butter, rounded side down. Place frozen rolls over pecans and allow them to rise as per package directions. Blend together dry butterscotch pudding mix, brown sugar and cinnamon. Sprinkle all of the mixture over the rolls. Pour melted butter over all. Bake at 375 degrees for 30 minutes or until sugar is well dissolved and bubbly. Turn onto cake plate that will catch the dripping syrup.

Spinach Potato Stack

1 pkg. frozen chopped spinach, thawed	1/4 tsp. black pepper
1 cup cottage cheese	1 pkg. frozen hash browns, thawed
1 cup onion, chopped	1/2 cup mozzarella cheese, shredded
2 tsp. Italian seasoning	1/2 cup cheddar cheese, shredded
1/2 tsp. garlic salt	15-oz. jar spaghetti sauce, heated

Drain spinach and combine with cottage cheese, onions and seasonings. Mix well. Set aside. In large casserole dish, layer half of hash browns in bottom. Spread spinach mixture over potatoes. Top with remaining potatoes. Sprinkle with cheeses. Bake at 375 degrees for 45 minutes. Cut into squares. Serve with spaghetti sauce.

Nutty Microwave Apples

4 medium apples	4 tsp. orange juice
4 Tbsp. raisins	1 Tbsp. lemon juice
4 Tbsp. chopped nuts	1/2 tsp. cinnamon
4 Tbsp. brown sugar	

Remove apple cores but do not cut all the way through to the bottom. (To do this, cut from top around core then dig core out with spoon.) Peel a one-inch strip around the top of each apple. Place apples around the edge of a 9-inch microwave dish. In small bowl, combine raisins, nuts, brown sugar and orange juice. Spoon mixture into apples. Sprinkle apples with lemon juice and cinnamon. Cover with plastic wrap. Microwave on high for six to seven minutes. Let sit. Serve warm.

Sausage Cheddar Muffins

Cornmeal	1/4 tsp. ground red pepper
1 3/4 cups all-purpose flour	1 egg, beaten
1/2 cup sharp cheddar cheese, shredded	3/4 cup milk
1/4 cup sugar	1/3 cup cooking oil
2 tsp. baking powder	6 sausage links, cooked and crumbled
1/4 tsp. salt	

Grease muffin cups and top of pan. Sprinkle cups with cornmeal. In medium bowl, stir together flour, cheese, sugar, baking powder, salt and red pepper. Make a well in the center. In small bowl, combine egg, milk and oil. Add egg mixture all at once to flour mixture. Stir just until moistened (batter should be lumpy). Fold in the crumbled sausage. Fill muffin cups even with the top of the pan. Bake at 400 degrees for 20 to 25 minutes or until muffins are golden. Serve warm.

---

*D*ad says:
Everybody loves hash browns. To keep shredded potatoes from going brown, grate them into a bowl of cold water. Take out as much as you will cook at one time. Drain shredded potatoes on a folded paper towel, then push them into a skillet with hot oil. Let one side brown, then flip to the other side. To preserve nutrients, grate clean potatoes with the skin on. To save time, buy frozen hash browns, potato patties or freshly sealed shredded potatoes sold near the eggs in most grocery stores.

Quick Potato Pancakes

1 pkg. frozen hash browns, thawed
1/4 cup onion, chopped
1 egg
2 Tbsp. flour
1 tsp. dill weed

3/4 tsp. salt
Dash pepper
1/4 cup vegetable oil
3/4 cup sour cream

In medium bowl, mix hash browns, onions, egg, flour, dill weed, salt and pepper. Heat two tablespoons oil in non-stick skillet over medium heat. Drop 1/2 cup of potato mixture in hot skillet and flatten into pancake shape with spatula. Cook three to four minutes or until golden brown. Turn over and cook other side. Serve with sour cream.

Baked Canadian French Toast

16 slices 1/2-inch thick firm white bread,
    crusts removed
2 Tbsp. butter, melted
12 slices Canadian bacon
2 cups sharp cheddar cheese, shredded
8 eggs

3 cups half-and-half cream
1 tsp. salt
1/4 tsp. pepper
3 large fresh tomatoes

In large baking pan, place bread in single layer. Brush bread with butter. Turn slices over and butter other side. Arrange bacon over bread. Sprinkle with half the cheddar cheese. Set aside. In large bowl, lightly beat eggs, cream, salt and pepper until well blended. Slowly pour over bread and cheese. Bake at 350 degrees for 15 minutes. Core tomatoes. Cut off a thin slice from the top and bottom of each tomato. Discard. Cut each tomato into four slices. Arrange tomato slices over top of bread. Bake until set, about eight minutes. Sprinkle with remaining cheese. Place under broiler until cheese bubbles. Cut into squares and serve.

All-American French Toast

3 eggs
1/3 cup milk
2 Tbsp. brown sugar
1 tsp. vanilla
2 tsp. cinnamon

1 loaf Italian or French bread, cut into
    1-inch thick slices
Cooking oil
Maple syrup, warmed
Butter or margarine

Whisk together eggs, milk, sugar, vanilla and cinnamon. Mix well. Heat oil in medium skillet on medium heat. Place bread in egg mixture until saturated, turning once. Cook in skillet three to four minutes until one side is golden brown, then flip and cook the other side. Serve with butter and syrup.

Egg Nog French Toast

6 English muffins, split
3 eggs
3/4 cup prepared eggnog
1/2 tsp. grated lemon peel

1/2 tsp. cinnamon
1/4 tsp. nutmeg
4 Tbsp. butter or margarine
Powdered sugar

In lightly-greased baking pan, place English muffin halves in a single layer with split side up. Beat together eggs, egg nog and lemon peel. Pour over muffins. Sprinkle with cinnamon and nutmeg. Let stand 20 to 30 minutes. Heat skillet or griddle over medium heat. Melt one tablespoon butter at a time and cook French toast on both sides until golden brown. Transfer to large, ovenproof baking dish in single layer and keep warm in 200 degree oven while finishing remaining French toast. Dust with powdered sugar and serve warm with syrup.

Gooey Caramel French Toast

Italian bread
1 egg
1/3 cup milk
1/2 tsp. salt

Butter or margarine
1/3 cup packed brown sugar
8-oz. container plain yogurt

Diagonally cut eight 1-inch-thick slices from Italian bread. In pie plate, mix egg, milk and salt. In medium skillet over medium heat, melt two tablespoons butter or margarine. Dip bread slices into egg mixture to moisten both sides, then fry in hot butter or margarine until browned on both sides, turning once. Place toast on warm platter. In same skillet, heat brown sugar and two tablespoons butter or margarine until sugar is completely dissolved. Return toast to skillet to coat both sides with sugar mixture. Spread yogurt on top of toast. Serve immediately.

Orange Cinnamon French Toast

6 eggs
1/3 cup orange juice
1/3 cup milk
3 Tbsp. granulated sugar
1 Tbsp. orange peel, grated
1 Tbsp. vanilla

3 tsp. cinnamon
1 loaf French bread, 1-inch thick slices
Cooking oil or butter
Powdered sugar
6 thin orange slices
Maple syrup

Whisk together eggs, orange juice, milk, sugar, peel, vanilla and cinnamon. Arrange bread in single layer in shallow dish. Pour egg mixture over bread. Let stand until saturated, turning once, about 30 minutes. In large skillet, heat butter or cooking oil. Add bread slices and cook, turning once, until golden brown. Arrange on serving platter. Top each slice with a pat of butter or margarine. Sprinkle with powdered sugar. Garnish with orange slices. Serve with maple syrup.

Best Basic Pancakes

2 eggs
5 Tbsp. butter, melted
1 cup milk
1 1/4 cups all-purpose flour

1 Tbsp. sugar
4 tsp. baking powder
3/4 tsp. salt

In mixing bowl, beat eggs until well blended. Add butter and milk. Mix well. In a separate bowl, use a fork to combine the flour, sugar, baking powder and salt. Slowly add the egg mixture just until the batter is thoroughly moistened. Heat a skillet or griddle until drops of water sizzle on it. Lightly grease the hot griddle. Drop two to three tablespoons batter in the skillet for each pancake. Cook until bubbles form, turn and cook until the bottom is lightly browned. Serve immediately.

Fruity German Pancakes

For batter:
4 eggs
1/2 cup flour
1/2 tsp. baking powder
1 Tbsp. granulated sugar
Pinch salt
1 cup milk
1 tsp. vanilla

2 Tbsp. butter, melted
1/8 tsp. nutmeg
For filling:
4 Tbsp. butter
1/2 cup sugar
1/2 tsp. cinnamon
1/8 tsp. nutmeg
1 large apple, sliced thinly

For batter: In medium bowl, mix eggs, flour, baking powder, sugar and salt together. Add milk gradually. Add vanilla, butter and nutmeg. Mix thoroughly. Let stand for at least 30 minutes. *For filling:* In ovenproof skillet, melt butter. Brush onto sides, too. Sprinkle 1/4 cup sugar and spices over butter. Spread apple slices evenly in pan. Sprinkle remaining sugar over apples. Heat over medium heat until mixture bubbles. *For pancakes:* Slowly pour batter over apples in skillet. Bake at 425 degrees for 15 minutes. Reduce oven to 375 degrees and bake an additional ten minutes. Slide onto serving platter. Cut into wedges. Makes three to four servings.

True Buttermilk Pancakes

2 cups all-purpose flour
2 Tbsp. sugar
2 tsp. baking powder
1 tsp. baking soda
1/2 tsp. salt

2 eggs
2 cups buttermilk
1/2 cup milk
1/4 cup butter, melted

In large bowl, combine flour, sugar, baking powder, baking soda and salt. In another bowl, lightly beat the eggs, buttermilk, milk and melted butter. Add liquid ingredients to dry ingredients all at once, stirring just to blend. The batter should be slightly lumpy. Heat a lightly oiled griddle or heavy skillet over medium heat. Place 1/4-cup batter portioned out onto the hot griddle, spacing them apart. When bubbles cover the surface of the pancakes and their undersides are lightly browned, turn them over and cook about 2 minutes more until the other sides are browned. Serve warm.

Whipped Belgian Waffles

1 cup sour cream
1/2 cup milk
3 Tbsp. butter, melted
1/4 tsp. vanilla
2 egg yolks, beaten
1 cup flour
1 tsp. baking powder

2 tsp. sugar
1/2 tsp. salt
1/4 tsp. baking soda
1 egg white, beaten stiff
1 cup strawberries, washed and halved
1 cup whipped cream
Syrup

In medium bowl, combine sour cream, milk, butter, vanilla and beaten egg yolks. In another bowl, combine all dry ingredients and mix well. Blend sour cream mixture into dry ingredients until smooth. Carefully fold in beaten egg white. Pour about half of the batter into greased or buttered hot waffle maker. Serve with fresh strawberries, whipped cream and syrup of choice. Makes two large waffles.

Peanut Butter Waffles

1 1/2 cups whole-wheat flour
1/4 cup uncooked quick-cooking oatmeal
1 Tbsp. baking powder
1/2 tsp. salt
1/4 cup peanut butter

1/2 cup packed brown sugar
2 eggs, lightly beaten
2 cups milk
2 tsp. vanilla

In large bowl, combine flour, oatmeal, baking powder and salt. Set aside. In another bowl, combine peanut butter, brown sugar, eggs, milk and vanilla. Mix well. Add liquid ingredients to dry ingredients. Mix just until dry ingredients are moistened. Do not overmix. Spoon 1/2 cup batter into preheated waffle iron and cook for about seven minutes or until golden brown and waffle stops steaming.

Waffle Ham Sandwich

3/4 cup honey, divided
1/4 cup apple juice
2 Tbsp. butter or margarine

2 crisp red apples, cored and sliced
8 frozen waffles, toasted
8 thin slices ham

For syrup: Heat 1/2 cup honey and apple juice in small saucepan. Set aside, keeping warm. In large skillet, melt butter with remaining 1/4 cup honey over medium heat. Add apples and cook about four minutes, stirring constantly, until apples are lightly caramelized and crisp-tender. *For each serving,* place two waffles on a plate, slightly overlapping. Top each waffle with a slice of ham, apple mixture and drizzle with syrup.

DAD'S Specialties

Super Sandwiches

Classic Tuna Sandwich

7-oz. can water-packed tuna,
    drained and flaked
1 tsp. lemon juice

1 Tbsp. sweet pickle relish
1/4 cup mayonnaise
6 slices bread

In medium bowl, combine tuna, lemon juice, pickle relish and mayonnaise. Spread evenly on three slices bread and top with remaining bread. Garnish with lettuce leaves, if desired. Serves three.

Broiled Ham & Swiss Dijon

2 Tbsp. Dijon mustard
1 Tbsp. honey
1 Tbsp. vegetable oil

12 oz. cooked ham, sliced
4 slices rye bread, toasted
4 slices Swiss cheese

In small bowl, combine mustard and honey. Set aside. In large skillet, heat oil. Add ham and cook over medium-low heat until ham is heated through. Spread honey mustard sauce on each slice of bread. Layer with slice of ham and slice of cheese. Broil on a cookie sheet until cheese melts. Serves four.

Caesar Served Up

2/3 cup mayonnaise
3 Tbsp. lemon juice
1 tsp. garlic, minced
1/4 tsp. pepper

12 slices multi-grain bread
1 small head Romaine lettuce, torn
1/2 cup fresh Parmesan cheese, grated
6 hard-boiled eggs, sliced

In large bowl, combine mayonnaise, lemon juice, garlic and pepper. Mix well. Spread one teaspoon on one side of each slice of bread. Set aside. Add lettuce and cheese to remaining mayonnaise mixture and toss to mix well. Heap one cup lettuce mixture on each of six slices of bread. Top with egg slices and remaining slices of bread. Serves six.

Cheesy Tuna Burgers

1 can water-packed tuna
1/2 cup cheddar cheese, shredded
1 small onion, chopped

1 cup celery, chopped
1/4 cup mayonnaise
6 hamburger buns

In medium bowl, mix tuna, cheese, onion, celery and mayonnaise. Spread an equal amount on each of six split buns. Bake at 350 degrees for 15 minutes, or until bubbly. Serves six.

Chicken Bacon Club

18 thin slices of white bread, lightly
   toasted and buttered
12 slices deli chicken
Mayonnaise

12 slices bacon, cooked crisp
12 slices tomato
Salt and pepper
Lettuce leaves to garnish

Arrange 2 slices chicken each on six pieces of toast. Spread chicken with mayonnaise and cover with another piece of toast. Spread with mayonnaise. Arrange two slices bacon and two slices tomato on each. Sprinkle with salt and pepper. Top with lettuce and remaining piece of toast. Secure with wooden toothpicks. Cut each sandwich into four triangles. Serves six.

Easy Chicken Salad

3/4 cup cooked chicken, diced
1/2 cup mayonnaise
2 Tbsp. celery, chopped
2 Tbsp. almonds, chopped

1 Tbsp. fresh parsley, chopped
4 slices whole wheat bread
1/4 cup jellied cranberry sauce

In medium bowl, combine chicken, mayonnaise, celery, almonds and parsley. Set aside. Spread bread with cranberry sauce and top with chicken salad mixture. Makes two sandwiches.

---

*D*ad *says:*
For a change from regular lettuce and tomato garnish, try topping your sandwich with bean sprouts, alfalfa sprouts, fresh spinach leaves, watercress or even fresh, raw vegetables, such as sliced cucumbers, green peppers, cabbage, celery, carrots or red onion.

Fancy French Dippers

1 1/2 lbs. cooked roast beef, thinly sliced
1 cup mushrooms, sautéed
6 slices mozzarella cheese

1 loaf French bread, split in half
   crosswise and warmed in oven
1 cup beef broth, heated

Layer thin slices of beef on half of French loaf. Top with mushrooms and cheese. Cover with other half of bread and slice into sandwich-sized portions. Serve with hot beef broth. Dip sandwich into broth while eating. Serves six.

Granny's Apple-Raisin Treat

4 Tbsp. Dijon mustard
2 Tbsp. honey
1 medium sweet red pepper, sliced
2 Granny Smith apples, cored and
   thinly sliced

1/2 cup bleu cheese, crumbled
Watercress to garnish
8 slices raisin bread, lightly toasted

In small bowl, combine mustard and honey. Stir to mix well. Spread honey mustard evenly on one side of each slice of bread. Layer watercress, apple slices, red peppers and bleu cheese. Repeat layering of apple slices and red peppers. Top with remaining slice of bread. Serves four.

Bavarian Beef Rolls

1 lb. ground beef
1/2 cup onion, chopped
1/4 cup green pepper, chopped
2 Tbsp. butter or margarine

10-oz. can beef gravy
2 cups cabbage, shredded
6 hard rolls, split and toasted
1/4 cup cheddar cheese, shredded

In medium skillet, cook ground beef, onions and green peppers in butter until beef is browned and vegetables are tender. Stir in gravy and cabbage. Cook over medium heat for ten minutes. Spoon 1/2 cup mixture on bottom half of each roll. Sprinkle with cheese and cover with top half of rolls. Serves six.

Bleu Mushroom Burgers

2 lbs. lean ground beef	Salt and pepper
1 medium onion, chopped	1/4 lb. bleu cheese, crumbled
1 Tbsp. bottled steak sauce	1/2 lb. mushrooms, thickly sliced

In large bowl, combine ground beef with onion, steak sauce, salt and pepper. Form into 12 thin patties. Top six patties with crumbled bleu cheese and mushroom slices. Top with remaining six patties and press edges together to seal. Grill, fry or broil to desired doneness. Serve on hamburger buns. Serves six.

Chili Burgers

1 lb. lean ground beef	Two 8-oz. cans chili or pinto beans
1/2 tsp. salt	3 slices cheddar cheese, quartered
1/4 tsp. pepper	4 hamburger buns, split and toasted
1 tsp. chili powder	

In medium bowl, combine ground beef, salt, pepper and chili powder. Mix well. Form into four patties. In baking pan, broil to desired doneness. Top burgers with 1/4 of the beans. Bake at 375 degrees until beans are bubbly hot. Top with three cheese quarters and broil until cheese melts. Serve on buns.

Cucumbers & Cottage Cheese

2 cups low-fat cottage cheese	Dash salt
1 cucumber, peeled, seeded and chopped	8 slices sourdough bread
1/4 cup green onion, chopped	Lettuce leaves

In medium bowl, combine cottage cheese, cucumber, green onions and salt. Mix well and refrigerate until well chilled. Spoon onto sourdough bread and garnish with lettuce, if desired. Serves four.

---

*D*ad says:
For a real switch, don't limit yourself to sliced white bread in a sandwich. Try sourdough, cracked wheat, multi-grain, rye, pumpernickel, brown and specialty flavored or herbed breads. Try rolls, buns, pita bread, English muffins, croissants, popovers, onion rolls, bagels and tortillas.

Grilled Italy Special

8 slices bread
Softened butter or margarine
4 slices Mozzarella cheese
2 Tbsp. onion, chopped
2 medium tomatoes, sliced

1/3 cup sour cream
2 tsp. oregano
Salt to taste
8 slices bacon, fried crisp and drained

Spread both sides of each slice of bread with butter. For each sandwich, top a slice of bread with one slice cheese, a dollop of sour cream, onions, a sprinkle of oregano, several tomato slices and a dash of salt. Arrange two pieces of bacon on each. Top with remaining slices of bread. Place each sandwich in a skillet. Grill each side of bread until golden and cheese is melted. Makes four sandwiches.

Ham Crescent Rollups

1 egg, slightly beaten
1/2 cup cheddar cheese, shredded
3/4 cup ham, cooked and chopped

8-oz. can refrigerated crescent rolls
2 tsp. sesame seeds

Set aside one teaspoon beaten egg. Combine remaining egg with cheese and ham. Separate crescent roll dough into four rectangles. Press perforated edges firmly to seal, flattening the dough slightly. Place 1/4 of the ham mixture along the long edge of each rectangle. Roll up jelly-roll style, overlapping the ends of the roll slightly. Press ends together to seal. Brush with reserved egg and sprinkle with sesame seeds. Bake at 375 degrees for 15 minutes.

Hawaiian Ham & Pineapple

4 1/2-oz. can deviled ham
1/2 cup crushed pineapple, drained well
1/2 cup low-fat cottage cheese

3 Tbsp. mayonnaise
4 slices cracked wheat bread

In medium bowl, combine deviled ham, pineapple, cottage cheese and mayonnaise. Mix until well blended. Spread on cracked wheat bread. Garnish with lettuce if desired. Makes two sandwiches.

Hot Chicken Buns

2/3 cup mayonnaise
1 Tbsp. lemon juice
Dash hot sauce
2 cups cooked chicken, diced
3/4 cup sliced pitted olives

1 cup cheddar cheese, shredded
1/2 cup celery, chopped
1/4 cup green onions, chopped
1/4 cup green pepper, chopped
4 hamburger buns, split in half

In medium bowl, combine mayonnaise, lemon juice and hot sauce. Stir until well blended. Stir in chicken, half the olives, half the cheese, green onions, green pepper and celery. Spread buns with chicken mixture. Top with remaining olive slices and cheese. Bake at 400 degrees for ten minutes. Place under broiler until cheese bubbles. Serves four.

Italian Soupburgers

1 lb. lean ground beef
1/4 cup onion, chopped
1/8 tsp. oregano
1 can condensed minestrone soup

1/3 cup water
1/3 cup ketchup
6 hamburger buns, split and toasted
12 slices Mozzarella cheese

In skillet, cook ground beef, onion and oregano until meat is browned and onion is tender. Stir in soup, water and ketchup. Simmer for ten minutes, stirring occasionally. Spread on toasted buns. Top with cheese slices and broil until cheese is bubbly. Serves six.

Monte Cristo Stacks

For each sandwich:
2 slices bread
Butter or margarine, softened
1 thin slice cooked ham
1 thin slice Swiss cheese
1 thin slice baked chicken
1 thin slice cheddar cheese

1 egg
Dash salt and pepper
1 Tbsp. cold water
1 Tbsp. vegetable oil
Vegetable oil for frying
Butter or margarine for frying
Raspberry jam

Spread both slices of bread with butter. On one slice, layer ham, Swiss cheese, chicken and cheddar cheese. Cover with second slice of bread. Press sandwich firmly together, wrap in plastic wrap and refrigerate until well chilled. In small shallow bowl, combine egg, salt, pepper, cold water and oil. Whisk until well blended. Unwrap sandwich. Holding firmly together, dip into egg mixture, first one side, then the other. Fry in heavy skillet in mixture of oil and butter 1/4 inch deep. When browned on both sides, remove from skillet, drain on paper towels. Next, bake the sandwiches at 350 degrees for eight to ten minutes. Cut each one in half. Serve hot with raspberry jam.

Really Sloppy Joes

1 lb. ground beef
1 can condensed chicken gumbo soup
2 Tbsp. brown sugar
1/2 cup ketchup

1 small onion, chopped
1 Tbsp. mustard
2 Tbsp. Worcestershire
2 Tbsp. flour

In medium skillet, cook ground beef until browned. Drain fat. Stir in remaining ingredients and simmer for ten minutes, or until thickened. Serve on split hamburger buns. Serves six.

Roast Beef on Rye

1 lb. cooked roast beef, thinly sliced
6 slices rye bread
1/4 cup sour cream
1 Tbsp. vinegar
3/4 tsp. Dijon mustard

3/4 cup sugar
1/4 tsp. salt
1 small red onion, thinly sliced
6 cherry tomatoes, thinly sliced

Arrange sliced beef on bread. In small bowl, combine sour cream, vinegar, mustard, sugar and salt. Mix well. Spread sour cream mixture on beef. Top with onion and cherry tomato slices. Top with remaining slices of bread. Serves six.

Open-Face Skinny Sandwiches

2 cups Swiss cheese, shredded
1 1/4 cup biscuit mix
1 medium tomato, chopped
1/2 cucumber, chopped

1/2 cup mayonnaise
1 hard-boiled egg, chopped
1/4 tsp. salt
6 slices whole wheat bread

In large bowl, combine cheese, biscuit mix, tomato, cucumber, mayonnaise, hard-boiled egg and salt. Stir until well mixed. Spread on slices of bread. Bake at 450 degrees for ten to 12 minutes or until cheese is bubbly. Serves six.

Southwestern Beef

4 Tbsp. mayonnaise
3 Tbsp. prepared horseradish
8 slices black bread, lightly toasted
1 ripe avocado, peeled and sliced

12-oz. cooked roast beef, thinly sliced
1 small red onion, thinly sliced
Sprouts to garnish

In small bowl, combine mayonnaise and horseradish. Mix well and set aside. Spread mayonnaise-horseradish sauce evenly on one side of each slice of bread. Layer avocado slices, roast beef, onion slices, sprouts and top with remaining slice of bread.

Spicy Chicken Pitas

1/2 cup sour cream
3 Tbsp. mayonnaise
1 Tbsp. lime juice
1 1/2 tsp. salad oil
3/4 tsp. salt
1/2 tsp. ground red pepper

3 cups cooked chicken, diced
1 cup tomato, chopped
1/2 cup avocado, diced
3 Tbsp. green onions, chopped
1 cup lettuce, shredded
6 pita breads

In large bowl, combine sour cream, mayonnaise, lime juice, oil, salt and red pepper. Stir to mix well. Add chicken, tomato, avocado and green onions. Toss well. Split pitas one-third of the way. Stuff with equal portions of shredded lettuce and chicken salad mixture. Serves six.

The Classic Hero

1 loaf French bread, cut in half horizontally
4 Tbsp. mayonnaise
3 Tbsp. Dijon mustard
6-oz. cheddar cheese, sliced
1 medium green pepper, cut into rings

2 dill pickles, sliced
1 red onion, sliced
6-oz. Swiss cheese, sliced
6-oz. ham, sliced
Lettuce to garnish

In large bowl, combine sour cream, mayonnaise, lime juice, oil, salt and red pepper. Stir to mix well. Add chicken, tomato, avocado and green onions. Toss well. Split pitas one-third of the way. Stuff with equal portions of shredded lettuce and chicken salad mixture. Serves six.

Hot Chili Recipes

Homestyle Chili

3 cups dried kidney beans
6 cups water
1 1/2 lbs. ground beef
1 large onion, chopped
4 tsp. salt
1 cup celery, chopped
1 tsp. black pepper

4 tsp. chili powder
1 large can stewed tomatoes,
  pureed in blender
Two 8-oz. cans tomato sauce
1/2 cup ketchup
1 tsp. celery salt

Wash beans. Cover with water and soak overnight. In large skillet, cook beef and onions until meat is browned and onions are tender. Combine with beans in heavy kettle. Stir in remaining ingredients except celery. Bring to boil, reduce heat and simmer four to six hours, stirring occasionally. Add more water if necessary to keep chili from scorching. Add celery and simmer 30 minutes more. Serves 12.

Add Zest To Canned Chili

If you don't have time to cook chili from scratch, canned chili can be a good alternative, if you take a minute to dress it up. The next time you open a can of chili, try making some of these improvements:
• Water down too-thick chili with tomato juice, beer or red wine.
• Add chopped fresh or canned tomatoes with liquid.
• Sautee chopped onions, chopped green pepper and minced garlic in a little vegetable oil, then stir them into the canned chili.
• Stir in tomato sauce and top with shredded cheese and avocado chunks.
• Too make it hotter, add hot sauce or crushed dried red peppers.

Best Chili Toppers

Offer these fresh toppings to accompany a steaming bowl of chili: finely chopped green or white onions, chopped chili peppers and red, green or yellow bell peppers, dried crushed red pepper, dollop of sour cream, shredded cheddar and Monterrey Jack cheeses, shredded carrots, shredded raw celery, sliced or cubed avocado sprinkled with fresh lime juice, slivers of sweet or dill pickles, raisins (really, give it a try) or coarsely chopped almonds.

Freeze-Ahead Chili

5 lbs. lean ground beef
3 onions, chopped
1 quart tomatoes
1/2 cup flour
1/2 cup quick-cooking oatmeal
2 Tbsp. chili powder

2 Tbsp. paprika
1 Tbsp. oregano
4 Tbsp. sugar
4 Tbsp. salt
1 1/2 tsp. garlic powder

In skillet, cook ground beef and onions until beef is lightly browned and onions are tender. Add tomatoes and cook mixture slowly until well done. Combine flour, oatmeal and seasonings and mix well. Add flour-oatmeal mixture to meat mixture. Press mixture into loaf pans. Cover with foil, seal tightly and freeze. When frozen solid, remove from pans, wrap in waxed paper then in foil. Seal and label. When ready to make chili, thaw one block of mix. Add equal amounts of drained canned beans and simmer until heated through. Use a heavy pan to prevent scorching or heat in a double-boiler.

Easy Mexican Chili

1 lb. ground beef
1 medium onion, chopped
1 clove garlic, minced
2 Tbsp. fresh cilantro, chopped
1 tsp. chili powder
1/2 tsp. salt

1/4 tsp. ground cumin
1 can whole tomatoes with juice, chopped
4-oz. can chopped green chiles
8-oz. can pinto beans, undrained
2 Tbsp. masa (corn flour)
1/4 cup warm water

In skillet, brown beef with onion, garlic, cilantro and seasonings. Drain. In large kettle, combine beef with tomatoes and chiles. Bring to a boil. Cover and simmer for 30 minutes. Add beans. Bring to boil. Cover and simmer for 15 minutes. To thicken chili, dissolve masa in warm water, then add mixture to chili, stirring constantly over medium heat until it reaches desired thickness. Add more if necessary. Serve topped with grated cheddar cheese, diced fresh tomatoes and chopped green onions.

Chili with Beans

Chili is a savory meat and tomato dish usually spiced up with hot peppers or chiles, onions, garlic, and green peppers simmered together for hours. Chili often includes beans. Thus, you will find canned chili labeled simply "chili" or "all-meat chili" which does not include beans or "chili with beans." However, some of the best chili usually includes at least two types of beans, such as kidney beans, red beans and pinto beans. To take the gas out of beans and make sure they cook up tender, soak dried beans over night in water, then drain and rinse well before adding. You will have to simmer chili longer when using dried beans. If you are in a hurry, use canned beans.

Chicken Chili

2 pounds skinless, boneless chicken breasts, cubed
1/4 cup vegetable oil
1 cup white or yellow onion, chopped
3 cloves garlic, minced
1 sweet red pepper, seeded and diced
4-oz. can mild green chiles, drained and chopped

16-oz. can whole tomatoes with liquid, chopped
1 1/2 Tbsp. tomato paste
3 tsp. chili powder
1 tsp. oregano
1 cup chicken broth
1/4 tsp. salt

In large kettle, sauté chicken in oil, stirring frequently, until chicken is white and firm. Reduce heat to medium. Add onion and garlic, cooking until onion is transparent. Add remaining ingredients and stir well. Bring to boil. Reduce heat and simmer uncovered for 30 minutes or until chicken is tender, stirring occasionally. Serves six.

Cincinnati Parlor Chili

1 lb. ground beef
1 medium white or yellow onion, chopped
1 clove garlic, minced
Two 8-oz. cans tomato sauce
1 cup water
1/2 oz. unsweetened chocolate
1 Tbsp. red wine vinegar
1 Tbsp. chili powder

1 tsp. allspice
1/2 tsp. cinnamon
1/2 tsp. salt
15-oz. can red beans, drained
Hot cooked spaghetti noodles
Shredded cheddar cheese
Chopped fresh onions

In large kettle, brown beef, onion and garlic. Drain. Add tomato sauce, water, chocolate, vinegar and seasonings. Bring to boil. Reduce heat, cover and simmer for 45 minutes, stirring occasionally. Add beans and continue simmering for 15 minutes. Serve chili ladled over noodles. Top with cheese and onions. Serves four.

Midwestern Chili

1/2 lb. lean ground beef	8-oz. can tomato sauce
1 medium onion, chopped	2 Tbsp. chili powder
1 small green pepper, chopped	1/2 tsp. salt
1 clove garlic, minced	15-oz. can kidney beans, red beans or
28-oz. can whole tomatoes with liquid, chopped	pinto beans, drained

In large kettle, brown ground beef with onion, green pepper and garlic. Add remaining ingredients, except beans. Bring to boil. Reduce heat and simmer covered, stirring occasionally, for 30 minutes. Add beans. Simmer for 15 minutes. Serves six.

The Heat Of Fresh Chiles

What kind of hot pepper or fresh chile should you chop up and toss in the kettle? The answer depends on how spicy you want the dish to be. Do consider adding fresh chiles to your chili because they not only add heat but also flavor. As a rule, the smaller the fresh chile in size, the hotter it is. The hottest peppers are also the narrowest with the pointiest ends. Larger, broader chiles with blunt ends are milder.

No matter what you might have heard, color doesn't always determine heat. Red chiles are usually red because they have been ripened by the sun. Even though you should discard the seeds, they aren't the hottest part. The spicy heat comes from capsaicin in the veins of the chile. To make a chili milder, scrape out the membranes. Always discard the tops with the stems. If chiles are plump, firm and blemish-free when you buy then, you can usually store them in a plastic bag in the refrigerator for about two weeks. Red chiles will not store as long as green chilies will. Look for these varieties:

Serrano. These are some of the hottest chiles. They are bright green, very thin and very long. You can also find them canned in the Mexican section of the grocery store.

Jalapeño. These are also extremely hot, especially the fresh ones. They are dark green, thin skinned and about two to three inches long. Most stores also have them canned or pickled. As a rule, the fresh ones taste better.

California or Anaheim. These are mild, medium green, longer, broad at the tops and blunt on the ends. When canned, they are usually called simply "green chiles." This is what many people use chopped to top their nachos. You can usually find them either whole or chopped in a can. These fresh chiles give chile verde its color and unique taste.

Poblano. Another mild chile, these look like a green pepper. You can't find them canned, but some stores have them in dried form.

A word of warning: Fresh chiles, especially the hot varieties, can be very irritating to your skin and may injure your eyes if you touch them with your fingers after handling. Wash hands with soap and water immediately after chopping chiles. Avoid prolonged contact with the juices or oils of hot peppers. If your skin is sensitive, wear rubber gloves. Remember, too, not to touch a loved one, especially children, until after you've washed your hands.

Put Out The Fire

Spicy chili perks up your taste buds, but it can also set your mouth afire. Remember, every individual has his or her own unique tolerance to heat in food. It's best to make a less spicy chili, then offer sides to heat it up, like crushed dried red pepper, bottled hot sauce, or chopped fresh jalapeños. Always serve bread with chili—that will calm the blaze. Serve warm, tasty French bread, homemade sweet cornbread, homestyle biscuits or moist soda bread. A cool gelatin salad helps take the gas out of beans.

Also serve some kind of icy drink like good old reliable water or a specialty fruit drink. Many chili connoisseurs swear by cold milk to take the edge off, but other professional spicy pepper eaters say milk makes things worse. Do what works for you and yours. Give your dinner guests a choice of grated cheese or sour cream to top the chili—both work well to dampen the flames.

Savory Pork Chili

2 Tbsp. vegetable oil
4 strips bacon, diced
2 lbs. stewing pork, cubed
1/2 cup flour
1 cup onion, chopped
3 cloves garlic, minced
3 Tbsp. chili powder

1 jalapeño pepper, stemmed,
   seeded and chopped
2 cups chicken broth
1/4 tsp. salt
Two 15-oz. cans pinto beans,
   drained and rinsed

Heat oil in kettle. Add bacon and cook until crisp. Remove bacon with slotted spoon. Drain on paper towels and set aside. Put flour in paper bag. Add pork cubes and shake to coat well. Remove pork and shake off excess flour. Sautee pork in bacon drippings until evenly browned. Reduce heat to medium. Stir in cooked bacon, onion and garlic. Cook eight minutes or until onion is transparent and garlic is soft. Add chili powder, jalapeño peppers and chicken broth. Heat to boiling, reduce heat and simmer uncovered for two hours or until pork is tender and sauce is thick. If sauce gets too thick during cooking, add water to thin slightly. Stir in salt. To serve, heat beans, then ladle chili over beans.

San Francisco Veggie Chili

1 medium onion, chopped
1 medium green pepper, chopped
2 cups mushrooms, sliced
1 clove garlic, minced
Two 16-oz. cans stewed tomatoes
   with liquid, chopped
8-oz. can tomato sauce

1 cup red wine or beef broth
1 Tbsp. chili powder
1 tsp. cumin
1 tsp. oregano
1/4 tsp. red pepper sauce
1 medium zucchini, chopped
15-oz. can red beans, drained

In large kettle, sauté onion, green pepper, mushrooms and garlic in a little vegetable oil until tender. Add remaining ingredients, except zucchini and beans. Bring to boil, reduce heat and simmer covered for 45 minutes, stirring occasionally. Stir in zucchini and beans. Continue simmering for 15 minutes until zucchini is crisp-tender. If desired, garnish each serving with sour cream, sliced avocado and shredded Monterey Jack cheese. Serves six.

Sweet Dixie Chili

1/2 lb. pound ground sausage
1 medium onion, chopped
1 medium green pepper, chopped
1 cup celery, chopped
16-oz. can tomato juice

16-oz. can whole tomatoes
   with juice, chopped
1 Tbsp. chili powder
1 Tbsp. brown sugar, firmly packed
1 bay leaf
15-oz. can red beans, drained

In large kettle, brown sausage with onion, green pepper and celery. Drain. Add remaining ingredients except beans. Bring to a boil. Reduce heat, cover and simmer 45 minutes, stirring occasionally. Add beans and continue simmering for 15 minutes. Remove bay leaf before serving. Serves six.

Tasty Chile Verde

2 Tbsp. vegetable oil
1 small pork roast
1/2 tsp. ground cumin
1/2 tsp. dried cilantro
1/2 tsp. salt
3 large Anaheim peppers, seeded and diced
1 small onion, chopped

1 clove garlic, minced
1 to 2 cups water to cover
2 Tbsp. masa (corn flour)
1/4 cup warm water
4 cups cooked white rice
Flour tortillas

In large pan, brown pork roast in vegetable oil, adding seasonings during browning process. Add peppers, onion and garlic. Sautee in oil until onion is transparent and garlic is soft. Cover meat and vegetables with water. Bring to boil. Reduce heat and cook on low, covered, for two hours, stirring occasionally. Cook until peppers have dissolved, meat breaks apart easily and all ingredients have combined to make a meaty sauce. Dissolve masa in warm water. Add to sauce to thicken as desired. Serve over rice with tortillas.

Vegetable-Beef Chili

1 Tbsp. vegetable oil
1 lb. ground beef
1 cup onions, chopped
1 clove garlic, minced
1 1/2 tsp. cumin
1 1/2 tsp. oregano
1 1/2 tsp. Serrano pepper,
    seeded and chopped
1 1/2 cups water

2 cups mushrooms, sliced
2 medium tomatoes, chopped
1/2 cup green pepper, chopped
1/2 cup sweet red pepper, chopped
1/2 cup zucchini, diced
1/4 cup celery, diced
1/4 cup carrot, coarsely shredded
1 Tbsp. chili powder
16-oz. can kidney beans, drained

In large kettle, heat oil. Add beef, onions and garlic. Cook until beef is browned and onions are tender. Add cumin, oregano, Serrano pepper and water. Bring to boil. Add all remaining ingredients, except beans. Bring to boil. Reduce heat and simmer for one hour. Add the beans and heat through. Serves four.

Vegetarian Chili

1/2 cup dried kidney beans
1/2 cup dried pinto beans
8 cups cold water
1 1/2 cups onion, chopped
3 cloves garlic, minced
1/2 cup carrot, diced
1/2 cup celery, diced
1/3 cup vegetable oil
1 cup dried lentils, washed
4 Tbsp. chili powder

1 Tbsp. oregano
2 tsp. dried cilantro leaves or coriander
2 Tbsp. paprika
16-oz. can whole tomatoes with liquid, chopped
1 sweet red pepper, seeded and chopped
2 cups fresh mushrooms, sliced
1/4 cup soy sauce
1/4 tsp. salt

Wash red kidney beans and pinto beans, discarding any stones or misshapen beans. Place beans in large bowl. Cover with five cups cold water. Soak overnight. Rinse and drain. Set aside. In large kettle, sauté onions, garlic, carrots and celery in oil until onion is transparent. Add drained beans, lentils, chili powder, oregano, coriander, paprika, tomatoes and three cups cold water. Stir to combine well. Bring to a boil, reduce heat and simmer uncovered for two hours, stirring occasionally. Add sweet red pepper, mushrooms and soy sauce. Simmer another two hours, adding more water if necessary, until beans are tender. Stir in salt. Serves six.

DAD'S Specialties

Dad's Specialties

Doing Dutch Oven

Season Your Oven

Before you use your Dutch oven for the first time, you need to season it. This is absolutely necessary. And you can't do it with a salt shaker. "Seasoning" a Dutch oven means to ready the cast iron for cooking. First, wash your oven thoroughly with hot, soapy water. It will remove residual oils from manufacturing if your oven is new and will remove any cooking residue if your oven is used. Rinse and dry well. Next, bake your oven in a preheated 350-degree conventional oven for 30 minutes. This will dry out any moisture in the pores. Let cool. Now, rub the inside with shortening, being careful to completely cover the entire surface. Return to a 350-degree oven for another 30 minutes to complete the seasoning process. Finally, wipe any excess shortening or oils from the oven, and you're ready to go!

Checklist

Dutch Oven Essentials

❒ 12-inch or 14-inch cast iron Dutch oven with lid.
❒ Firewood and palm-size stones or commercial barbecue briquettes
❒ Matches or lighter
❒ Small hand shovel
❒ Long-handled metal tongs
❒ Heavy duty aluminum foil
❒ Heavy oven mitts

Chickaree Chicken

1 cup flour
1 Tbsp. salt
1 Tbsp. coarsely ground black pepper
4 skinless, boneless chicken breasts

1 Tbsp. butter or margarine
1 tsp. hickory or smoke flavoring
Milk for gravy

In a paper sack, combine flour, salt and pepper. Shake to mix. Drop chicken pieces in bag, one at a time, and shake to coat completely with flour. Melt butter in medium or 14-inch Dutch oven and sprinkle with smoke flavoring. Brown chicken in butter, turning to brown both sides. Cover oven and place coals on top of lid. Cook over medium coals for one hour, or until chicken is tender. Remove chicken from oven. Stir two to three tablespoons of flour mixture into drippings and whisk with enough milk to make a thickened gravy. Serve with hot biscuits, if desired. Serves four.

Outdoor Clam Chowder

Two 6-oz. cans minced clams, drained (reserve juice)
3/4 cup onion, chopped
3/4 cup celery, diced
1 1/2 cup potatoes, diced
Water

1/3 cup butter or margarine
1/3 cup flour
2 cups half & half or light cream
Salt and pepper as desired
1 Tbsp. red wine vinegar
1 1/2 tsp. fresh parsley, chopped

Place onion, celery and potatoes in medium Dutch oven. Cover vegetables with juice from canned clams. If vegetables are not completely covered, add enough water to cover. Simmer until potatoes are tender. In a second oven, melt butter. Stir in flour and cook for two minutes. Add cream and whisk until smooth and thick. Stir in vegetables, clams and seasonings. Heat through. Serves six.

Inside-Out Sloppy Joes

3 lbs. lean ground beef
1 medium onion, chopped
3 3/4 cup water
Three 6-oz. cans tomato paste

3 pkgs. dry Sloppy Joe seasoning mix
4 cups biscuit mix
1 1/3 cups water

In medium Dutch oven, cook ground beef and onion until beef is browned and onion is transparent. Add tomato paste, 3 3/4 cups water and seasoning mix. Stir to combine. Cover and bring to a simmer. Simmer ten minutes. In large bowl, combine biscuit mix and 1 1/3 cups water to make soft dough. Drop by spoonfuls onto simmering sloppy joe mixture. Cover and place coals on lid. Bake until golden brown or until an inserted knife comes out clean. Serve in bowls.

Bacon Steak & Mushrooms

1/2 lb. bacon, cooked until brown
2 cups fresh mushrooms, sliced

4 beef steaks
Salt and pepper to taste

In small or 12-inch Dutch oven over medium coals, cook bacon and brown mushrooms in grease. Remove from oven and set aside. In oven, brown steaks on both sides. Set aside. Place two steaks in bottom of oven. Cover with a layer of mushrooms and bacon. Place other two steaks on top of mushrooms and top with remaining mushrooms and bacon. Season with salt and pepper. Cover. Place on low fire with coals on top of oven lid. Bake for 20 to 30 minutes. Serves four.

Chops & Scalloped Potatoes

4 large pork chops
Vegetable oil or bacon grease
4 large potatoes, sliced thin

2 large onions, sliced thin
1 can cream of mushroom soup
1 cup cheddar cheese, grated

Trim pork chops to remove bones and excess fat. In medium Dutch oven, brown chops on both sides in vegetable oil or bacon grease. Remove meat from oven. Layer half the potatoes in the bottom of the oven, then half the onions, then two chops, then half the cream of mushroom soup. Repeat the layers. Sprinkle grated cheddar cheese on top and cover. Place oven on coals and arrange coals on lid. Cook one to two hours, until potatoes are tender. Serves four.

Veggie Beef & Rice

1/3 lb. bacon, cut in small pieces
1 cup onion, chopped
4 stalks celery, chopped
1 lb. lean ground beef
1 cup uncooked long-grain rice
1 quart stewed tomatoes with juice

1 cup water
1 tsp. salt
1/2 head of broccoli, cut into spears
2 carrots, thinly sliced
1/2 cup fresh mushrooms, sliced
1 cup water

In Dutch oven, combine bacon, onion, celery, and ground beef. Cook over hot coals until ground beef is browned and bacon is crisp. Drain grease. Stir in rice, tomatoes, water and salt. Add vegetables. Cover and cook over hot coals with coals on lid for 30 minutes, stirring occasionally. Add another cup of water, cook for 20 more minutes. Serves six.

Beefy Baked Beans

1/4 lb. bacon
1/2 lb. lean ground beef
1 small onion, chopped
1 small green pepper, chopped
1/4 cup brown sugar, packed

1/4 cup ketchup
8-oz. can homestyle chili sauce
1 Tbsp. prepared mustard
1/4 lb. cooked ham, cut into cubes
31-oz. can pork and beans

In medium Dutch oven, brown bacon and ground beef. Add onion and green pepper. Cook until tender. Drain fat. Add brown sugar, ketchup, chili sauce and mustard. Simmer for 15 minutes. Add beans and ham. Cover and simmer for two hours with coals on lid. Serves six.

It's The Pits

The best way to cook Dutch oven is in a specially made fire pit. With a little preparation, you can virtually forget your food for hours on end. This is especially great on a camping trip or at a family gathering because you don't have to babysit the food. You and yours can go about having fun while your lunch or dinner cooks. Then when you come back hungry, foods on! NOTE: Always be safe around fire pits or campfires and make sure children stay far away from the hot oven. If you want to Dutch oven cook more often than the occasional camping trip, make a pit in your backyard near the concrete back porch or deck.

Of course, you don't need a fancy pit to cook with a Dutch oven. A cleared area of dry dirt or concrete, a campfire ring or a barbecue pit, and a bunch of coals will do the trick. Simply gather the coals under and around the oven, then place some on top. Dinner will be done in no time.

To make a Dutch oven fire pit: In a well-drained area, dig a pit that is about six inches deeper than your oven with its lid on and about one foot bigger around than your oven. Line the bottom and sides of the pit with dry flat stones. If you can get it, dry lava rock is ideal. When you are ready to start cooking, lay a fire in the bottom of the pit with plenty of dry firewood. Toss in enough extra rocks to cover the lid of your oven. Light the fire. Once it has burned down to the coals, remove the coals and the extra stones from the pit. Lower your Dutch oven into the pit, cover the lid with the hot stones from the fire, rake the hot coals on top of the pit and cover the whole thing with the dirt you removed when you dug the pit. Depending on the recipe, you can relax for two or three hours and let the hot rocks do the cooking. All you have to do is eat! *For safety reasons, do not leave an oven or fire pit unattended.*

Wilderness Beef Stew

2 lbs. stew meat	4 stalks celery, sliced
Vegetable oil or bacon grease	1 can whole-kernel corn, drained
2 large potatoes, cut into cubes	1 pkg. dry onion soup mix
4 carrots, cut in thick slices	2 cups hot water

In medium Dutch oven, brown stew meat on all sides in vegetable oil or bacon grease. Add vegetables. Sprinkle onion soup mix over meat and vegetables. Stir. Pour in hot water, cover, and place coals on top of lid. Cook over medium heat for two to three hours or until meat is tender. Serves six.

Campfire Potatoes

6 strips bacon	2 large onions, thinly sliced
4 large potatoes, thinly sliced	Salt and pepper

Line bottom of medium Dutch oven with bacon strips. Fry until bacon is crisp. Layer potato and onion slices in oven. Add salt and pepper to taste. Cover and cook for about 30 minutes with coals on lid. Rotate oven often to avoid hot spots. Serves six.

Fish Roll Ups

3 carrots, cut into strips
6 broccoli spears
6 fillets of white fish

3 Tbsp. butter or margarine, melted
1 tsp. crushed dill weed
Cooking string

In medium Dutch oven, steam carrots and broccoli until tender. Wrap a broccoli spear and some carrot strips with fish fillet. Tie with string. Place in oven, sprinkle with dill. Cook turning as needed, until fish flakes easily with fork. Baste with melted butter. Serves six.

Candied Yams

6 strips bacon
4 large sweet potatoes or yams,
    thinly sliced

1 1/2 cup brown sugar, packed
1/2 cup mini-marshmallows

In medium Dutch oven, cook yams until fork-tender but still firm. Peel and slice into 1/2-inch slices. Melt butter in oven, brown yams on both sides. Sprinkle with sugar and dot with additional butter. Cover and bake for 30 minutes. Pour marshmallows over top. Cover until marshmallows melt. Serves six.

Ham Hocks & Beans

3 cups dried beans
4 ham hocks

2 medium onions, chopped
1 cup cheddar cheese, grated

In a large Dutch oven, cover beans with water. Soak overnight. Drain. Place ham hocks in bottom of oven. Add onions, beans, cheese and enough water to cover all ingredients. Place lid on oven and cover with coals. Cook for three to four hours, or until beans are tender. Serves six to eight.

Cheesy Green Beans

2 cans French-cut green beans, drained
1 can cream of mushroom soup

1/2 cup cheddar cheese, shredded
1 Tbsp. bottled pimentos, chopped

Place green beans in bottom of small Dutch oven. Add remaining ingredients and stir well. Cook until mixture is heated through and cheese melts. Serves six.

Magic Dinner Rolls

1 cup lukewarm water	1 egg
1/4 cup butter or margarine, melted	1 Tbsp. yeast or 1 yeast cake, dissolved
1/4 cup sugar	in 1/4 cup lukewarm water
1 tsp. salt	3 cups flour

In large bowl, combine all ingredients. Beat well, form into a large ball, cover and let rise for one hour. Knead for ten minutes and shape into desired rolls. Spray the bottom of a 12-inch Dutch oven with vegetable spray. Cover bottom of oven with rolls. Cover and bake for about 12 minutes or until tops and bottoms of rolls are brown. If bottoms brown first, remove Dutch oven from coals and keep lid on to complete cooking. Serves six.

Easy Peach Cobbler

2 large cans sliced peaches	Cinnamon to taste
1 1/2 pkg. dry yellow cake mix	

Completely line a 12-inch Dutch oven with foil. Put the peaches in the bottom of the oven. Sprinkle with dry cake mix over the peaches. Sprinkle with cinnamon as desired. Cover and bake for 35-45 minutes. Serve with ice cream or top with milk or cream.

Cinnamon Apple Cobbler

1 cup butter or margarine	2 cups biscuit mix
1 cup brown sugar, firmly packed	1/4 cup brown sugar, firmly packed
1 can apple pie filling with sliced apples	Water

In large Dutch oven, melt butter. Stir in one cup brown sugar. Cover with apple pie filling. Bring mixture to a boil. In large bowl, stir together biscuit mix and 1/4 cup brown sugar, adding enough water to make a batter. Pour batter over apples in oven. Cover and bake ten minutes. Remove lid, sprinkle top of cobbler with additional brown sugar, replace lid. Cook an additional ten minutes. Serve warm with cream.

Real Sourdough Biscuits

1 1/4 cups warm water
1 Tbsp. active dry yeast
1 tsp. salt
1 Tbsp. shortening

1 Tbsp. sugar
1 cup sourdough starter batter
   (see recipe below)
4 cups flour

Dissolve yeast in warm water. Add salt, shortening, sugar, sourdough starter and two cups flour. Beat until smooth. Add enough of the remaining flour to make a soft dough. Blend well and knead lightly until well mixed. Cover and allow to double in bulk, about one hour. Punch down. Pinch off golf-ball sized pieces and roll into balls. Place side-by-side in greased cake pans that will fit in the bottom of Dutch oven. Cover and again allow to double in bulk. Place three pennies along bottom of oven to allow for airflow under cake pan. Put cake pan on the pennies. Cover with lid and lid with hot coals. Bake the biscuits until golden brown on the top and bottom, checking every few minutes. Check often as biscuits burn easily.

Sourdough Starter

1 Tbsp. dry yeast
2 Tbsp. honey

2 cups warm water
2 cups white flour

Dissolve yeast and honey in warm water in a large glass or plastic bowl. Stir in flour. Cover bowl with a towel and let sit in a warm place for several days, or until foamy and soured. Empty contents into a jar, cover tightly and store in the refrigerator. If you don't use your starter for a week or so, you'll need to feed it. Remove 1/2 to one cup of the original starter. Use it, give it away or throw it away. Stir in a mixture of one cup flour, one cup warm milk or water and a little sugar. Let sit at room temperature for a few hours, then stir and refrigerate. Prepare starter at least one week before you plan to use it in a recipe.

Chocolate Pudding Cake

1 yellow or chocolate pudding-type
  cake mix

3 to 4 chocolate candy bars

Spray the bottom and sides of 12-inch Dutch oven with vegetable spray. Sprinkle a few teaspoons of dry cake mix in the bottom of the oven and shake back and forth to coat the bottom evenly. Mix the cake according to package directions and pour into the oven, checking to make sure the oven is level. Cover and bake with coals on lid until cake pulls away from the sides of the oven and is springy to the touch. Remove from heat. Place chocolate bars on cake. When melted, spread over cake.

Dutch Oven Fudge

1/2 cup butter or margarine
1 can evaporated milk
5 cups granulated sugar

2 cups chocolate chips
1 cup chopped nuts (optional)
1 heaping cup marshmallow creme

Melt butter in bottom of medium Dutch oven, turning oven as butter melts so entire inside is coated. Add milk and sugar. Cook and stir until thickened. The mixture should make a sucking noise when you stir it. Remove from heat. Pour into a large bowl. Quickly stir in chocolate chips, nuts and marshmallow creme. Beat until the mixture is stiff. Scrape bowl and pour mixture into greased or foil-lined cookie sheet. Spread quickly. When cool, cut into pieces.

Fruited Baked Apples

4 apples
2 oranges, peeled, seeded and separated
   into segments

4 Tbsp. brown sugar
2 Tbsp. butter or margarine

Slice the top fourth off each apple. Set aside tops. Hollow out the core and seeds, being careful not to puncture the bottom of the apple. Fill each apple with orange segments. Set aside. Melt butter or margarine in Dutch oven. Place apples in oven. Sprinkle with brown sugar. Replace the top on each apple. Cook in covered oven until apples are soft. Let cool slightly before serving. Serves four.

Pineapple Upside Down Cake

Vegetable spray
3 cans pineapple chunks, drained
   (reserve juice)
1/4 cup butter or margarine

1 cup brown sugar, firmly packed
1 lemon cake mix
1/2 cup brown sugar, firmly packed

Completely line a large Dutch oven with foil, shiny side up. Spray foil with vegetable spray. Melt butter in oven. Stir in one cup brown sugar and pineapple chunks. Bring to boil. In large bowl, combine dry cake mix, 1/2 cup brown sugar and enough reserved pineapple juice to make a batter. Pour batter over boiling pineapple chunks. Cover with lid and bake until cake is browned and pulls away from sides. Invert cake and remove foil. Serve warm.

DAD'S Specialties

Choosing & Cooking Meats

Meat can be one of the most expensive items on your grocery list. You should know what to look for in selecting quality poultry, fish, pork, lamb, veal and beef. A general rule when choosing any meat is to check the color and the odor. After meat has been stored in the refrigerator for a few days, always check the smell. If it has a foul odor, throw it out.

Pathogens—germs and bacteria—found in meat and poultry can cause serious illness in humans. Raw meats, especially those being thawed, should be stored covered on a plate on the bottom shelf of the refrigerator to avoid spilling meat juices and contaminating other foods. Cooking to proper internal temperatures, usually to 170 degrees or more, is the primary way to kill pathogens in meat. When cooking meats, check the internal temperature with a meat thermometer. Cook meat within a few days of purchase or within a day of thawing to assure it does not go bad. *Thawed meats should not be refrozen.* Fresh fish should be in the refrigerator for only a day before using.

Poultry: Chicken is the most popular choice of poultry for dinner, but turkey, duck and game hens also make great picks for the supper table. Whether fresh or frozen, look for well-shaped, plump birds that have blemish-free, light, even-colored skin. The flesh of fresh birds should look moist but not wet as wetness can indicate the bird has been partially frozen. When selecting younger birds, gently bend the tip of the breastbone, which should be flexible. There should be no signs of bruising or feathers. Make sure the legs are pliable and the skin is intact. The body should be compact and well-rounded with plump, firm breasts. The bird should smell fresh, and the smells from the wrapping should disappear quickly. If poultry has a foul smell, do not cook or eat it. Throw it out.

Thaw frozen poultry in the refrigerator overnight before cooking. Do not thaw meat on counter or in sink as this encourages bacteria growth. A whole chicken

*D*ad says:
The best way to thaw frozen meat is covered on a plate or in a pan for a few days in the refrigerator. So, plan ahead.

should be baked in a 350-degree oven for about one hour (15 minutes per pound), depending on the size of the bird. Follow directions printed on packaging for larger birds, such as turkey. Poultry is done when the internal temperature reaches 170 degrees, meat is white and juices run clear.

Fish: When choosing whole fish, look for clear, bright eyes that are not sunken, and bright, red gills.

Scales should not be missing and should be firmly attached. The tail should be stiff and the flesh should be firm with a sea-fresh smell. When choosing fillets, look for neat, trim cuts with firm flesh. White fish should have a white, translucent color with no discoloration. Smoked fish should have a glossy appearance with firm flesh that is not sticky, and a pleasant, smoked smell. When choosing frozen fish, make sure that the selection is frozen hard with no signs of thawing and no evidence of freezer burn. There should be no ice crystals or dull, white, dry patches on the fish.

When choosing shellfish, shells should not be cracked or broken. Shells of mussels and oysters should be tightly shut. Discard Open shells that do not close when tapped sharply. Lobsters, crab and prawns should have a good color and be heavy for their size. Lobsters and crabs should have all their limbs intact.

Pork: The meat from a pig should be slightly pink with an overtone of gray. The fat is white but much softer than that of other meats. The flesh is usually streaked with fat. Organically cured hams and bacon done with natural smoking and organic grains will appear gray in color. The shoulder, loin, tenderloin, leg, side, spare rib, shoulder, and hock all provide delicious cuts of pork. The best pork is firm and pink. It should not be too red, too white or too fat. It should not be damp or slimy. *For different cuts of pork, see illustration Cuts of Pork on page 139.*

Lamb: The flesh of a young sheep should be pinkish and the fat should be firm and white. It is usually roasted. Chops and cutlets are often grilled. Mutton, the flesh of more mature sheep, is a darker red than lamb, but the fat is very similar in appearance. Tenderness and taste depend on the age of the lamb when slaughtered. Older lambs provide meat with a stronger flavor than younger animals. Lamb should be firm to the touch and range in color from pink to dark pink. *For different cuts of lamb, see illustration Cuts of Lamb on page 139.*

Veal: This is the flesh of very young calves, usually up to one year old. Veal should be moist and appear white or slightly pink. It has little fat but what there is should be clear white. Veal doesn't have as pronounced a flavor as meat from more mature cattle. Cooked veal is white, tender, and very lean, but quality can vary depending on how the calf was reared. Today, the best veal calves are raised on mother's milk. *For different cuts of pork, see illustration Cuts of Veal on page 140.*

Beef: The best beef is shiny and bright red, firm to the touch, with a light scent. The fat should be clear white and very firm from grain-fed beef, and slightly yellow and very firm on grass-fed beef. The most tender meat has a network of white fat and has been aged for a minimum of 21 days. The hindquarter provides cuts which can be cooked quickly. Slow-cooking and boiling cuts come from the forequarter. Remove meat from the paper or vacuum pack as soon as possible. Put it in the refrigerator, covered on a glass or china plate. When ready to cook, do not wash meat or valuable juices will be lost. Merely wipe it with a damp paper towel.

Never pierce the meat while it is cooking or valuable juices will be lost. As a general rule, the best results are obtained if the surfaces of meats are seared (browned) as soon as possible when cooking starts. This locks in the juices. After searing, cooking should be slower to develop the finest flavor and tenderness. Tougher cuts should be cooked very slowly for a long time. To sear meats, heat a heavy skillet on the stove, add a small amount of oil and quickly brown all sides of meat in hot oil. Transfer to roasting or cooking pan and cook as desired.

Dad says:
If you want to make sure meat is cooked properly, invest in and use a meat thermometer to check internal temperature before serving.

Timing per pound for roasting meats in 350-degree oven

Meat Type	Doneness	Internal Temp	Minutes Per Pound
Beef	rare	140 degrees	22 min. per pound
	medium	160 degrees	26 min. per pound
	well done	170 degrees	33 min. per pound
Chicken	medium	170 degrees	15 min. per pound
Cured ham	well done	150 degrees	20 min. per pound
Lamb	medium	170 degrees	40 min. per pound
	well done	182 degrees	45 min .per pound
Mutton	medium	170 degrees	30 min. per pound
	well done	182 degrees	35 min. per pound
Pork	well done	185 degrees	40 min. per pound
Veal	well done	170 degrees	35 min. per pound

Knowing Grades of Beef

It's an old-fashioned notion, but you really should talk to your butcher. Tell the butcher what type of beef you want and how you'd like to prepare it. Most of them will be happy to share their knowledge and advice. They likely will be able to give you great tips on cooking your selection. The best meats will be found at a meat market, if you plan to spend a lot of money and preparation time on your meat selection. Otherwise, the larger grocery stores and supermarkets will have a fine selection of meats, too. You'll likely find knowledgeable and helpful butchers there as well. Don't be afraid to ask.

All beef sold in the United States must be inspected by the United States Department of Agriculture (USDA) to insure the meat is wholesome and free from disease. Grading by the USDA, to tell the quality of a particular cut of beef, is voluntary, and meat plants must pay to have meat graded. USDA-graded beef sold at the retail level is Prime, Choice and Select. Lower grades *(Standard, Commercial, Utility, Cutter, and Canner)* are mainly ground or used in processed meat products. *Be aware that retail stores may use other terms, which must be different from USDA grades.*

USDA Prime: Prime grade beef is the ultimate in tender, juicy and flavorful meat. It has abundant marbling flecks of fat within the lean, which enhances both flavor and juiciness. Prime steaks and roasts work the best for broiling and roasting. Don't expect to find Prime meat in the supermarket. Top restaurants and hotels purchase most wholesale Prime meat and the rest is sold to top butchers.

USDA Choice: Choice grade beef has less marbling than Prime but is of very high quality. Choice roasts and steaks from the loin and rib will be very tender, juicy and flavorful. They, like Prime, are suited for roasting and broiling. Good cuts are found in meat markets and most grocery stores.

USDA Select: Select grade beef is very uniform in quality and somewhat leaner than the higher grades. It is the most popular grade overall, and often bears a brand name. It is fairly tender, but because it has less marbling, it may lack some of the juiciness and flavor of the higher grades. Only the tender cuts should be roasted or broiled. Tougher cuts should be marinated before cooking or cooked with moisture, such as pot roasting or stewing, to obtain maximum tenderness and flavor.

Try to obtain meat from younger animals. The prices are higher, but so is the tenderness and taste. *Aging* does help to tenderize cuts of beef from older cattle.

Selecting Cuts of Beef

Quality beef is separated into four major cuts: loin, rib, round and chuck. Packages of fresh beef from the supermarket usually are labeled with the cut as well as the product, such as "chuck roast" or "round steak." This helps consumers know what type of heat is best for cooking the meat. *Generally, round and chuck are less tender and require moist heat, such as pot roasting, braising or simmering, while loin and rib can be cooked by dry-heat methods, such as broiling, roasting or grilling.* The tenderness, juiciness and flavor of the meat also depends on the area of the cattle the beef is cut from. *For different cuts of beef, see illustration Cuts of Beef on page 140.*

*D*id you know? *Aging describes the holding of beef at a temperature of 34 to 36 degrees for a period of time to break down the tough connective tissues through the action of enzymes. This process increases tenderness.*

Ask Mom

For quick main dish microwave recipes, see *Where's Mom Now That I Need Her?*, pages 225 to 234 "Easy Microwave Cooking."

Ask Mom

For more cooking definitions, see *Where's Mom Now That I Need Her?*, pages 52 to 54 "Common Cooking Terms."

Ground Beef: The ground beef on display in a grocery store can come from any part of the steer, including the trimmings. If you want the best burgers or meatloaf and are willing to pay a few cents extra per pound, choose round, chuck or sirloin beef and have it freshly ground by the butcher. *Round* has practically no fat and makes for a fine low-fat burger. *Chuck's* higher fat content makes for tasty, juicy burgers. *Sirloin* that is well-marbled makes tender, flavorful, deluxe hamburgers. Grill, broil or pan-broil for burgers or bake for meatloaf.

Cooking Definitions

Baste: To brush marinade or drippings over meat during cooking or roasting.

Braise: A method by which tougher cuts of meat are browned in fat, then cooked, tightly covered, in a small amount of liquid at low heat for a lengthy period of time. Braising can be done on top of the range or in the oven.

Broil: To cook thinner cuts of meat by placing them on an oven-proof pan on the rack that is directly under the source of heat. It is best to keep oven door open slightly when broiling. Turn meat so both sides cook evenly.

Grill: To cook meat on a rack directly over the source of heat such as on an outdoor barbecue or over the hot coals of a campfire.

Marinate: To make meat more flavorful and tender by letting it stand totally covered in liquid marinade for several hours or overnight before cooking.

Pan Broil: To cook meat in a heavy, ungreased skillet on top of the stove. Grease from the meat is poured off while cooking so that it doesn't fry.

Pot Roast: To brown a roast or other large piece of meat in fat quickly, then cook it in a covered pan on top of the stove or in the oven. A small amount of liquid is added to make the roast tender.

Roast: To cook meat in an oven, uncovered and with no added liquid, allowing the dry heat to surround the item.

Saute: To cook small chunks of meat quickly in melted butter or oil until brown and tender.

Sear: To brown meat rapidly by using extremely high heat.

Simmer: To cook meat in hot liquid just below the boiling point. Bubbles will form slowly, but break just before reaching the liquid's surface.

Stewing: To simmer tough cuts of meat in liquid for hours to become tender.

Cuts of Meat

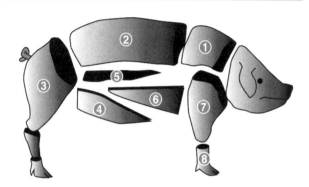

PORK

1. Blade Shoulder
2. Loin
3. Leg
4. Side
5. Tenderloin
6. Spare rib
7. Arm Shoulder
8. Hock

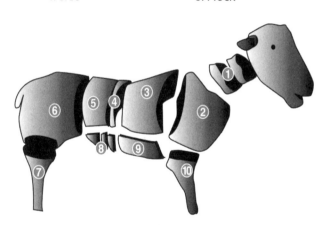

LAMB

1. Neck Slice
2. Shoulder
3. Rib
4. Loin Chop
5. Loin
6. Leg
7. Hind Shank
8. Riblets
9. Breast
10. Fore Shank

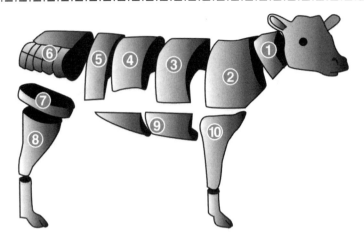

VEAL

1. Blade
2. Shoulder
3. Rib
4. Loin
5. Sirloin

6. Boneless Rump
7. Round Steak
8. Leg (round)
9. Breast
10. Fore Shank

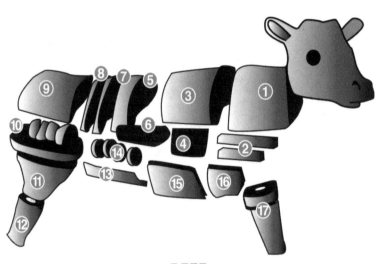

BEEF

1. Chuck
2. Flanken Ribs
3. Rib
4. Back Ribs
5. Short Loin
6. Porterhouse

7. Tenderloin
8. Sirloin
9. Round
10. Rump Roast
11. Round Steak
12. Hind Shank

13. Flank
14. Flank Steak Rolls
15. Short Plate
16. Brisket
17. Fore Shank

DAD'S Specialties

From The Grill

Dad's Three-Meat Kabobs

1/2 lb. lean beef, cut into cubes
2 boneless, skinless chicken breasts,
    cut into cubes
1/2 lb. pork, cut into cubes
1 medium onion, cut into chunks
2 green peppers, cut into chunks

8 cherry tomatoes
8 mushroom caps
3 Tbsp. vegetable oil
3 Tbsp. lemon juice
Dash salt and pepper

Alternate beef, onion, chicken, pepper, pork, tomato and mushroom on skewers. Brush with oil and lemon juice. Sprinkle with salt and pepper. Grill for 20 minutes, turning skewers often. Serves four.

Grilled Stuffed Steaks

6-oz. pkg. long grain and wild rice mix
6 New York strip steaks
1 egg, beaten

1/4 cup green onions, sliced thinly
Easy Barbecue Sauce (See recipe below)

Cook rice according to package directions and set aside. Using sharp knife, cut a pocket in side of each steak. Combine cooked rice, egg and green onions. Mix well. Stuff about 1/2 cup rice mixture into the pocket of each steak. Grill over hot coals, basting frequently with barbecue sauce. Cook 6 minutes on each side for medium-rare steak, longer for more well-done steak. Serves six.

Easy Barbecue Sauce

1/4 cup sugar
1 Tbsp. flour
1 tsp. salt
1 tsp. ginger

1/2 cup ketchup
3 Tbsp. soy sauce
1 tsp. Worcestershire
1 Tbsp. white vinegar

In large bowl, combine sugar, flour, salt and ginger. Mix well. Add ketchup, soy sauce, Worcestershire and vinegar. Mix until well blended. Use on any meats on outdoor grill. Makes enough to barbecue three pounds meat.

Dad says:
Marinate beef in the refrigerator up to five days. Boil used marinade before brushing on cooked beef. Discard any uncooked leftover marinade.

Preparing Meats

Before placing meat on the grill, trim off excess fat to prevent a fire flare-up. There's nothing worse than blackened meat that you didn't intend to serve blackened. To keep steaks, pork chops or ham slices from curling as they cook, make shallow cuts about 1/4 inch apart on the surface of the meat with a sharp paring knife.

How Much Per Person? For the average appetite, allow 1/4 to 1/2 pound of boneless meat per person or 3/4 to one pound of meat on the bone. Usually two hamburgers, hotdogs, pieces of chicken, and chops or three to four ribs per adult.

How Thick? Steaks and chops should be at least one inch thick. Thinner cuts will get too done before they brown on the grill. In general, grill tender cuts of meat only. You can barbecue less tender cuts if you marinate or pound them first.

No Sticking: When you cook meat that might stick to the grill, such as fish, chicken or other lean meats, brush the grill with a little vegetable oil before you start. Cooking time will vary with the cut, thickness and shape of the meat, what temperature it is when placed over the coals, the position of the meat on the grill and desired degree of doneness.

When To Season: When barbecuing, season the meat after you turn it. Salting raw meat draws the juices from it. Use tongs instead of a fork to turn meat—piercing the meat with a fork lets delicious juices escape.

Test For Doneness: To decide when a piece of meat is done, use a sharp knife to make a small slit near the bone. Check the color of the meat. Chicken should be white and juices clear. Pork should be white with no pink. Most fish should be white and flaky. Cook beef according to desired doneness: medium rare (brown on the outside, red and juicy inside,) medium (browned outside, not as red inside) and well done (well browned outside and cooked through inside).

Don't Forget To Baste: To baste meats with barbecue sauce or butter, use a thick, wide brush. Actually, a new paint brush will work well. Some sauces can be used throughout the cooking time, while others should be used only during the last 15 to 30 minutes. Sauces that contain tomato sauce or sugar tend to burn easily and should be used only during the last 15 minutes.

Brown Sugar Chicken

1/3 cup brown sugar
1/3 cup soy sauce
1/4 cup water

3 Tbsp. vegetable oil
1/2 tsp. dry mustard
3 lbs. chicken breasts

In small saucepan over low heat, stir together brown sugar, soy sauce, water, oil and dry mustard until sugar is dissolved. Let mixture cool. Place chicken in a bowl. Pour cooled sugar mixture over chicken, cover and marinate at room temperature for two hours or overnight in the refrigerator. Turn chicken two to three times during marinating. Grill, basting with marinade, until done, about 10 minutes each side.

Lemon Ginger Chicken

1/4 cup lemon juice
1 tsp. grated lemon peel
1 tsp. vegetable oil
1/2 tsp. salt
1/2 tsp. ginger

1/2 tsp. paprika
1/4 tsp. onion salt
1/4 tsp. pepper
3-lb. fryer chicken, cut into pieces

In shallow baking dish, combine all ingredients except chicken. Mix thoroughly. Add chicken pieces, turning to coat well. Cover and refrigerate for at least three hours. Grill chicken over medium coals for 45 minutes, turning and basting frequently.

Barbecued Pork Chops

1/2 cup ketchup
1 cup water
1/3 cup vinegar
1/2 tsp. nutmeg

1 tsp. salt
1 tsp. celery seed
4 pork chops

Combine ketchup, water, vinegar and spices. Place pork chops in shallow dish. Pour sauce over chops. Marinate for two hours at room temperature, or cover bowl and marinate in refrigerator overnight. Barbecue chops on the grill, basting with marinate, until done.

Starting the Fire

Start your barbecue briquettes about one hour before you plan to cook. Lay a crumbled up piece of brown sack paper along the bottom of the barbecue. Stack the coals in the center of the paper in a pyramid shape. Douse the coals with starter fluid, then wait two to three minutes to allow the starter to penetrate the coals. Light the coals in several places on the pyramid. Wait 40 to 45 minutes until coals are ashen gray around the edges and red hot in the centers. Using a long-handled fork or tongs, spread the coals in a tight, even layer over the bottom of the barbecue. Food should be completely underlined with coals. For a special flavor, soak wood chips in water for 30 minutes and scatter them over hot coals. Use sparingly as they add a strong smoked flavor. For variation, try hickory, mesquite, cherry, apple or alder chips. Start cooking when the chips begin to smoke. Wood chips and ready-light (or pre-soaked) coals can be found in the barbecue and grilling section of most supermarkets.

How Hot Are Those Coals? Want to figure out how hot your coals are? It's easy—all you need is your hand. No! Don't pick them up. Simply hold your hand, palm side down, above the coals at the height your food will be cooking. Then count seconds, saying "one one thousand, two one thousand, three one thousand"" If you have to move your hand after two seconds, the coals are hot. If you need to move your hand after three seconds, the coals are medium-hot; four seconds, medium; five seconds, medium-low; and six seconds, low.

Gas Barbecues & Grills: When using a gas barbecue or grill, make sure you preheat your grill on the high setting with the lid open for 10 to 15 minutes before you start to cook. Once the grill is preheated, turn the control to the desired setting, usually medium. Close the grill cover if you want foods to cook faster and have more of a smoked flavor. The heat pattern on a gas grill will change with the wind direction and the grill location. For the most even cooking, place grill in a sheltered area. Keep a spray bottle filled with water to put out flames if you have a flare-up on a gas grill. The finer the mist, the better. If you sprinkle water over a wide cooking area, you will lower the temperature of the coals too much and your food will steam instead of grill.

Clean-Up Tips: Before you start cooking, brush vegetable oil on the grill. Foods won't stick and clean up will be easier. If you use skillets or pans on the grill, coat the bottom of each with a thin layer of bar soap. It will be simple to clean off the soot after barbecuing. To clean a dirty grill, let it cool, then use a stiff wire brush to scrape off all particles. If you have a stubborn mess, let the grill cool completely, then put it in an extra-strong garbage bag. Sprinkle dishwashing powder over it and pour in enough steaming hot water to cover the grill. Tie the bag closed, and let it sit for an hour or two on a flat surface. Take out of the bag and easily scrub off soot and burned on food with wire brush. Rinse and allow to dry.

Barbecue In A Wheelbarrow?: If you don't have a barbecue or fancy grill, don't despair. An old wheelbarrow will do the trick, really! Convert an old wheelbarrow into a low-cost, versatile, portable barbecue. Fill it with six inches of dirt, sand or gravel, then simply stack bricks up along the sides and place your barbecue grill across the bricks. Vary the heat by stacking fewer or more bricks. Scatter your coals over the dirt or sand and there you have it! One must: Make sure you cover your wheelbarrow barbecue with a waterproof tarp when it's not in use to keep out small animals and the rain. If the sand gets wet, you'll need to change it. Leaving wet sand in the wheelbarrow will rust out the bottom.

> **CAUTION:** Never use gasoline or kerosene to start coals. This is quite dangerous and the toxins from this type of fuel will spoil your food. Always place your barbecue in an open area, not under a roof or in a shed. Do not douse hot coals or an open fire with more lighter fluid. If there is a spark, the fire can travel up the lighter fluid trail and explode the can in your hands. Keep children away from hot barbecue or grill. Place in area where people can see and steer clear of the lit barbecue.

Grilled Drunk Salmon

4 salmon steaks, cut one inch thick
1/4 cup vegetable oil
1/4 cup white wine
1 tsp. shredded lime peel

2 Tbsp. lime juice
1/4 tsp. pepper
2 cloves garlic, minced

Place salmon steaks in shallow dish. In small bowl, combine oil, white wine, lime peel, lime juice, garlic and pepper. Mix well. Pour mixture over salmon. Turn salmon to coat well with marinade. Cover and refrigerate for at least six hours or overnight. Drain salmon, reserving marinade. Use paper towels to pat excess moisture from salmon. Grill over medium-hot coals for seven minutes, brushing occasionally with marinade. Turn and grill for another eight minutes. When done, salmon should flake easily when tested with a fork. Serves four.

Orange Shrimp Kabobs

18 large shrimp, peeled and deveined
12 strips bacon
18 cherry tomatoes
1 large zucchini, halved and cut into 12 chunks

18 large mushrooms
1/4 cup honey
4 tsp. orange juice
3 cups cooked rice

Thread three shrimp on each of six skewers, alternating with two strips of bacon, three cherry tomatoes, three mushrooms, and two chunks of zucchini. Spiral-wrap the bacon around the vegetables and shrimp as you thread them on the skewers. In a small bowl, combine honey and orange juice. Brush mixture generously over kabobs. Grill six inches from coals for ten minutes or until shrimp is bright pink and bacon is golden crisp, turning and basting frequently. Serve kabobs over rice if desired.

The Skinny on Skewers:

For meat kabobs, use metal skewers that are long enough to fit completely across the width of the grill. If you use bamboo skewers, soak them in water for 30 minutes before threading food onto them to keep them from burning. To keep food from sticking to skewers, lightly oil the skewers before threading food onto them. When threading foods, leave a small gap between all pieces of food to allow for complete cooking. Leave at least four inches between the food and the skewer handle to allow for proper heat penetration. Use a whole water chestnut, a chunk of raw potato or a chunk of raw carrot on the end of the skewer to keep food from slipping off as it cooks. To keep track of skewers and keep them out of the reach of children, remove food from skewer and place on plate to serve, then place all empty skewers in one bowl or basket for cleaning.

Mushroom Stuffed Chicken

2 Tbsp. margarine
1/2 cup fresh mushrooms, chopped fine
1/3 cup green onion, chopped
1/4 cup tomato sauce

1 1/2 cups cooked rice
3 lb. fryer chicken, cut into quarters
2 cups Tangy Barbecue Sauce
  (See recipe on page 153.)

In a large frying pan, melt margarine. Stir in mushrooms and green onions, and sauté over low heat until vegetables are still slightly crisp. Stir in tomato sauce and cooked rice. Heat through. Loosen the skin on each chicken quarter, forming a pocket between the chicken and the skin. Spoon one-fourth of the rice mixture into each pocket and secure with toothpicks or skewers. Grill chicken on greased grill, skin-side up, five inches from low coals, for 20 minutes. Turn chicken, brush with barbecue sauce, and grill for another 40 minutes, basting with barbecue sauce every ten minutes.

Island Teriyaki Steak

1 1/2 lbs. sirloin steak
1/2 cup soy sauce
1/4 cup brown sugar
1 tsp. ginger

1/4 tsp. cracked black pepper
15-oz. can pineapple chunks
1 can whole water chestnuts

Cut steak into one inch wide strips. In a deep bowl, combine soy sauce, brown sugar, ginger and pepper. Mix well. Add steak strips and stir to coat steak well. Cover bowl and marinate for two hours at room temperature, or overnight in the refrigerator. Lace steak accordion-style on four skewers, alternating with pineapple chunks. Place a water chestnut on the end of each skewer to hold meat in place. Grill over medium coals for 15 minutes, turning and basting frequently with marinade. Serves four.

Barbecued Turkey Breast

1 1/2 pounds boneless turkey breast,
  sliced one-inch thick
1 cup white wine
1/2 cup soy sauce

1/2 cup vegetable oil
1 1/2 Tbsp. lemon juice
2 garlic cloves, crushed

In medium bowl, combine wine, soy sauce, oil, lemon juice and garlic. Mix well. Arrange turkey slices in a shallow dish. Pour marinade over turkey. Cover and marinate in refrigerator at least six hours or overnight. Drain turkey, reserving marinade. Grill over hot coals 30 minutes, turning frequently and brushing with sauce. Serves four.

Peachy Pork Chops

1/2 cup peach jam
1 Tbsp. soy sauce
1 Tbsp. water

1 Tbsp. dry onion flakes
1/2 tsp. Tabasco sauce
8 thinly sliced pork chops

In large bowl, combine all ingredients except pork chops. Mix well. Place pork chops in shallow pan. Pour sauce over chops until they are evenly covered. Refrigerate for at least one hour. Grill over hot coals for 30 minutes, turning often and basting with sauce. Heat remaining sauce and serve with pork chops. Serves four. If desired, you can substitute other fruit jam, such as apple, apricot or pineapple preserves.

Japanese Shish Kabobs

1 boneless, skinless chicken breast,
    cut into cubes
1/2 lb. cooked ham, cut into cubes
2 fresh zucchini, cut into cubes
1 cup pineapple chunks, drained

1/4 cup pineapple juice
3 Tbsp. soy sauce
1 Tbsp. vegetable oil
1 tsp. cornstarch

On long metal skewers, alternate chicken, zucchini, ham and pineapple chunks until skewer is full. Combine pineapple juice, soy sauce, oil and cornstarch in a jar. Screw on lid and shake until all ingredients are well combined. Place skewers in shallow pan. Pour pineapple juice mixture over the skewers. Rotate skewers until all food is coated. Broil over grill for five minutes on each side, basting with pineapple juice mixture.

Tasty Zucchini Kabobs

4 small zucchini, cut into lengthwise slices
3 cloves garlic, crushed
1/2 cup vegetable oil

1 Tbsp. basil
Pinch salt
Dash freshly ground black pepper

Place zucchini in shallow dish. In small bowl, mash garlic with two tablespoons oil until smooth. Whisk in remaining oil, basil, salt and pepper. Pour over zucchini and marinate for 30 minutes. Drain. Grill over hot coals for five minutes each side.

Cheese Dip on a Grill

1/2 lb. cheddar cheese, shredded
1/2 lb. Monterey Jack cheese, shredded
1/2 cup butter or margarine

4 ounces fresh salsa
1 small loaf French bread,
    cut into bite sized cubes

In a cast-iron skillet, combine cheeses and butter. Place on grill over medium-hot coals. Whip constantly with wire whisk until cheeses and butter are melted and smooth. Stir in salsa. Keep skillet at edge of grill, stirring occasionally. To serve, dip bread cubes into cheese mixture.

Cheesy Grilled Broccoli

1 1/2 lbs. broccoli
1/3 cup vegetable oil
2 1/2 Tbsp. lemon juice

1/4 tsp. salt
1/8 tsp. black pepper
3/4 cup fresh Parmesan cheese, grated

Peel broccoli stalks and trim to 3 1/2-inch pieces. Cut each stalk in half vertically, cutting through flowerets. Place broccoli spears in shallow dish. In another bowl, combine oil, lemon juice, salt and pepper. Pour over broccoli and toss to coat. Cover and marinate at room temperature for 30 minutes. Drain. Put Parmesan cheese in plastic bag. Place broccoli, one spear at a time, in bag and shake to coat with cheese. Grill over medium coals for ten minutes on each side. Serves four to six.

Creamy Corn & Peppers

4 ears fresh corn
1 sweet red pepper, seeded and
    finely chopped
1/2 cup heavy cream

1/8 tsp. salt
Dash pepper
Dash Tabasco sauce

Using a sharp knife, cut kernels from each ear of corn. In large bowl, combine corn with all other ingredients. Mix well. Divide corn mixture evenly onto six nine-inch-square pieces of foil. Fold foil over and seal tightly so that steam cannot escape. Grill over medium-hot coals for 15 minutes. Serves six.

Fruited Chicken Bundles

4 chicken breasts, skinned and boned
1/2 cup raisins
1/3 cup dried apricots, snipped into
    fine pieces
1/4 cup unsweetened flaked coconut

1/4 cup water chestnuts, diced
2 Tbsp. butter or margarine, softened
2 Tbsp. light corn syrup
6 Tbsp. butter or margarine, melted
Orange slices

Place each chicken breast between two pieces of plastic wrap. Pound until meat is about 1/4-inch thick. Set aside. In small bowl, combine raisins, apricots, coconut, water chestnuts, softened butter and corn syrup. Place 1/4 cup fruit mixture on top of one end of each chicken breast. Roll chicken breasts up and secure with wooden picks. Grill over medium coals for 45 minutes, turning and basting occasionally with melted butter. Garnish with slices of orange. Serves four.

Lime-Glazed Chicken & Beef

1 Tbsp. lime peel, finely shredded
1/2 cup lime juice
4 Tbsp. vegetable oil
1/4 tsp. salt
2 chicken breasts, skinned and boned
    cut into cubes

1/2 lb. sirloin steak, cut into cubes
1 sweet red pepper, cut into chunks
1 small summer squash, cut into chunks
1 medium onion, cut into chunks
2 Tbsp. honey
1 tsp. sesame seeds

In large bowl, combine lime peel, lime juice, oil and salt. Mix well. Add chicken and beef cubes. Stir until well coated. Cover and refrigerate for three to four hours, turning once each hour to distribute marinade. Thread chicken and steak on four skewers, alternating with pepper, squash and onion. In small saucepan, combine 1/4 cup marinade, honey and sesame seeds. Warm through. Grill skewers over medium-hot coals for six minutes. Turn kabobs, brush with marinade/honey mixture. Grill six more minutes. Brush with mixture again before serving. Serves four.

Grilling Essentials

Clean barbecue grill *(gas, electric or coals)*

Metal tongs *(preferably those that open and close like scissors)*
Use tongs to spread coals, turn meats and grasp hard-to-grip foods

Metal spatula *(preferably one with a long handle)*
Use spatula to turn meats instead of piercing them with a fork

Basting brush *(a new 1 1/2" paint brush works well)*

Skewers *(sturdy 16-inch metal skewers with large, easy-to-grip handles work best)*
Avoid skewers that are hooked together—you should turn them individually.

Small grill basket *(for small foods like vegetables or foods that crumble like fish)*
Choose one with a hinged lid that allows you to turn it during cooking.

Aluminum foil *(great for cooking fish and vegetables with cheese or sauces)*.

Butterflied Short Ribs

4 lbs. beef short ribs
3/4 cup soy sauce
1/4 cup water
3 green onions, sliced thin

2 cloves garlic, minced
2 Tbsp. sesame seeds
2 Tbsp. brown sugar
1/4 tsp. ginger

Butterfly the ribs by cutting the meat lengthwise down to the rib, then spreading the meat out so it can be laid flat on the grill. Spread the ribs in a shallow dish. In another bowl, combine soy sauce, water, green onions, garlic, sesame seeds, brown sugar and ginger in a jar. Screw on lid and shake until all ingredients are combined well. Pour sauce over ribs and let marinate for two hours at room temperature. Grill for five minutes each side, basting with marinade. At five minutes, ribs will be brown and crusty on the outside but still slightly pink on the inside.

Tangy Barbecue Sauce

1 cup ketchup
4 Tbsp. brown sugar
1/2 cup white vinegar
4 Tbsp. Worcestershire

2 tsp. celery seed
1 tsp. chili powder
1 tsp. seasoned salt

In mixing bowl, combine all ingredients in the order listed, mixing with a wire whisk until well blended.

Three Barbecued Peppers

1 sweet red pepper, seeded and quartered
1 green pepper, seeded and quartered

1 sweet yellow pepper, seeded and quartered
1 Tbsp. vegetable oil

Brush the skin side of each pepper quarter with oil. Grill over medium-hot coals for ten minutes, or until peppers are tender and slightly charred. Serves four.

Sweet & Sour Sauce

8-oz. can crushed pineapple, undrained
1 cup ketchup
1 cup unsweetened pineapple juice

1/2 cup brown sugar, firmly packed
1/2 cup vinegar

Put undrained pineapple in blender. Cover and blend until finely chopped. In saucepan, stir together pineapple, ketchup, pineapple juice, brown sugar and vinegar. Bring to a boil, stirring constantly. Reduce heat and simmer, uncovered, until sauce thickens. Makes about three cups. Especially good on beef and hamburgers.

Smokey Barbecue Sauce

1 can tomato soup
1/4 cup sugar
1 Tbsp. vinegar
Dash pepper
1/4 tsp. ground cloves
1 1/2 tsp. liquid smoke

1/2 soup can water
1 Tbsp. Worcestershire
1 tsp. salt
1/4 tsp. cayenne pepper
1/4 tsp. allspice

In mixing bowl, combine all ingredients in order listed, mixing with wire whisk until well blended. Let stand for at least one hour before using. Makes two cups.

Cheesy Pizza Burgers

1 1/2 lb. lean ground beef
Salt and pepper as desired
1 cup shredded mozzarella cheese

1/3 cup olives, chopped
1/4 cup prepared pizza sauce
1 1/2 Tbsp. basil

In large bowl, combine all ingredients. Form into four patties. Grill over hot coals for three minutes on first side and eight minutes on other side (longer for well-done burgers). Top burgers with additional pizza sauce, olive slices and strips of mozzarella cheese.

Brie Onion Burgers

1 1/2 lbs. lean ground beef
1 tsp. salt
1/4 tsp. pepper
2/3 cup onion, coarsely chopped

1 tsp. thyme
4 slices Brie cheese
4 Tbsp. Dijon mustard

Sauté onion until tender. In large bowl, combine ground beef, salt, pepper, onions and thyme. Mix well and form into four patties. Grill over hot coals for four minutes on first side and eight minutes on other side. Top each burger with a slice of Brie and a tablespoon of Dijon mustard.

New Orleans Creole Burgers

1 1/2 lbs. lean ground beef
1 tsp. salt
1/4 tsp. pepper
1/2 cup yellow bell pepper, finely chopped
1/2 cup tomato, finely chopped

2 Tbsp. green onion, finely chopped
2 Tbsp. ketchup
1 tsp. garlic, minced
1 tsp. oregano

In mixing bowl, combine all ingredients. Mix well and form into four patties. Grill over hot coals four minutes on first side and eight minutes on other side (longer for well-done burgers). Top burgers with more chopped tomato, yellow bell pepper and Three-Alarm BBQ Sauce.

Three-Alarm BBQ Sauce

1/2 cup onion, finely chopped
4 cloves garlic, minced
2 Tbsp. crushed red pepper
1 Tbsp. vegetable oil
1 cup beef broth

6-oz. can tomato paste
3/4 cup honey
1 tsp. thyme
1 tsp. oregano
1 tsp. salt

In medium saucepan, cook onion, garlic and hot pepper in oil until the onion is tender. Add broth, tomato paste, honey and spices. Bring to boil, stirring constantly. Reduce heat and simmer uncovered, for 30 minutes. Strain through a sieve or fine strainer and discard any onion and garlic solids. Makes 1 1/2 cups.

True Tex-Mex Burgers

1 1/2 lbs. lean ground beef
1 tsp. salt
1/4 tsp. pepper
1/2 cup canned refried beans
1/2 cup shredded cheddar cheese

1/2 cup crushed corn tortilla chips
2 Tbsp. canned green chiles, drained
   and chopped
2 Tbsp. prepared taco sauce

In large bowl, combine all ingredients. Form into four patties. Grill over hot coals for four minutes on first side then eight minutes on other side (longer for well-done burgers). Top burgers with additional heated refried beans, taco sauce, shredded cheese, sliced and seeded green chiles and whole tortilla chips, as desired.

Rodeo Hot Dogs

1 loaf French bread
1 tsp. prepared mustard
1 Tbsp. butter or margarine, softened
6 large beef frankfurters

6 slices American cheese
6 tomato slices
2 Tbsp. ketchup

Cut loaf of bread into thirds horizontally. On bottom layer of bread, spread mustard and butter. Cut frankfurters in half lengthwise and place on bread. Top with middle layer of bread. Arrange cheese and tomato slices on middle layer. Spread top layer of bread with ketchup. Put top layer over middle layer. Wrap the loaf in foil, sealing edges. Grill over medium-low coals for 30 minutes. Serves six.

Stuffed Hot Dogs

4 hot dogs
4 thick slices American cheese

4 slivers sweet pickle
4 slices bacon

With a sharp knife, split hot dogs almost through. Stuff one slice of cheese and one sliver of pickle into each. Wrap one slice bacon loosely around each wiener and secure with wooden picks. Place the wieners cut-side down on grill. Grill over medium-low coals six minutes on each side.

Chicago-Style Topper

4 tsp. prepared spicy brown mustard
1/2 cup sweet pickle relish

1 cucumber, peeled and chopped
1 tomato, chopped

Grill eight hot dogs and buns. Spread brown mustard on one side of bun. Place hot dog in bun. Spoon pickle relish onto other side of bun. Top with cucumbers and tomatoes. Serves eight.

Italian Two-Pepper Topping

1 green pepper, cubed
1 sweet red or yellow pepper, cubed
1 garlic clove, minced

1/2 tsp. oregano
1 tsp. olive oil
4 slices mozzarella cheese, cut into fourths

In small frying pan, stir-fry peppers, garlic and oregano in olive oil for three to five minutes. Top each grilled hot dog with two slices of cheese and a spoonful of pepper topping. Makes enough topping for eight franks.

Dad's Specialties

Great Tailgating Grub

True tailgating success stories start and end with food. Good food. Tailgating involves a bunch of other f-words, too, like fun, football, fans, family and friends. Sure, the game, the traveling, the party atmosphere and the extra-curricular activities all add to an awesome tailgating experience, but the food is number one. To make sure your friends and family enjoy their meals and talk about the delicious treats long after, take time to prepare your cooking tools and utensils, picnic essentials and tried-and-true recipes in advance. The hard-core tailgater has food and beverages ready for the pre-game, half-time and postgame party, and enough to go around for those fellow tailgaters who spend the entire game-day in the parking lot (some really do).

Patriots Parmesan Popovers

2 eggs
1 cup milk
1 cup flour

1/2 tsp. salt
1 Tbsp. vegetable oil
1/2 cup fresh Parmesan cheese, grated

Make ahead. In large mixing bowl, combine eggs, milk, flour and salt. Beat until smooth. Add oil and beat again until well blended. Sprinkle Parmesan cheese in a thin layer in the bottoms of a well-greased muffin tin. Pour batter to fill tins half full. Bake at 475 degrees for 15 minutes. Reduce heat to 350 degrees and bake for an additional 25 minutes. Remove from tins and let cool. Split and fill with tuna salad.

Dolphin Safe Tuna Filling

1 can water-packed tuna, drained
   and flaked
1/2 cucumber, peeled and chopped
1/4 cup plain, non-fat yogurt
2 tsp. lime juice

1 tsp. poppy seeds
1 Tbsp. green onion, chopped
Salt and pepper
Dash of garlic powder
Alfalfa sprouts

Assemble filling on site. In mixing bowl, combine tuna, cucumbers, yogurt, lime juice, poppy seeds, onion, salt, pepper and garlic powder. Mix well. Spoon into popovers. Add small amount of sprouts to each sandwich. Serves four.

Raiders Jack & Tomato Salad

1 1/2 cups Monterey Jack cheese, cubed
2 medium tomatoes, halved, seeded
   and cubed
1 pickled jalapeño pepper, seeded and
   sliced thin

2 Tbsp. fresh parsley, chopped
2 Tbsp. vegetable oil
1/2 clove garlic, minced

Make ahead but take out of cooler and let sit before serving. In medium bowl, combine all ingredients. Toss together until well combined. Cover and refrigerate for at least two hours. Bring to room temperature before serving. Salt to taste. Serves four.

Steelers Carrot Cake

1 cup sugar
1 cup mashed ripe banana
   (about 3 bananas)
1/2 cup vegetable oil
3 eggs
1 1/2 cup flour
2 tsp. baking powder

1 tsp. salt
1/2 tsp. baking soda
1 tsp. cinnamon
1/4 tsp. ground cloves
1 cup quick-cooking oats
1 cup shredded carrots (about 3 carrots)

Make ahead. In large bowl, beat together sugar, bananas and oil. Add eggs, one at a time, beating well after each. Combine flour, baking powder, salt, baking soda, cinnamon and ground cloves. Add this to banana mixture. Mix well. Stir in oats and carrots. Pour into greased 9-inch square baking pan. Bake at 350 degrees for 40 to 45 minutes or until knife inserted into middle comes out clean. Serves eight.

Dreamy Cream Frosting

1/2 cup butter
8-oz. pkg. cream cheese, softened
1 tsp. vanilla

1 lb. powdered sugar, sifted
8-oz. bowl whipped cream, thawed

Combine butter, cream cheese and vanilla in large bowl and beat until well blended. Add powdered sugar gradually, beating vigorously. When creamy and light, fold in whipped cream. Spread over cool carrot cake.

Tailgate Is A Verb

tail·gate `tA(&)l-"gAt (noun) a board or gate at the rear of a vehicle that can be removed or let down for loading; the back hinged end of a truck or stationwagon. It all started when some hungry football fans threw down the tailgate, sat down there and had an impromptu picnic – sandwiches, chips and a cold drink—before the game or during halftime. It has grown into a nationwide pastime complete with tables and chairs, TVs, radios, grills, camp stoves, travel trailers and, most importantly, famous tailgating recipes.

Tail·gate `tA(&)l-"gAt (verb) to party and feast at pre-game, halftime and post-game; to celebrate in the parking lot before an event.

Vikings Stuffed Vegetables

3 oz. cream cheese, softened
2 oz. bleu cheese, crumbled
1 tsp. onion, finely chopped
1 tsp. fresh lemon juice

2 small cucumbers, peeled
2 celery stalks, washed and trimmed
2 oz. snow peas, stem ends removed

Make ahead and refrigerate for one day. In small bowl, combine cream cheese, bleu cheese, onion and lemon juice. Set aside. Cut cucumbers into thick slices. Scoop out seeds to create a small cavity. Spoon filling into each. Cut open snow peas carefully along curved edge. Lay open and spoon filling into each. Clean, trim and cut celery stalks. Spoon filling into each. Arrange vegetables in shallow airtight container lined with damp paper towels. Cover vegetables with more damp paper towels. Refrigerate until chilled, up to 24 hours. Pack in an insulated container. Serves four.

'49ers Potato Salad

6 medium potatoes, boiled until tender
1 apple, peeled, cored and diced
1/2 cup celery, chopped
2 hard-boiled eggs, chopped
1/3 cup green onions, chopped

1/2 cup sour cream
1/2 cup mayonnaise
2 Tbsp. chopped dill
Salt and pepper as desired

Make ahead so flavors can incorporate. Peel boiled potatoes and cut into cubes. In large bowl, combine potatoes, apples, celery, eggs and green onions. Toss together. In small bowl, combine sour cream, mayonnaise, dill, salt and pepper. Mix until well blended. Pour dressing over potato-apple mixture and stir to coat well. Chill at least two hours before serving.

Cardinals Confetti Meatloaf

1 Tbsp. vegetable oil	1 egg, slightly beaten
3/4 cup chopped carrot	1/3 cup bottled chili sauce
1/4 cup chopped green pepper	1 cup fresh bread crumbs
1/2 cup chopped onion	1/4 tsp. salt
1/4 tsp. sage	Dash pepper
1 1/2 lbs. lean ground beef	1/2 cup cheddar cheese, grated

Make ahead and refrigerate overnight. In medium skillet, heat oil over low heat. Add carrot, green pepper, onion and sage. Cover and cook for 10 minutes, or until vegetables are tender. In mixing bowl, combine beef, egg, chili sauce, bread crumbs, salt and pepper. Gently stir in vegetables and cheese. Line a lightly greased loaf pan with aluminum foil, leaving an overhang on sides. Lightly grease foil. Spoon meat mixture into prepared pan, packing lightly and smoothing top. Bake at 375 degrees for one hour. Cool on a wire rack for ten minutes. Lift meatloaf and foil from pan, allowing juices to drain back into pan. Cover with hanging foil. Place on plate and refrigerate. When completely cooled, carefully peel off foil. Slice meatloaf then place back in shape of loaf and wrap in clean foil. Refrigerate until ready to serve.

Fly A Flag?

Some tailgaters go out of their way to fly a huge flag to let friends and family know where they are. This works. But for those who don't want to go to the trouble of setting up the flagpole and all, buy one or more large mylar balloons of one solid color and mark them with your name or symbol using an extra-large black permanent marker. Tie this to your bumper or vehicle antennae. Your folks will find you.

Packers Poppyseed Bread

3 cups flour	1 1/2 cups milk
2 1/2 cups sugar	1 1/4 cups vegetable oil
1 1/2 tsp. baking powder	3 eggs
1 1/2 tsp. salt	1 tsp. almond extract
2 1/2 Tbsp. poppy seeds	1 1/2 tsp. vanilla

Make ahead. In large bowl, mix all ingredients. Beat until smooth. Bake in a greased and floured loaf pan at 350 degrees for one hour 15 minutes. Remove from pan while hot. Serve warm with whipped cream on top or cool, slice and serve.

Buckeneers Buttered Mushrooms

1 lb. large firm mushrooms,
   stems removed
1/4 cup butter, melted

1/2 tsp. onion powder
1/2 tsp. garlic salt
1/2 tsp. pepper

Make these on site or prepare ahead, refrigerate, then simply grill foil packages on game day. Clean and cut mushrooms into thick slices. Divide evenly onto four nine-inch square pieces of foil. In small bowl, combine butter, onion powder, garlic salt and pepper. Mix well. Drizzle evenly over mushrooms. Fold foil over and seal tightly. Grill over medium-hot coals for 15 minutes. Serves four.

Giants Big Meatballs

1 pound lean ground beef
1/4 cup green onions, minced
1/4 cup onion, chopped
1 clove garlic, minced
3 Tbsp. beef broth
1 Tbsp. vegetable oil

1/4 tsp. salt
1 Tbsp. flour
1 cup beef broth
1 cup milk
Salt and pepper

Make meatballs a day ahead and refrigerate overnight, then pack on ice until ready to grill. In large bowl, combine beef, onions, garlic, beef broth, oil and salt. Mix well. Set aside 1/4 cup of meat mixture. Shape remaining mixture into one-inch balls. Cover and refrigerate at least one hour. Thread meatballs on skewers, leaving some space between each. Grill six minutes per side. To make gravy, brown reserved 1/4 cup meat mixture in skillet. Stir one tablespoon flour into meat and meat drippings. Add one cup warm beef broth, stirring constantly, until well-combined and boiling. Add milk gradually, stirring constantly. Reduce heat. Add salt and pepper to taste. Serve meatballs with gravy and biscuits.

Avoid Food Poisoning:

Pack food in a well-insulated cooler with ice or ice packs to maintain a temperature of below 40 degrees. When temperatures outside are above 90 degrees, transport the cooler in the back seat of an air-conditioned car instead of the trunk. Buy a refrigerator thermometer for the cooler to make sure perishable items such as potato salad, cole slaw, pasta salad and all things made with eggs or mayonnaise will not spoil. Also invest in a meat thermometer to ensure burgers, steaks, bratwurst and chicken are adequately cooked on the grill. Burgers and brats should reach an internal temperature of 160 degrees, while chicken should be cooked to 170 degrees. Beware of food that has been sitting out or goes unrefrigerated for more than two hours. Many dishes may not taste or smell spoiled but the bacteria have had a chance to grow enough to make someone ill. When in doubt, throw it out.

Keep Out The Elements

Too much sun or inclement weather will send even the most-avid tailgater hunting for shelter. If you plan to tailgate a lot, invest in a small instant canopy. A great tip to keep the canopy on the ground during high winds: Fill two-liter soda bottles with water and use duct tape to secure the bottles to the bottom of the poles to keep the canopy anchored. Tent stakes don't work in a parking lot.

Bears Beer Biscuits

3 cups biscuit mix
3 Tbsp. sugar

1 egg
12-oz. can beer at room temperature

Make these ahead unless you have an oven in a travel trailer on site. The beer gives these biscuits a fluffy texture and unique flavor. In large bowl, mix all ingredients until moistened. Spoon into greased muffin tins, filling two-thirds full. Bake at 400 degrees for 18 minutes or until golden.

Broncos Buttermilk Cake

1 cup butter or margarine
4 Tbsp. cocoa
1 cup water
2 cups sugar
2 cups flour

2 eggs
1/2 cup buttermilk
1 tsp. baking soda
1 tsp. vanilla

Make ahead. In large saucepan, melt butter. Stir in cocoa and water. Bring to boil. Sift together sugar and flour. Add to hot mixture. Beat in eggs, buttermilk, soda and vanilla. Bake in greased sheetcake pan at 375 degrees for 15 minutes or in greased round cake pan for 35 to 40 minutes. Frost while hot.

Hot Cocoa Frosting

1/3 cup butter or margarine
4 Tbsp. cocoa
4 Tbsp. canned evaporated milk

1 tsp. vanilla
1 pound powdered sugar

In small saucepan, combine all ingredients. Cook until butter is melted and mixture is smooth. Pour onto hot cake.

> *D*ad says:
> If you plan to use a generator, make sure it's full of gas before you get there. If it's an early game, whip up some breakfast foods for pre-game grubbing. Creative finger foods will always be a hit. For instance, if you want steak, make it an easy-to-eat kabob. Think disposable everything. Bring plenty of heavy-duty plastic garbage bags and set aside at least one for recycling aluminum. Totally clean up your site after all the revelry.

Cowboys Orange Smokies

1/3 cup onion, chopped	1 Tbsp grated orange peel
3 Tbsp. butter or margarine	1 tsp. salt
1/3 cup honey	3/4 cup orange juice
3 Tbsp. lemon juice	1 1/2 Tbsp. cornstarch
3 Tbsp. soy sauce	1 pkg. miniature smoked hotdogs

Make ahead, then warm in pan on grill or camp stove. In small saucepan, saute onion in butter until tender. Add honey, lemon juice, soy sauce, orange peel and salt. In small bowl, blend orange juice into cornstarch. Gradually stir orange juice mixture into hot mixture. Heat, stirring constantly, until sauce thickens. Add mini hotdogs. Cook until warmed through.

Saints Jambalaya

1/2 cup celery, chopped	1/4 cups ketchup
1/2 cup onion, chopped	1 Tbsp. Worcestershire
1/2 cup green pepper, chopped	1/4 tsp. salt
3 Tbsp. butter or margarine	2 cups shrimp, cooked and peeled
8-oz. can chicken broth	Hot cooked rice

Prepare on site. In kettle, saute celery, onion and green pepper in butter until tender. Add broth, ketchup, Worcestershire and salt. Simmer, covered, for ten minutes, stirring occasionally. Add shrimp and simmer for five additional minutes. Add rice and stir. Serves four.

Seahawks Halibut Kabobs

6 Tbsp. butter or margarine, melted
1/4 cup red wine vinegar
1/4 cup ketchup
3 Tbsp. brown sugar, firmly packed
1/2 tsp. salt
1/4 tsp. pepper
1/8 tsp. garlic salt

1/2 cup unsweetened pineapple juice
2 tsp. cornstarch
3/4 lb. one-inch thick halibut steak
18 chunks green pepper
18 large mushrooms
18 cherry tomatoes

Make sauce ahead, then grill marinated halibut on site. In small saucepan, combine melted margarine, vinegar, ketchup, brown sugar and spices. Heat to boiling, stirring occasionally. In small bowl, stir pineapple juice into cornstarch until smooth. Gradually stir into hot mixture. Bring to a boil again, stirring frequently. Boil two minutes or until thick. Cover and chill until sauce is completely cooled. Cut halibut steaks into one and a half inch cubes. Marinate in cooled sauce at room temperature for at least one hour. Drain, reserving sauce. Thread six skewers with alternating fish, green peppers, mushrooms and cherry tomatoes. Warm sauce in pan on camp stove or grill. Brush kabobs generously with sauce. Grill kabobs over medium coals for ten minutes, turning and basting frequently with sauce. Serve immediately with remaining sauce.

Jets Marshmallow Popcorn

3/4 cup light corn syrup
1/4 cup butter or margarine
2 Tbsp. water

1 lb. powdered sugar
1 cup miniature marshmallows
5 quarts popcorn

Make ahead. In heavy saucepan, combine corn syrup, butter, water, powdered sugar and marshmallows. Stir over low heat until mixture begins to boil. In large bowl, pour mixture over popped corn. Shape into balls. Makes about 30 balls.

Checklist

Tailgating Essentials

Cooking
- ❏ Cooler with pre-prepared food
- ❏ Cooler with food to be prepared
- ❏ Cooler filled only with fresh ice
- ❏ Many beverages in cans or plastic bottles
- ❏ Cushioned cup holders
- ❏ Grill and/or campstove
- ❏ Aluminum foil
- ❏ Cooking utensils
- ❏ Briquettes and lighter

Picnic
- ❏ Strong folding chairs
- ❏ Card table or long-narrow folding table
- ❏ Container with lid to hold paper products and plastic utensils
- ❏ Heavy-duty paper plates and large capacity paper soup bowls
- ❏ Heavy-duty plastic knives, forks and soup spoons
- ❏ Large platic cups or large styrofoam cups for hot drinks
- ❏ Roll of heavy-duty paper towels to use as napkins
- ❏ Tarp or instant canopy

Clean-up
- ❏ Clean, damp kitchen towels sealed in plastic zip-lock bags
- ❏ Two gallons of water
- ❏ Anti-bacterial soap for hands
- ❏ Paper towels
- ❏ Large, heavy-duty plastic trash bags
- ❏ Pre-moistened cleaning cloths

Personal
- ❏ First-aid kit
- ❏ Antacids
- ❏ Pain reliever
- ❏ Sunblock
- ❏ Toilet paper
- ❏ Jumper cables
- ❏ Rain gear
- ❏ Camera and film
- ❏ Football
- ❏ Pen or pencil and index cards

Bulldogs Fruit Kabobs

For kabobs:
6 wooden skewers
Large white grapes
Swiss cheese, cut into cubes
1 can pineapple chunks, drained
Mild cheddar cheese, cut into cubes
Small strawberries

For dip:
8 oz. cream cheese, softened
8 oz. sour cream
8-oz jar marshmallow creme
1 Tbsp. lemon juice
1/8 tsp. nutmeg

Prepare on site. *For kabobs:* Thread one grape, Swiss cheese, pineapple chunk, cheddar cheese and strawberry alternately on skewer until filled. *For dip:* Combine cream cheese, sour cream, marshmallow creme, lemon juice and nutmeg. Mix until smooth. Let sit for one hour. Chill and serve.

Sun Devils Breakfast Sandwich

2 eggs, lightly beaten
2/3 cup milk
1/4 tsp. salt
2 Tbsp. sugar

8 slices white bread
1 cup strawberry preserves
Butter or margarine
1/2 cup powdered sugar

Prepare on site. In shallow bowl, combine eggs, milk, salt and sugar. Beat with fork to mix until well blended. Spread four slices bread with strawberry preserves. Top with remaining bread slices. Dip sandwiches in egg mixture to coat both sides. On a griddle, melt butter or margarine. Grill sandwiches over low heat for four to five minutes, browning both sides. Sprinkle with powdered sugar and serve warm. Serves four.

---

*D*ad says:
Place pre-prepared foods in disposable containers such as heavy-duty foil baking pans, ziplock bags and plain old aluminum foil so you don't have to clean up reusable plastic containers.

Cup-of-Joe Longhorns

1/4 cup fresh ground coffee beans
4 top-sirloin steaks, cut into
   half-inch cubes

1/4 cup fresh ground pepper corns
Vegetable oil
Sea salt

Prepare on site. Grind the coffee beans and pepper corns to fine granules. If you don't have a grinder, many grocery stores have coffee grinders available for use. Pick out your favorite robust coffee beans and grind them there. Place steak cubes on skewers. Brush steak with vegetable oil. Mix ground coffee beans and pepper on a large plate. Roll and press steak kabobs in mixture until coated. Grill to desired tenderness. After grilling, sprinkle with salt and let rest for five minutes before serving.

More Tailgating Tips

- Call the stadium ahead of time to see what accommodations and rules exist for tailgaiters.
- Will beer or other alcoholic beverages be allowed?
- What is the cost per vehicle to park?
- When does the lot open and close on game day?
- Share preparation, clean-up and expenses with other buddy tailgaters.
- Bring playing cards or small board games to keep you and yours busy while you wait out the after-game exodus.

Bangin' Badgers Cheese Soup

3 Tbsp. butter or margarine
1/2 cup cooked ham, chopped
1 medium carrot, finely chopped
1 medium onion, finely chopped
1 celery stalk, finely chopped
1/2 green bell pepper, seeded
   and finely chopped
4 cups chicken broth

1/2 cup white flour
2 Tbsp. cornstarch
4 cups milk
1/2 tsp. paprika
1/2 tsp. ground mustard
1/4 tsp. cayenne pepper
1/2 lb. sharp cheddar cheese, grated
Salt and pepper

Make ahead then warm on grill or campstove. In large heavy kettle, melt butter or margarine. Add ham, carrots, onion, celery and green pepper. Cook over medium heat until vegetables are crisp tender, about ten minutes, stirring occasionally. Add three cups chicken broth. Bring to boil. In small bowl, mix one cup chicken broth with flour and cornstarch until well blended. Add flour/broth mixture to kettle, stirring constantly, until soup is slightly thickened. Reduce heat to medium. Add milk, paprika, mustard and cayenne pepper. Stir in cheese gradually, stirring until melted. To avoid curdling, do not allow soup to boil after cheese is added. Season with salt and pepper.

Crimson Tide Hot Tips

2 lbs. sirloin steak
4 beef bouillon cubes
1-2 Tbsp. water
3 tsp. cayenne pepper

1 tsp. black pepper
1/2 tsp. salt
3 Tbsp. vegetable oil

Prepare steak the night before you plan to cook it. Cut the steak into 1/2 inch cubes. In bowl, crumble bouillon cubes into water and stir until a thick paste is formed. Stir in cayenne pepper, black pepper and salt. Pour into large zippered plastic bag. Add steak cubes. Toss thoroughly to coat. Place meat onto skewers, place in plastic container or gallon sized freezer bags and refrigerate. When ready to grill, brush meat with vegetable oil. Also brush grill with oil. Place skewers on grill and cook two to three minutes per side.

Cornhuskers Grilled Cobs

4 fresh ears of corn
2 Tbsp. butter, melted

Salt and pepper
Paprika

Prepare on site. Peel back husks enough to remove cornsilk. In large pan, cover corn in husks with water and soak for 30 minutes. Drain. Grill over medium-hot coals for 25 minutes, turning frequently. Remove husks. Brush butter all over corn. Season with salt, pepper and paprika. Serve warm.

Hawkeyes Nutty Popcorn

2 quarts popped popcorn
1/3 cup raisins
1/2 cup almonds

1/2 cup sunflower seeds
1/4 cup butter or margarine, melted
1/4 cup grated Parmesan cheese

Make ahead. In large bowl or kettle, combine all ingredients until well mixed or until popcorn is evenly coated with butter and cheese. Store in tightly covered container. Makes 12 individual servings.

*D*ad says:
To keep the cooler dry, clean and organized, freeze bottled water and place in the cooler along with packed perishable foods and beverages.This will keep your food cold, and cut down on spills and clean up. Plus,as the water melts, you'll have cool liquid available for parched tailgaters.

Cougars Cub Sandwich

Two rolls of 8-piece ready-to-bake popup crescents

8 slices deli white turkey breast, sliced thick

8 slices bacon, cooked crisp and broken in half

8 slices Alpine Swiss cheese

Make ahead. On greased baking sheet, lay out crescent dough, making a square with two pieces. You should have eight squares. Place Swiss cheese on top of square, then layer with turkey and bacon. Fold over and press edges of dough together with fork to seal. Bake according to crescent package directions or until are golden brown. Serve hot or cold.

*D*ad says:
Make plenty of extra food to share with visiting tailgaters. If there's a favorite recipe that everyone always asks for, print it out on some index or recipe cards to share with all those askers.

Aggies Edible Footballs

1/4 cup butter or margarine
10-oz. pkg. mini marshmallows
6 cups chocolate flavored crispy rice cereal

1 cup peanut butter chips
1/2 cup chopped peanuts
One tube white cake frosting

Make ahead. Grease 13 x 9-inch pan. In large saucepan over low heat, melt butter and add marshmallows, stirring occasionally until melted and smooth. Remove from heat and stir in crispy rice cereal, peanut butter chips and peanuts. Mix until well-coated. Press mixture into pan. When cool enough to handle and still pliable, scoop out a handful of mix and shape into football. This will be easier if you rub some butter on your hands first. Lay footballs on wax paper to cool completely. With frosting, make football ties. Makes about 20 mini-footballs.

Hoosiers Hot Wings

For the dressing:
4 slices bacon
2 Tbsp. white onion, diced
1 clove garlic, minced
Salt and pepper
6 oz. bleu cheese, crumbled
2/3 cup plain yogurt
1/2 cup milk

For wings:
4 lbs. chicken wings, about 24 pieces
Vegetable oil for frying
4 Tbsp. butter or margarine, melted
1 Tbsp. vegetable oil
1/2 cup hot sauce
1/4 cup honey

For dressing: Cook bacon in skillet until barely crisp. Remove, drain, crumble and set aside. Add onion to bacon drippings and cook just until softened. Remove from heat. Pour onion with bacon drippings into medium bowl. Stir in garlic, salt, pepper, blue cheese, yogurt and milk. Mix well. Stir in crumbled bacon. Set aside.

For wings: Clean and separate chicken wings at joint. Pat dry. In heavy saucepan, heat oil. Fry chicken wings in three separate batches without crowding until golden brown and cooked through, about eight minutes. Drain wings on paper towels. In medium bowl, combine butter or margarine, one tablespoon vegetable oil, hot sauce and honey. Mix thoroughly. Toss wings in hot sauce mixture. Serve with dressing on the side.

Sooners Corn Sticks

1 egg
1 1/2 Tbsp. shortening
1 tsp. sugar
1 tsp. salt

1 1/2 tsp. baking powder
1/2 cup whole-wheat flour
1 cup corn meal
1 cup buttermilk

Make ahead. In large bowl, beat together egg, sugar and shortening until smooth. Set aside. In another bowl, sift together flour, cornmeal, salt and baking powder. Gradually add flour mixture to shortening mixture, alternating with buttermilk. Mix until well blended. Pour batter into greased cast-iron cornstick pans. Bake at 400 degrees for 20 minutes. Serve warm or at room temperature. Makes one dozen.

Fighting Irish Stew

1 lb. lamb or beef	1 Tbsp. brown sugar
2 onions, chopped	2 cups beef broth
Vegetable oil	1/4 cup barley
4-6 large potatoes, peeled and cubed	4 bay leaves
2 medium carrots, cubed	1 tsp. basil
2 parsnips, cubed	Salt and pepper

Make ahead and heat in large kettle on game day. Cut meat into one-inch cubes. Also cube potatoes, carrots and parsnips. Heat vegetable oil in skillet and brown meat and onions. Set aside. Saute carrots and parsnips for a few minutes and add a bit of brown sugar to glaze them. Place meat, onions, potatoes, carrots and parsnips into large casserole dish. Add beef broth. Add barley, bay leaves, basil, salt and pepper. Stir until well combined. Cover dish and bake at 350 degrees for about one hour or until potatoes are tender. Mash some potatoes into liquid when reheating to make a thick and delicious stew.

Rebels Apple Snacks

1 cup whole-wheat flour	1/3 cup vegetable oil
1 cup quick-cooking oats	1 tsp. vanilla
3/4 tsp. baking soda	6-oz. pkg. dried apples, chopped
1/2 tsp. cinnamon	1 cup bran flakes cereal, crushed
1 cup applesauce	2 Tbsp. butter or margarine
1/2 cup honey	

Make ahead. In large mixing bowl, combine flour, oats, soda and cinnamon. In another bowl, combine applesauce, honey, oil and vanilla. Stir applesauce mixture into flour mixture until well blended. Stir in dried apples. In small bowl, combine crushed bran flakes and butter. Sprinkle half the bran flake mixture over bottom of greased 9 x 13 pan. Spoon batter over bran, spreading evenly. Sprinkle with remaining bran mixture. Bake at 350 degrees for 25 to 30 minutes. Cool and cut into bars. Makes 24 bars.

No Flyaways

Use a three-drawer rubber or plastic storage box that can sit out on the table or the tailgate to hold paper plates, bowls, cups, napkins and utensils. A large toolbox will work in a pinch. At the very least, find a couple of clean rocks to hold down paper products and keep them from flying across the parking lot when caught by the wind.

Gophers Easy Guacamole

2 ripe avocados
1 small tomato, diced
1 small onion, diced
1 clove garlic, crushed

1 Tbsp. lemon juice
1/2 tsp. salt
1/2 tsp. chili powder
1/4 tsp. ground cumin

Prepare on site. Peel avocados and remove pit. Cut in half and mash in bowl with fork. Stir in tomatoes, onions, garlic, lemon juice and spices. Mix until well blended. Cover tightly and refrigerate until chilled. Serve with white corn chips.

Food Safety Tips:

Wash hands before, during and after preparing food for a tailgate. Pack moist towelettes to clean up before eating. Always defrost meats in the refrigerator or in the microwave at home — never after arriving at the parking lot. Keep thawed meats in cooler below 40 degrees before grilling. Tightly seal raw or thawed meat in plastic wrap to prevent juices from contaminating other food items. Consider packing meat products in one cooler and additional foods in another. Keep raw meats and ready-to-eat foods separate. When grilling, use one plate to hold raw meats and another clean plate to serve cooked meats. Always use a meat thermometer. Don't forget that carry-out and/or pre-prepared foods are also susceptible to food poisoning. Foods should not be left outside for more than two hours. In temperatures above 90 degrees, the time is reduced to one hour.

Boilermakers Grilled Potatoes

4 large baking potatoes
1/4 cup butter, melted

Salt and pepper
Dried parsley

Prepare on site. Scrub potatoes. Cut in half lengthwise. With sharp knife make slashes through flesh only (without cutting skin) 1/4-inch apart in grid pattern. Place potato, cut side up on flat surface. Squeeze gently so that the flesh spreads slightly. Brush each half with melted butter so that butter drips into grids. Grill skins down over medium-hot coals for 35 minutes, turning over once during last ten minutes. To reduce grilling time, boil whole potatoes until tender but firm, cut in half, slash and butter, then grill flesh-side down for ten minutes. Salt and pepper to taste. Garnish with parsley.

Runnin' Utes Native Tacos

For fry bread:
2 cups all-purpose flour
2 tsp. baking powder
1/4 cup granulated sugar
1/2 cup instant nonfat dry milk
1/4 tsp. salt
1 cup water
Vegetable oil, for deep-frying

For filling:
1 small onion, chopped

2 Tbsp. vegetable oil
2 fresh red chiles, seeded and chopped
1 tsp. chili powder
Salt and pepper
1 cup water
1 pound lean ground beef
2 cups canned pinto beans, drained
8 squares traditional fry bread
Cheddar cheese, grated
Lettuce, grated
Tomatoes, chopped

For frybread: In large bowl, mix together flour, baking powder, sugar, dry milk and salt. Stir in the water to make sticky dough. Turn the dough out onto floured surface. Sprinkle with flour and roll out to a large rectangle, about 1/2-inch thick. Cut into eight to twelve four-inch squares. Cut 1/2-inch slit in middle of each square. In deep cast-iron skillet or deep-fat fryer, heat oil until piece of dough sizzles in pan. Fry squares of dough, turning once, until golden brown on both sides, about three minutes total. Drain on paper towels. Serve warm topped with taco fixings. *For filling:* In medium skillet, saute onion in oil until soft. Add chiles, chili powder, salt, pepper and water. Bring to boil, reduce heat and simmer for 30 minutes. Let cool. Place mixture in blender and puree until smooth. Saute beef until browned. Drain oil. Add chile sauce and beans, mashing some beans until mixture reaches desired consistency. Heat through. Place meat/bean mixture on fry bread. Top with cheese, lettuce and tomatoes.

Lobos Bread Pudding

1 cup brown sugar, firmly packed
1 1/2 cup water
2 Tbsp. butter or margarine
1 tsp. ground cinnamon
1 tsp. orange peel, grated

5 cups toasted French bread cubes
1/2 cup almonds, chopped
1/2 cup raisins
1 apple, chopped
1 cup Monterey Jack cheese, shredded

Make ahead. Heat brown sugar, water, margarine, cinnamon and orange peel to boiling. Reduce heat and simmer, uncovered, for five minutes. In ungreased casserole dish, layer half the bread cubes, nuts, raisins, apples and cheese. Repeat layers. Pour hot brown sugar syrup over the top. Bake uncovered at 350 degrees for 30 minutes or until syrup is absorbed. Serve with milk or topped with whipped cream. Serves six.

DAD'S Specialties

179

Dad's Specialties

Homemade Ice Cream

Certainly, you can buy numerous flavors of premium ice cream in any grocery store, but homemade ice cream is a treat that few of us experience anymore. The process of making ice cream at home is fun, and the results taste much fresher than store-bought. So try your hand at one of Dad's favorite past-times – making delicious ice cream from scratch without much fuss.

You can make homemade ice cream using an electric ice-cream maker or an old-fashioned manual churner. You can even make ice cream in coffee cans or zipper lock freezer bags. The secret is to get the ice cream to freeze at below normal freezing temperatures. You have to get the right mix of rock salt to ice surrounding the mixture because when salt comes into contact with ice, it lowers the freezing point. *When using an ice-cream maker that requires rock salt and ice, use a ratio of one cup salt for every six cups of ice.*

Kid's Quick Ice Cream

1/2 cup milk	4 Tbsp. table salt
1/2 tsp. vanilla extract	Two quart-sized zipperlock freezer bags
1 Tbsp. granulated sugar	1 gallon-sized zipperlock freezer bag
4 cups crushed ice	Gloves

Pour milk, vanilla and sugar in one quart-sized bag. Seal tightly, pushing out as much air as possible. Knead bag to mix ingredients until well combined. Place this bag inside second quart-sized bag. Seal this bag, pushing out as much air as possible so that the bag will not open. (Double-bagging helps ensure that salt and melting ice will not leak into ice cream.) Place these two bags inside gallon-sized bag. Fill large bag with crushed ice and sprinkle salt on top. Push air out and seal bag. Put gloves on. Shake and massage bag, making sure ice surrounds cream mixture. It will take only five to eight minutes for mixture to freeze into ice cream. Makes one serving.

Coffee Can Ice Cream: An alternative to using zipper lock plastic bags is to use clean coffee cans instead. The recipe is the same but can be doubled or tripled because the coffee can will hold more. Put the milk mixture into a standard-sized coffee can. Seal with the plastic lid. Place that can inside a larger "economy size" can. Pack the large can with ice and salt, and seal with the lid. Now, get a friend, and roll the can back and forth on the ground in a shady place until the ice cream sets. Check after ten minutes, then roll for an additional five to ten minutes until desired consistency.

Old-Fashioned Churned Vanilla

6 eggs
2 cups granulated sugar
1/4 tsp. salt

1 Tbsp. vanilla
13-oz. can evaporated milk
1 gallon whole milk

In large mixing bowl, beat eggs. Add sugar gradually, stirring constantly. Add salt, vanilla and canned evaporated milk. Add about two cups fresh milk and mix together well. Pour mixture into ice-cream maker. Add enough remaining milk to fill about two-thirds full. Add chipped ice and rock salt to barrel around freezer can. Crank freezer until ice cream begins to freeze, adding more ice and salt as needed. When handle becomes almost impossible to turn, remove top and dasher. Replace top. Cover can with more ice and salt. Cover ice with old towel to allow the ice cream to "cure" for at least one hour. For an electric freezer, follow manufacturer's directions.

Lemon Custard Treat

Finely grated peel of three lemons
1/2 cup fresh lemon juice
3/4 cup granulated sugar
2 cups half-and-half cream

4 large egg yolks
Pinch of salt
2 cups heavy cream

In heavy bowl, combine lemon zest, lemon juice and sugar, stirring until well mixed. Let stand for 30 minutes. In saucepan, scald half-and-half over medium heat. Let cool and set aside. In small bowl, whisk egg yolks and salt until well blended. Slowly add about half of the cream to egg yolks, stirring gently. Pour mixture into saucepan. Cook over medium to low heat, stirring constantly until mixture thickens enough to cover back of spoon. Do not boil. Immediately remove custard from heat. Strain into large bowl. Stir in lemon mixture and heavy cream. Lay sheet of wax paper or plastic wrap directly on surface to prevent skin from forming, then refrigerate until thoroughly chilled. Pour chilled ice-cream mixture into ice-cream maker. Freeze according to manufacturer's directions. When ice cream is thickened and frozen, cover and place in the freezer until firm.

---

*D*ad says:
For a higher yield and creamier texture, make and chill the ice-cream mixture the day before you plan to freeze it. A chilled mixture freezes faster. After freezing the ice cream in your ice-cream maker, "ripen" the ice cream by leaving it covered in the freezer of your refrigerator for at least four hours to fully develop its flavor and texture.

Only-Two-Eggs Vanilla

2 1/2 cups milk
2 large eggs
1 tsp. cornstarch
1/2 cup granulated sugar

2 tsp. vanilla extract
1/4 tsp. salt
1 cup heavy cream

In medium saucepan, bring two cups milk to boil. In medium bowl, beat eggs until light, then beat in remaining 1/2 cup milk and cornstarch. Stir egg mixture into hot milk and cook, stirring, until thickened. Stir in sugar, vanilla and salt. Cook one minute longer. Set custard aside to cool to room temperature. Refrigerate until well chilled. In medium bowl, beat heavy cream until soft peaks form. Fold custard mixture into cream. Pour into ice-cream maker and freeze. Once frozen, pack in freezer container and allow to ripen in refrigerator freezer for several hours.

*D*ad says:
To avoid the formation of crystals, add an envelope of unflavored gelatin for every six cups of liquid. Let gelatin soften in 1/4 cup of liquid, then heat until gelatin dissolves and stir into remaining liquid. Ice cream will have a lighter texture if given room to expand during the churning and freezing process; only fill the canister two-thirds full.

No-Kidding Avocado Ice Cream

3 quarts orange juice
3 oz. can pre-sweetened lemonade mix
1/3 cup sugar

5 Tbsp. fresh lemon juice
3/4 cup heavy cream

Peel and pit avocados. Cut into chunks and blend in blender. With blender on low, add salt, sugar, lemon juice and heavy cream. Blend until well mixed. Pour mixture into bowl of ice-cream maker and freeze according to manufacturer's directions.

*D*ad says:
As the ice melts during churning, add more salt and ice to keep the temperature cold enough. The faster the freezing process of ice cream, the smoother its texture. Before opening a canister of ice cream, remove the ice and water to well below the level of the lid. Wipe the lid well to make sure that no salt or water gets into the ice cream as you remove it.

Elegant Avocado Zest

4 egg yolks
3/4 cups sugar
1 1/2 cups milk
1/2 cup whipping cream
4 ripe avocados

1/2 cup orange juice
2 tsp. lime juice
1 tsp. lemon juice
Fresh mint to garnish

Beat egg yolks and sugar until ribbons form. Set aside. Heat milk to boiling, stirring frequently. Pour two tablespoons hot milk slowly into egg mixture, stirring so that it will not curdle. Pour egg mixture into remaining hot milk. Heat mixture over low heat, stirring constantly. Remove from heat and continue to stir a few more times. Stir in cream to form custard. Thoroughly chill mixture. Pit and peel avocados. Place in blender with orange, lime and lemon juices. Blend well. Whisk avocado mixture into chilled custard. Freeze in ice-cream maker as per directions. Garnish with sprigs of mint.

Still-Freeze Method

Still freezing" means you simply freeze your ice-cream mixture in the refrigerator freezer. The process is more time consuming, but, if you are diligent, the results can be tasty. No special ice cream maker is required. Just pour the mixture into cake pan or freezer trays then place it in the freezer. When a frozen crust forms around the sides, take the mixture out and stir it, do this three or four times during the freezing process. Or you may simply want to freeze the mixture without stirring. Generally, the texture of still-frozen ice creams is good when sufficient air has been whipped into the mix prior to freezing or at some point during the freezing.

Still-Freeze Peppermint

1/2 large peppermint candy cane
2 cups heavy cream

1 cup milk

Dissolve candy in milk in double boiler. Chill this mixture. Now, pour into refrigerator tray and freeze until firm. Remove to ice cold bowl and beat quickly. Add heavy cream during the beating process. Return mixture to tray and finish freezing in freezer.

Powder Punch Ice Cream

1/2 cup sugar
2 cups milk
1 cup whipping cream

1 packet unsweetened powder punch
    mix, any flavor

In a large bowl mix together sugar, milk and powder punch mix. Stir until dissolved. Place mixture in freezer until slushy. In medium bowl, whip cream until stiff. Remove milk mixture from freezer and fold in whipped cream until just combined. Return to freezer for about two hours until firm.

Buying An Ice-Cream Maker

If you don't want to go to the trouble of still-freezing, you can hunt around for a manual churner or an electric ice-cream maker. Be prepared to spend anywhere from $40 to $120 depending on how fancy you want to get. The main difference between units is their means of freezing power. Traditional methods call for placing the ice-cream mixing bucket into a larger wooden bucket, then filling the cavity in between with ice and rock salt. Depending on how much energy you want to put into it, you can choose a manual or electric churning process. Newer models use plastic outer buckets along with ice and table salt. The very newest offering is the insulated freezing chamber—a bucket with liquid suspended between inner and outer walls, which, when frozen, acts as a chilling agent to freeze the ice cream. These new units make rock salt and ice obsolete.

Coffee Ice Cream

1 cup strong black coffee
1/2 cup sugar

1 tsp. gelatin
1 cup evaporated milk

In saucepan, combine coffee, sugar and gelatin. Heat until gelatin is dissolved. Place in refrigerator until completely cooled. Beat mixture until very light. In saucepan, scald evaporated milk. Chill. Beat milk until very light. Gradually beat milk into coffee mixture. Freeze as desired.

Irish Cream Ice Cream

1/2 cup sugar
3 egg yolks
2 cups whipping cream

3 Tbsp. Irish cream liqueur
3 crunchy chocolate bars, chopped

In large bowl, combine eggs and sugar until creamy. Add whipping cream and beat until light. Add Irish cream liqueur and crushed crunchy bar bits. Stir well to incorporate. Pour into container and freeze as desired.

Cookies & Cream

1 cup sugar	2 eggs, beaten
1/4 cup flour	3 cups whipping cream
1/4 tsp. salt	1 Tbsp. vanilla extract
2 cups milk	12 chocolate sandwich cookies, crumbled

In saucepan, combine sugar, flour and salt. Gradually stir in milk. Cook over medium heat about 15 minutes or until thickened, stirring constantly. In bowl, beat eggs. Stir about 1/2 cup hot milk mixture into beaten eggs. Add egg mixture to remaining hot mixture in saucepan, stirring constantly. Cook one minute. Remove from heat. Refrigerate one hour. In large bowl, combine whipping cream and vanilla, whisking together until light and fluffy. Add chilled mixture, stirring with wire whisk to combine. Add crumbled chocolate sandwich cookies before freezing. Freeze as desired.

Fresh Peach Ice Cream

2 cups peaches, finely chopped	2 eggs
1 cup sugar	1 cup heavy cream
1 Tbsp. lemon juice	1 cup milk

In medium bowl, combine peaches, 1/2 cup sugar and lemon juice. Cover and refrigerate for two hours, stirring mixture every 30 minutes. Remove from refrigerator. Whisk eggs in mixing bowl until light and fluffy. Whisk in remaining 1/2 sugar until completely blended. Pour in cream, milk and peaches. Stir until well combined. Pour into appropriate container and freeze as desired.

Sweet Strawberry Ice Cream

2 cups fresh strawberries, finely chopped	4 egg yolks
1 cup sugar	1 cup whipping cream
1/2 lemon, juiced	1 cup milk

In small bowl, combine strawberries, 1/2 cup sugar and lemon juice. Stir and let sit for at least one hour. In medium bowl, beat eggs yolks. Gradually add remaining 1/2 cup sugar. In saucepan, heat cream and milk together. Gradually stir into egg and sugar mixture. Cool completely. Add strawberries and stir until well combined. Pour into appropriate container and freeze as desired.

Very Chocolate Ice Cream

2 cups milk
1/2 cup chocolate syrup
1 cup sugar
3 Tbsp. flour

1/4 tsp. salt
2 eggs, slightly beaten
2 cups whipping cream
2 tsp. vanilla

Stir chocolate syrup into milk. In saucepan, scald milk. In bowl, mix together sugar, flour and salt. Add just enough of the scalded milk to flour mixture to form a thin paste. Stir paste into remaining hot milk. Over low heat, cook mixture about 15 minutes or until it thickens slightly. In medium bowl, beat eggs. Add milk mixture gradually to beaten eggs. Cook this over low heat for about two minutes, stirring constantly. Cool quickly in the refrigerator. Once cooled completely, whisk in whipping cream and vanilla. Freeze as desired.

No-Sugar Strawberry

1 1/2 cups nonfat dry milk powder
3 cups skim milk
3 Tbsp. margarine, melted
1/2 cup boiling water
12 individual packets artificial sweetener

1 small pkg. sugar-free vanilla
    pudding mix
2 cans sugar-free strawberry soft drink
8 oz. frozen strawberries, chopped

Blend dry milk powder, margarine, water and artificial sweetener in blender. Pour into ice cream freezer container. Slowly stir in pudding mix. Mix well. Slowly stir in soft drinks and strawberries. Add milk to fill line. Freeze. Makes two quarts.

Non-Dairy Coconut Banana

2 tsp. gelatin
1/4 cup guava nectar, or other tropical
    fruit juice
1/4 cup honey

2 1/4 cups vanilla soy milk
1 cup mashed banana
1 tsp. vanilla extract
1/4 cup finely shredded coconut

In a small bowl, sprinkle gelatin over juice. Let sit, stirring occasionally, until gelatin is dissolved and softened, about ten minutes. In a medium saucepan, whisk honey and two cups soy milk. Cook until just hot, stirring frequently; and remove from heat. Add softened gelatin to hot milk mixture, stirring until gelatin is completely dissolved. Stir in remaining soy milk, bananas and vanilla. Cool in refrigerator until chilled. Add coconut and stir to combine. Freeze as desired.

Non-Dairy Strawberry

2 tsp. kosher gelatin

1/4 cup apple-strawberry juice

2/3 cup all-fruit strawberry jam

3 cups vanilla soy milk

1 tsp. vanilla extract

In a small bowl, sprinkle gelatin over apple-strawberry juice. Let sit, stirring occasionally, until gelatin is dissolved and softened, about ten minutes. In medium saucepan, whisk together jam and two cups soy milk. Cook until just hot, stirring frequently. Remove from heat. Add softened gelatin to hot milk mixture, stirring until gelatin is completely dissolved. Stir in remaining soy milk and vanilla. Cool in refrigerator until well chilled. Pour into appropriate container. Freeze as desired.

Brain Freeze?

We've all experienced it—that turbo-cold, razor-sharp ache that zings right into your brain when you eat ice-cream really fast. Similar symptoms have been known to attack people who woof down slushees, snow cones, freezees, milk shakes and iced cappuccinos. Some researchers speculate that the headache sensation is caused by something icy freezing the roof of your mouth, chilling a nerve that goes directly to the brain. Others say the quick consumption of something cold triggers a dilation of blood vessels in the head, causing the body to try to regulate the temperature of the brain. How can you avoid brain freeze? Eat frozen concoctions slowly.

Ask Mom

See *Where's Mom Now That I Need Her?* for more than 350 easy recipes for breakfast, sandwiches, soups, salads, main dishes, vegetarian meals, side dishes, breads, beverages, desserts, cookies, candies and microwave meals.

Do Almost Anything

Carve a Turkey

Most men, at some point in their lives, will be asked to carve a turkey. For some reason, women at family holiday parties assume that any man present knows how to do this. It's a good thing for women to learn, too. When you spend time and money preparing a turkey, it's important to carve and present it well to your hungry guests.

Step 1: Let the cooked turkey sit for 15 minutes before carving. Meanwhile, gather your supplies and wash your hands. You will need a carving knife and fork, a kitchen towel and a serving platter. Poultry shears (kitchen scissors) are also helpful. You should choose a good carving knife with a serrated edge. The blade should be about an inch wide and 10 inches long. A long, two-pronged carving fork is a must to steady the bird while you carve.

Step 2: Carve bird in pan, then transfer meat to serving platter. Carving can be a messy business, so you'll want to move the meat onto a serving platter after you've carved the turkey. The turkey should already be breast side up. Place the kitchen towel on the counter and the turkey, still in its roasting pan, on the towel. Place the pan in front of you so that the end of the legs point toward your right. *(See Illustration A on page 190.)*

Step 3: Begin to carve. If you are right-handed, hold the carving fork in your left hand and the knife in your right. Place the fork into the bird between the leg and the breast, then slice the skin down to the thighbone. *(See Illustration B on page 190.)*

Step 4: Separate the leg and thigh from the body. Prodding gently with the tip of your knife at the joint, try to find the natural division where the thigh can be separated easily from the body, then remove the entire leg and thigh. If you can't find where the joints meet naturally, do not try to saw through the bone. Instead, use poultry shears. Now cut the drumstick from the thigh, again following the natural separation at the joint. *(See Illustration C on page 190.)*

Step 5: Place pieces on the serving platter. If the turkey is large, carve dark meat evenly off the drumsticks and thighs. Then, using your fork and knife—do not use your fingers—pick up the pieces, stabbing them with the fork and supporting the bottom with the knife. Transfer to the serving platter, laying them around the outer edges, leaving the middle of the platter free for breast slices. If the turkey is small, place the drumsticks and thighs on the platter without slicing off meat.

Step 6: Remove the wings. To remove the wings, follow the same process of gently prodding with the tip of your knife to find the joint where the wings can easily be severed from the breast of the turkey. *(See Illustration D on page 190.)*

Step 7: Carve the breast. Using the carving fork to steady the bird, cut the breast on one side in slanting slices, parallel to the rib cage. *(See Illustration E below.)* Use long, sweeping motions. Check the pieces to make sure they are even, not too thick at one end and too thin on the other. When you have finished one side of the turkey, repeat the process on the other side. Pick up the slices with your carving fork and knife and transfer them to the center of the serving platter. You may want to use some of the natural juices in the roasting pan to pour over the sliced turkey.

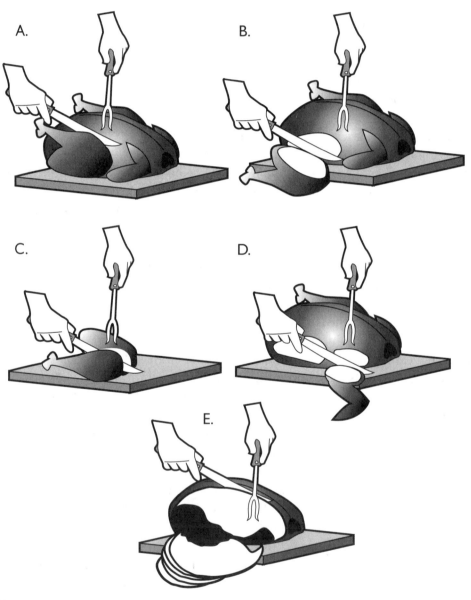

A.

B.

C.

D.

E.

Do Almost Anything

Fillet a Fish

Filleting a fish is a handy skill to know, especially if you go fishing or if you buy whole fish at the market. Whole fish usually are less expensive and often taste fresher than fish filleted by the grocer. To fillet a fish means to remove the rib bones and backbone from the edible flesh of the fish. You can leave the skin on or cut it off a fish fillet. You will need a long flexible fillet knife and a cutting board to accomplish this task.

Step 1: Begin by rinsing the fish in cool water and blotting it dry. Place the fish flat on the cutting board with the backbone nearest you and its head facing left. The fish will look like its swimming upside down. *(See Illustration A below.)*

Step 2: Cut in back of the gill. Hold the head with your left hand and, with the fillet knife, make a shallow vertical slit just behind the gill, coming straight downward toward the backbone. *(See Illustration B below.)* The shallow slit should go down to, but not through, the rib bones. Don't cut through the backbone.

Step 3: Cut along the backbone. At the bottom of the shallow slit, turn your fillet knife and, using the fine tip of the knife, make a horizontal slit along the backbone to the tail. Avoid cutting through the bone.

Step 4: Cut the first fillet. Placing the sharp edge of the knife along the first vertical slit, gently slice down the fish toward the tail, keeping the knife flat over the ribs *(See Illustration C on page 192.)* Peal the flesh back as you cut, allowing the tip of the knife to come out through the belly. Slice back just to the tail. Now cut the fillet loose from the rest of the fish. *(See Illustration D on page 192.)*

Step 5: Cut the second fillet. Turn the fish over so that the head now faces right, keeping the backbone nearest you. Repeat steps 2 through 4.

Step 6: Remove the skin from the fillets. Lay the fillet, skin-side down, with the narrow piece to your left. Cut through the flesh at the narrow end just to the inside of the skin. Keeping the blade flat on its side and close to the skin, slide it to the right, removing the skin from the fillet. *(See Illustration E on page 192.)* Repeat with second fillet.

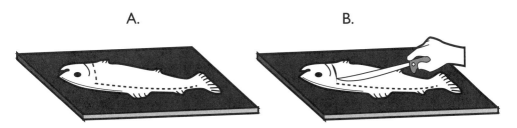

A.   B.

191

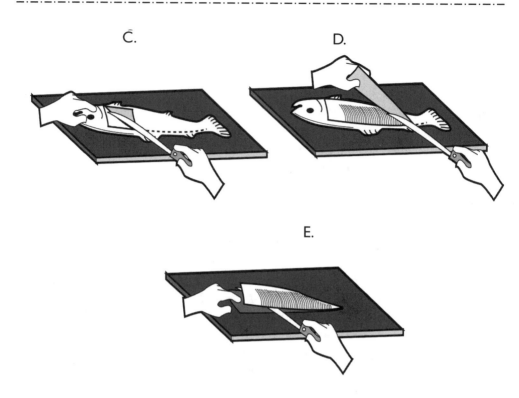

C.

D.

E.

Notes

Notes

Work to Live

Don't Live to Work

We begin our quest for knowledge from the time we learn to babble, stack blocks and memorize our ABCs. We haven't even lost our first tooth before we officially enter into formal education, which takes up most of the first two decades of our lives, and often longer.

We want to discover the world around us and our place in it. The big question we are all asked along this journey: "What do you want to be when you grow up?" The real question is: "When exactly do we grow up?" You will have many opportunities to change course throughout life, adjusting your activities as you fine-tune your lifestyle. The years you spend in high school, trade school and college give you the opportunity to discover what you'd like to do to make a living or make your mark on the world, but it's not the only time. Deciding what you want to be when you grow up is an on-going endeavor. And money, contrary to popular belief, is not the only consideration when you plan for a job or career. It does, however, have its place.

Finding Work You Like

Step 1: Think about what you enjoy doing. Research and learn about a lot of different subjects, jobs and career choices. Some people enjoy teaching, writing, singing, working on computers, drawing, crunching numbers, exploring math theories, astronomy, scientific experimentation, caring for other people, spending time outdoors or taking care of animals. Virtually any interest can grow into a profitable career. If you like to spend all of your time skateboarding, snowboarding, bicycling, dancing or pursuing similar activities—certainly there are people who make a living doing those things as well. If that's your choice, you need to know that you will have to work really hard at something you may have thought of as play. Many people choose to work in one field of relative interest so that they can afford to pursue their hobbies in their free time.

Step 2: Discover what you do well. Not only does your chosen career field have to be of interest to you—it also has to be something you will be good at. Fortunately people usually only like doing things they are good at doing. Maybe you have discovered that you are interested in and good at home construction. Do you have a knack for numbers? Do people seek you out for your excellent counseling and advice? Do you have a passion for medicine, science, the law, the environment, music, painting, writing or fixing the transmission in an old Chevy? Maybe you are adept at taking mechanical things apart, finding out what makes them tick and putting them back together. Can you inspire others, teach or speak in public? Do you have a special connection with children? Can you learn other languages, program a computer or design software?

Think about what you like to do and consider all of the various real-world jobs that might suit your interests and abilities.

Step 3: Decide the type of lifestyle you want. Gather information about how much money it will take to live the lifestyle you want. Research the five top paying careers in the location you'd most like to live. Find out what positions are in demand there. Career centers at high schools, colleges, universities and trade schools offer personality, interest and skills tests to help you make informed decisions concerning your future. The centers also have up-to-date information on professions, job responsibilities, qualifications, hours, benefits and pay. You will need to prioritize what you like to do, what you do well and how much money you want to make. It's best to do this before you even start college or trade school, but especially before you decide on a major, pay for years of schooling and graduate.

Step 4: Make a plan and put it in writing. Find out what kind of education and experience you will need and talk to professionals in that field. Careers in law and medicine, among others, take additional years of education and cost more in terms of tuition than other professions. You'll need to know all of the obstacles to decide if you have enough resources and commitment. Research which colleges and universities have the best programs for your selected career, then go for it.

Developing a Work Ethic

Step 1: Learn to work. When you were young, you had many opportunities to learn to work. Many children do chores to earn their allowance. By working you learned that doing a job well—cleaning a room, making a meal, completing a school project, planting a garden or mowing the lawn—is often a reward in and of itself. Odd jobs—such as the traditional newspaper route, babysitting, stocking shelves after school, waiting on tables, working at a fast food restaurant,

199

tutoring students or typing papers—provide work experience that teach basic skills that will always be in demand. Any workplace teaches the importance of being punctual, honest and dependable. As an employee you'll learn the satisfaction of doing a good job and earning a paycheck while developing a work ethic that will serve you well throughout your life. Always take pride in what you do and how well you do it.

Step 2: Don't be a slave for a paycheck. The worst kind of life is one of quiet desperation or aimless distraction. Your work will make up one-half of your waking hours every day of your life, so make sure the job you have is one you enjoy and have a talent for. You'll know it is a good job if you are successful at it and it pays the bills. The worst job is one you are forced to take because you have no other choices or opportunities. Stay in school. Get an education. A more directed and specialized education acquired as a young adult could make the difference between landing a fulfilling career and having to endure a miserable job.

Remember: "Work to live—don't live to work!" If you find at the end of your life that you spent more time at work and less time with your family and friends, and even less time actually experiencing the very stuff of life—the good stuff that goes on outside the office— then you will have wasted some quality time and missed out on some great experiences. Some people build spaceships for a living, discover cures for diseases, compose symphonies and change the course of the world. Others pick up garbage everyday, dig ditches, provide for their families and enjoy the simple pleasures of life. They, too, change the course of the world. No matter what type of work you do, look for something that enhances the life you dream of living. If you make wise and informed decisions in young adulthood, you will have more choices when you venture into the world of work.

We all have to work for a living. Work is much

better if you're doing something you like to do—something you are good at that pays the bills at the same time.

3: Take advantage of internship opportunities. Look into jobs, career opportunities and internships while you are in school. Many companies offer internships and apprenticeships to students in the hope that they will eventually join their team after graduation.

If you choose to attend a four-year university and earn a degree, start early to seek out and apply for an internship in your field. Internships are often offered over the summer for students who applied in the fall and were accepted in the spring. An internship is often your first and best opportunity to gain actual experience in your field. Find every opportunity to put the theory you study in the classroom into practice. If you cannot find a paying internship, then volunteer. This will not only expose you to the "real" world of your chosen career or profession—and reveal what you are getting into—but it will also provide you with references and experience to include on your resume for the real job hunt after graduation. Education coupled with experience is an unbeatable combination.

Preparing a Resume

Step 1: Gather all the information you need. A resume is a short synopsis of your educational and professional life. You'll need to know where you worked, the dates of your employment there, your supervisor's name and a brief summary of the skills you utilized and duties you performed in that position. In the educational summary you will list the names of the schools you've attended and when you graduated, or when you expect to graduate. Include volunteer work and extracurricular activities related to your field, as well as awards, achievements and recognition you have received. The rules for resumes are constantly changing. You may want to consult an Internet site

Dad's tip:
The sooner you decide on a course of study and begin to volunteer or work in that field, the sooner you will know if you have chosen something worth your time, money and energy. Even negative internships are helpful—you'll learn from your mistake and still have time to prepare for a career more to your liking. A positive internship puts you one step closer to being an employed college graduate in a timely manner.

before selecting a format to make sure you are in line with the latest preferred format. You'll want a resume that gets noticed for its professional look.

Step 2: Choose an easy-to-read font and type it all out. Resumes typed in Times New Roman or Arial look clean and readable. Include your name, address and phone number on separate lines, usually centered at the top of the page. (See Sample Resume on page 205.)

EDUCATION usually comes next. List the most recent institution first. Give the name of the university or college, city and state, grade point average (only if it's impressive – otherwise leave it out), degree earned, years attended and major course of study. Also list trade schools, additional courses and seminars. Give information about your high school years, too, such as the name of your high school, year graduated, grade point average (again, only if it's impressive) and any significant accomplishments.

The next thing to include is your career goal, sometimes captioned OBJECTIVE. Something like, "To secure an entry level position utilizing my skills in advertising that also offers an opportunity for advancement," or, "To secure a management position allowing for input into policy and the future of the company," or, "To have the opportunity to advance in a reputable company and find a permanent place through retirement." Let the company know exactly what you are looking for and what you can offer.

List WORK EXPERIENCE with most recent job first. Go back about five years. Give the name of company, its location, your job title, dates of employment and duties. If you have room you may want to include a brief summary of the skills you used or acquired in each position.

Next, most resumes usually offer a list of applicable abilities under the caption SKILLS. You might want to include: "Type 50 wpm, experience in research and development, human resources, payroll, and computer programs: MS Word, Excel, Quickbooks."

List all computer programs you have learned and used, unless they are obsolete. You may also want to include volunteer work.

On a separate page, list at least three solid REFERENCES. Most prospective employers will ask for them. You may want to include professional references (previous supervisors, mentors, etc.) and personal references, like a long time friend or neighbor. Personal references are especially important if you do not have a long work history. Give the reference's full name, title, company and phone number. Make sure that you call your references before including them so that they won't be surprised when your prospective employer calls about you. You want them to be ready to say some nice things about you. Offer this Reference page when the prospective employer asks for it.

Step 3: Do not include a photograph with your resume. A photo is considered tacky, unless your appearance is directly related to your job, such as being a model, an on-camera personality or selling beauty or health products. Do not list your age, marital status, personal family information or church affiliations. Include personal interests and hobbies only if they enhance your ability to do the job in question.

Step 4: Keep your resume to one page. Print it on a gray or beige high quality paper. Usually, you do not send your resume cold. Include a short cover letter that introduces yourself to the employer, states which position you are applying for, and summarizes the skills you could offer the company. Be sure to mention positive information about the company that compels you to join their team. Then give them contact numbers and a time frame you would like to meet for an interview. Keep this cover letter short and sweet. (See Sample Cover Letter on page 204.)

Step 5: Call the company for basic information. Get the name and correct spelling and title of the person to whom you will send the resume. Verify the

Dad says:
Don't overstate your abilities and experience.
You do not want to give your prospective employer false expectations.

Sample Cover Letter

Thursday, June 25, 2003

Ms. Eileen Hamilton
Human Resources Director
General Merchandise, Inc.
1234 Elm Avenue
City, State 55555

Dear Ms. Hamilton:

General Merchandise, Inc. is known for its innovation and excellence in product development and distribution. As my resume shows, I have a background in business which I hope to put to good use as a sales representative with your company.

I am completing my bachelors degree in business management. While at Favorite University, I have studied the importance of product placement and advertising. I particularly enjoyed building sales relationships with potential vendors during my internship at ABC Company.

My work as an office manager has taught me the importance of corporate communications. Staff development courses have broadened my awareness of current trends in organizational behavior.

As I graduate this month, I am confident that my experience and knowledge will allow me to make an immediate contribution at General Merchandise, Inc.. I am looking forward to meeting with you soon to discuss how my skills can meet your needs. I will call the week of July 1st to arrange an interview.

Sincerely,

Shirley U.Wantme
1234 Home St.
City, State 55555
(xxx)xxx-xxxx
shirleyuwantme@myserver.com

Enclosure

Sample Resume Format

SHIRLEY U. WANTME

1234 Home St.
City, State 55555
(xxx)xxx-xxxx
shirleyuwantme@myserver.com

EDUCATION
B.A., Favorite University, City, ST
Business Management. June 2003
List minor(s), academic honors, relevant memberships, significant presentations, group projects, reports, independent research.

OBJECTIVE
To secure an entry level position utilizing my skills in business that also offers opportunity for advancement.

EXPERIENCE
Organization Name, City, ST
Position Title. April 2000-June 2003
• Results, accomplishments, contributions and promotions.
• Positive difference or impact you made – specific, concrete, concise
  (3 lines or less).
• Begin sentences with action verbs.
• Indicate knowledge or skills you acquired if it's difficult to pinpoint specific
  contributions you made to the organization.

VOLUNTEER
Non-Profit Organization Name, City, ST
Fundraising Coordinator. January 1999-June 2003
• Results, accomplishments, contributions and promotions.
• Indicate the positive difference you made—specific, concrete, concise
  (3 lines or less).
• Begin sentences with action verbs.

RELATED SKILLS
Proficiency in business systems: Microsoft Word, Excel, PowerPoint.
Personnel management: Hiring, training, scheduling, budgeting.

address and phone number. Include this information and the date on your cover letter. Fax, mail or email your cover letter and resume to the person hiring. Call again to check if the company received it. Ask when they will be making a decision concerning interviews and when might be a good time to call back to check on their progress in the hiring process.

Ace the Interview

Step 1: Learn about the company ahead of time. Before you go to the interview you need to know a few things about the company. Find the company's web site and read about it or do some research on the company at the library. What kind of business does the company do? Who are their customers? What is its reputation? Who are its competitors? How many employees does it have?

When they call to invite you to the interview, ask who you will be interviewing with and his or her position. Inquire about the company's dress code—formal, business casual or casual. This information may seem trivial, but it is crucial that you dress appropriately for the interview. It is better to be slightly overdressed than underdressed for an interview.

Knowing this kind of information will give you an edge. You'll be able to talk knowledgeably with your interviewer. Once you have some facts about the company and the position you want, you can emphasize the things about your experience that make you especially suited for the job.

Step 2: Prepare your clothing the day before the interview. This will give you time for a trip to the dry cleaner, if needed. It will also give you time to launder, iron, sew buttons, fix hemlines, find matching stockings, polish shoes, etc. Pay attention to the little things. Carelessness with details can spoil your interview.

Choose crisp and polished clothing that is also comfortable. Do not wear anything too tight, too small or overly baggy. Look in a full-length mirror before

Ask Mom

For more on looking good and staying neat, see *Where's Mom Now That I Need Her?*, pages 239 - 257 "Laundry & Clothing Repair."

you walk out the door. Does everything hang well? Are hemlines even? Make sure you have enough room through your shoulders, across your hips, and through the rise of your slacks. Simply stated, you want to be able to concentrate on the interview, not on what you're wearing.

Step 3: Keep jewelry and accessories understated. Don't let your jewelry distract from you. Wear a watch that keeps accurate time. Go light on cologne or perfume. Don't chew gum. Wear one earring in each ear and make them conservative. Work is work, not a fashion show. Remember that if you are hired, you will be representing the company when you're on the clock.

Step 4: Spend time on personal hygiene and grooming. Above all, you should look and smell clean. Be sure to use deodorant. Hair and makeup should be conservative but attractive. Fingernails should be clean and shaped. If you wear polish, choose a subtle shade.

Step 5: Know where you are going. If you've never been to the office where you will be interviewed, go there a day or two before. You won't have to worry about finding the right building in addition to succeeding in the interview. You'll also know how much time to allot for driving and parking so that you aren't late.

Step 6: On the day of the interview, be on time. In fact, walk into the office ten minutes early. Many employers judge the work habits of a potential employee by whether he or she is on time and prepared for the interview. If you plan to arrive a few minutes early, you will be able to relax and wait, instead of arriving out of breath. Even if you mailed or delivered your resume ahead of time, take another copy with you. Also take your "References" page.

Step 7: During the interview, sit in a relaxed upright posture. Keep your hands relaxed and in your lap. Maintain good eye contact with your interviewer and smile. Answer all of the interviewer's questions in a positive, forthright manner. If you don't know the answer to a question, don't try to wing it. Just say you don't know but would be glad to get back to the interviewer with the answer promptly.

Dad says:
If you have body piercings (eyebrows, lips, tongue or nose), don't wear the jewelry to the interview. If you have tattoos, wear clothing that will cover them. You can express your individual style outside of work.

Step 8: You should ask some questions, too. You will seem much more motivated, intelligent and interested in the job and company if you ask some well-thought-out questions. There's another bonus, too—you'll find out more about the job and you might be able to spot some potential problems that could serve as red flags.

Don't ask more questions than your interviewer asks you. Ask what you need to know to make a decision. You should also look for clues as to how structured your position is, how much direct supervision you will have, what kind of training you will receive and to whom you will have direct responsibility.

Step 9: Close the interview with a firm handshake. A flimsy handshake is annoying to a prospective employer. Smile and make a brief statement that lets your interviewer know that you are looking forward to being part of the team.

Questions to Ask at an Interview

How do you see the company's future? Obviously, you don't want to get placed in a dead-end job or in a department that will be phased out during the next year. You are looking for a solid, competitive company that has a bright future. Asking about the company's position in the marketplace can alert you to problems and will let your interviewer know that you are aware of the company's product line.

Why are you looking for someone from outside the company to fill this position? Maybe the company is expanding and needs to bring in new employees. Your position might have been vacated by someone who was just promoted, or the company might have created a new slot that demands skills that present employees do not have. These are all legitimate reasons for seeking outside employees. You might be a little cautious, however, if you are replacing someone who was fired or who left because of difficulties with a supervisor or the company.

What kinds of job skills are you looking for in an applicant? As soon as you find out, you can emphasize the ones most important to your interviewer. You will also get a better sense of whether you are qualified and can meet the company's expectations.

What would my typical assignments be on this job? Try to pin the interviewer down to specifics. You want to get a feel for what the job will be like and whether it's something you will enjoy.

Will I be supervising other employees? If so, how many? Will you have responsibility for hiring, training and disciplining?

What kind of benefits does the company offer? At the first interview you can inquire casually about the company's employee benefits package, but specific questions might be reserved for a second interview or a job offer. Before you can make a final decision you'll need to find out about health insurance, life insurance, profit sharing, stocks or options and a pension plan. You'll also need to know about vacation and sick leave policies and when you will be paid.

Writing a Thank You

Step 1: To make a good impression, send a thank you. Mail it within two or three days after the interview. Make it a brief letter of thanks addressed to the person who interviewed you. The letter should be typed in business letter format on plain white paper or your own letterhead. Thank the interviewer for taking time with you and make one or two positive statements about the company. Close by letting the interviewer know when you will check back. Keep the letter brief—no more than two or three paragraphs—positive and complimentary. (See Sample Thank You on page 210.)

Step 2: If you don't want the job, bow out gracefully. What if you encounter a real stumbling block during the interview? Maybe you are clearly not qualified for the position or you can see that the

Dad says:
Avoid talking about money in the first interview unless the interviewer mentions it first.
If he or she asks how much you expect to be paid, ask instead, "What does this position usually pay?" When given a figure, if it's around what you had in mind, you reply should be, "That's within the range I had in mind." That way they know they can afford you, and you've left room for negotiating.

Sample Thank-You Letter

Friday, June 26, 2003

Ms. Eileen Hamilton
Human Resources Director
General Merchandise, Inc.
1234 Elm Avenue
City, State 55555

Dear Ms. Hamilton:

I appreciated the opportunity to interview at General Merchandise on Monday. The tour of the distribution center and the interaction with other sales reps gave me a clear picture of the kind of work I will be doing in the near future.

The entire experience has confirmed my desire to work as a sales representative for General Merchandise, Inc. My business training and experience have prepared me well for this position. Based upon my interviews, I am confident that I would fit in well with the entire staff.

Thank you again for the experience of getting to know your organization better. I would welcome the opportunity to work for General Merchandise, Inc. and look forward to hearing from you soon.

Sincerely,

Shirley U.Wantme
1234 Home St.
City, State 55555
(xxx)xxx-xxxx
shirleyuwantme@myserver.com

company is barely surviving. Or there might be some other situation—hours, pay scale, or no chance for promotion that keeps you from wanting to pursue the job. Yes, you need to be right for the job, but—just as importantly—the job needs to be right for you. You want to be successful in it.

In a courteous way, let the interviewer know that you are not the right person for the job. You may do this at the time of the interview or in your thank you note. You might say something like, *"I can see that a strong public relations background would be vital to success in this position. I don't have the experience in that area and as a result I wouldn't be able to meet the company's expectations."*

In another situation you might say, *"I am hoping to affiliate with a company that I can make a strong career commitment to. While your company is certainly an outstanding one, I am concerned about not being able to grow with the company."* Then thank the interviewer for taking time to talk to you. Wish the company success in finding a suitable applicant. Remember in business, never burn a bridge!

Negotiating Your Salary

Money is only a taboo topic of conversation if you treat it as such. Employers wanting to keep their budget down will hope you do. Don't be intimidated. Again, gather your information ahead of time. Knowledge is power. In the case of getting paid what you are worth, knowledge is cold hard cash. You will perform an essential task and should be paid well for that.

Step 1: Know what you are worth and how much to ask for. It pays to know in advance what the market will pay for your skills. Begin by evaluating your own salary history—you certainly want to make more with each successive job change, if at all possible. Check with a career counseling center, such as job service, before the interview to see what similar positions in

Dad says:
If your company offers employee stock options and retirement programs, like a 401K, buy into them from the outset. You won't miss the money, and you'll be putting it to good use. Most companies that offer employee stock purchase programs have a strong commitment to their workers. They will often match all or part of what you invest.

your area are paying. Remember to be realistic—you won't be paid as much as someone who has many years of expertise in the field. If an offer is extended, be polite. Before rejecting a low offer, find out the specific numbers in terms of salary and benefits. Ask about bonuses, health insurance, retirement programs, and anticipated cost-of-living and merit increases.

Step 2: Be confident, positive and ready to negotiate. When you return to the office for a second interview, you may receive a job offer on the spot—be ready to negotiate. If you've done your homework and feel confident that you know how much the position should pay for your skills and experience, you'll be ready to ask for the salary you deserve.

If your prospective employer offers less than you legitimately believe you should receive, tell him or her that you are interested in the job, but that you believe it should pay more. Back up your request with the specific reasons why you deserve to be paid at a higher starting wage than what has been offered. (Get information about average starting salaries for your particular position from business departments on university campuses, the Internet or market magazines.)

Prospective employers will generally offer the least amount necessary to get you on board. Some experts believe you should always ask for more, giving convincing reasons for your request. They reason that it is much easier to get a better starting salary than to try to catch up after a few months or years on the job when increases are more tightly regulated. The higher the salary you make in the beginning, the further ahead you will be when it comes to yearly cost-of-living and merit increases. If the employer refuses to budge and you still want the job, you've lost nothing.

Keeping Your Job

To get ahead in a job you'll need to be a top-notch employee. Build your career and avoid pitfalls by making the most of common sense, honesty and hard work.

Step 1: Be dependable and punctual. Get to work on time, or a little bit early, every day. Meet deadlines. Follow through with assignments. Be the kind of employee your boss can count on. Go the extra mile.

Step 2: Don't plan your social life at work. Make personal phone calls on breaks or at lunch, away from your desk. It's best to use your own cell phone for personal calls. Ask friends who want to drop in to confine it to your break or lunch hour. Planning a personal party, barbecue or dinner? Do it at home, not at the office.

Step 3: Try to leave problems at home. Don't talk about your personal problems with co-workers or your boss. Limit your conversations to business plans. Mingle with your colleagues, but steer the conversation away from your personal life. If you start to get moody or lose control, excuse yourself and visit the restroom. Take a few deep breaths, splash some cold water on your face and regain control.

Step 4: Talk to your boss when problems affect your work. If you run into serious personal problems, such as mental or physical health problems that negatively impact your job performance, talk to your boss privately right away. Most supervisors will help you create a plan to get through these obstacles and still keep your job, but do not ask for special treatment. Your boss will likely be more understanding and tolerant of your situation if you present him or her with a plan of action demonstrating that you are working to resolve the problem and get back to normal.

It may even be necessary to compose a written agreement that both of you sign. If personal or health problems threaten to jeopardize your job, talk with the human resources department. See what type of help is available. Some companies have employment counselors to help you through rough times, while others offer extended time off, a leave of absence or temporary disability. Address the problem early and honestly. Know that workers, supervisors, bosses and even CEOs are human, too.

Dad says:
Don't burn the candle at both ends. Meaning, don't party the night before work then expect to be at your best on the job. Eat well. Exercise. Get good sleep. The better you feel, the better employee you will be. And the more you will enjoy your job.

213

Step 5: Hone your skills. Improve typing, shorthand or accounting skills if applicable to your job. Keep up on the latest trends and computer programs. Visit the library and read trade magazines and journals that apply to your career field. Businesses often have tuition reimbursement programs in place for their employees to continue learning while working. Join professional organizations—employers will often pay the associated fees to join. You will learn more about your business while networking and associating with others who can give you valuable advice. As an added bonus, you may hear about jobs coming available through word-of-mouth rather than through the want ads of your local newspaper.

Step 6: Don't make excuses for why something can't be done. Instead, take on the challenge and find out how it can be done. Keep challenging yourself. If you don't feel challenged on the job, do something to improve yourself. Take a class in a new subject or learn a new job skill. Seize every opportunity for on-the-job training, special schooling or leadership seminars. You want to become indispensable to your company.

Step 7: Go out of your way to work well with others. Always try to get along with all of your co-workers and supervisors. You are a member of a team. If you demonstrate excellent people skills, you are much more likely to be promoted to a management level position. Acknowledge the help others give you on projects by giving credit where it's due. Work hard to hold up your end of the workload. Above all, avoid office gossip and squabbles.

Step 8: Respond quickly to questions and assignments. If your boss needs some figures, compile the figures the same day. If you can't get the actual figures together that day, deliver a memo outlining what you've done to date and when you will have the requested information.

Step 9: Be positive and smile. Attitude is often more important than aptitude. Don't be a complainer.

Laugh every once in a while and help lighten things up. Accept criticism in a positive way. Instead of leaping to your own defense, ask, *"How can I improve my job performance? I'd really appreciate your suggestions."*

Step 10: Keep up your personal appearance. Always be neat. Keep your work area clean. If you work at a desk, clear it off every night before you leave to go home—this gives the impression that you have your area under control. Always be well-groomed. Avoid clothes that are too tight, too baggy, soiled, discolored or wrinkled. Never wear clothing that needs to be repaired (a missing button, a ripped seam or a sagging hemline.) Be clean and smell good. And always observe the dress code.

Staying Out of Trouble

Step 1: Report sexual harassment. If someone in the office makes sexual advances, you can maintain your self-respect without jeopardizing your job. Politely ask the offender to stop hugging you, calling you "honey" or commenting about your body or sex life. If that doesn't work, tell the person that you feel uncomfortable with the behavior and that his or her remarks or actions negatively impact your ability to work. Tell the offender you want to be professional associates only.

If a person who holds a supervisory position and can prevent your promotion or threaten your job security insists on sexual performance to keep your job, immediately file a complaint with management or human resources. Make sure that you keep detailed notes on the offender's behavior so that you can report time, dates, witnesses and specific incidences to back you up. Do not ignore sexual comments or actions directed against you—often the offender will interpret your silence as an invitation to continue unacceptable and unprofessional behavior.

*D*ad says:
Even though you want to be one of the best employees, don't let people take advantage of you. Remember that this is a job and you should be compensated for repeatedly going above and beyond the call of duty. If you are being mistreated or under-appreciated, look for another job.

Step 2: Don't sexually harass others. You may be unaware of how your behavior affects others. Maybe you are a gregarious person who tells a lot of jokes or a touchy person who makes physical contact unintentionally. Be aware that these behaviors can be misinterpreted and may be offensive. Behavior that is acceptable when drinking beer with buddies on the weekends or gossiping on the phone with girlfriends does not fly on the job. Refrain from making sexual remarks of any kind. Always dress appropriately. Steer clear of sexist, racist or tasteless jokes. No flirting during working hours. If you find you have something in common with a co-worker, talk away from the office.

Step 3: Be aware of office politics. In the first few months of your new job, observe. Listen more than you talk. Keep opinions to yourself, at least while you are still new. Get to know people, ask friendly and polite questions, but don't get too personal. Develop conservative personal and professional boundaries. If you let everyone know your personal business, you have no personal business. If you are too quick to share your opinions about your co-workers or bosses, you may find that you've offended someone who could affect future salary increases and promotions.

There is a lot of truth in the statement: *"It's not what you know—it's who you know."* Make strong and smart professional contacts, then behave yourself so that they can recommend you to others.

Office Politics

Understanding office politics isn't difficult. In fact, your parents' simple advice when you were a kid in school works just as well in dealing with co-workers and management at a multi-million dollar company:

• Be courteous and kind.
• Keep your hands to yourself.
• Don't cuss, yell or whine.
• Treat others with respect.
• Don't tattle tell or gossip.
• Don't tell lies and don't take what isn't yours.
• Stay on task and get your work done.
• Don't be a chump—demand respect.
• If you can't say something nice, don't say anything at all.
• If you have a problem with someone, talk to them not everybody else.
• Decide your own personal values and don't compromise them for anyone else.

Asking for a Raise

Don't dread asking for a raise. You deserve one! With a little advance preparation, you can make a convincing case to your boss. Start planning for a raise in your own mind. Are you sure you deserve one? If not, don't ask for one. Before you approach your boss about a raise, you need to wipe any doubt from your mind. Be convinced of the salary you should be getting. Remember that it has nothing to do with your personal worth, but with the work you do for the company. Once you have resolved that in your mind, get ready to perform your own little "song and dance" – promote yourself.

Step 1: Document your successes. Keep a written record of your contributions and accomplishments. If you've found a solution to a difficult problem, record it. You may even have some written 'kudos' filed away from clients and co-workers who were particularly pleased with your service. Review this file carefully before asking for a raise. You may need to recall some details when you talk to your boss.

Step 2: Ask for regular feedback and follow suggestions. For several months before you plan on asking for a raise, ask your boss for regular feedback. You need to know how he sees you and what he thinks you could be doing better. React to all feedback in a positive, action-oriented way. If you can't get your boss to offer verbal feedback, ask for a written evaluation. Work on the things he or she suggests you work on to show some concrete accomplishments.

Step 3: Get ready to present your case. The best time to ask for a raise is soon after you've received professional recognition for a project you were working on. Gather up all your information ahead of time. Review your successes, rehearse some specific plans that will make you an ongoing value to the company. Type out a plan and give a copy to your boss when you meet. The plan should include a list of your achievements over the past year, plans for improvement in the next year and specifics about the raise you feel you deserve. You need numbers here. Back them up with statistics concerning the average or fair-market-value of your skills and experience.

Step 4: Make sure your timing is right. The optimum time to ask for a raise is three to four months before the budgets are prepared for the next year. If you wait until the budgets are done, your chances of getting a raise are slim.

Set an appointment with your boss at a time when you can both be relaxed. Avoid an appointment first thing in the morning when your boss must face the pressures of a full schedule. Steer clear of periods just before important meetings. An afternoon meeting toward the end of the week, when things wind down a bit, might be best. Ask for the meeting in your boss's office. Avoid going to a restaurant or any location away from the office.

Step 5: Be relaxed, friendly and forthright. Open the meeting by saying something like, *"I asked for this meeting to talk about a raise."* Realize that your boss will probably be uncomfortable and may initially turn you down. Don't take it personally—it's his or her job to save the company money and keep expenses down. Review your achievements of the past year together. Remind the boss of what you've done for the company while you've been on board. Then, to cement your value to the company, tell him or her some of the things you plan to improve in your department and the goals you'd like to accomplish.

Step 6: Present a copy of your written request with an amount. After you have spelled out your achievements and sketched your plans, tell your boss what kind of a raise you have in mind. Don't ask for a raise in general. Instead, tell your boss exactly how much money you would like to have. Asking for a raise involves negotiation and you need to spell out exact figures. Find out beforehand what the going rate is for a person in your position, with your years of experience and education. If you took the job at a lower salary, it may be that you need to move up to the going rate.

If the boss agrees to the raise, thank him or her immediately and ask when the new salary will be effective. Fill out the necessary paperwork immediately, if possible, so that your boss does not change his or her mind or forget.

Responding to Rejection

If, despite all of your reasoning, the boss turns you down for a raise, there are many possible responses to consider. Above all, remain polite and professional. Do not become angry or defensive.

If your boss says you need to improve in a certain area before he or she can give you a raise, and you agree with that assessment, say, *"I appreciate your feedback. I'll get back to you as soon as I have polished my skill in that area."*

If your boss says he can't make the decision, but has to defer to someone else, say, *"I'll be happy to make some notes to strengthen our position with your superior."* Saying this lets your boss know that you are confident he is on your side and will fight for you.

If your boss says the company isn't making enough money to give out raises this year, say, *"I understand the money is tight, but I'm sure the company will want to use its available resources on people who really produce in areas that count."*

If your boss hesitates, citing several past mistakes or shortcomings, say, *"Those things are in the past. I think my raise should be based on my ability to produce results now, which I have been doing consistently."*

If your boss listens to your arguments, presents the request to his superior and gets turned down, say, *"I appreciate your support. I'll think more about it and come up with a new approach. When the time is right, I'll get back with you and we can try again."*

Revving Up Your Work

Just like a marriage, you will experience a honeymoon phase in your new job. Everyone greets you pleasantly and puts their best foot forward. You may feel relieved and grateful to be working. Each day brings new challenges as you learn your job, get comfortable with the staff and show off your skills. Then . . . you get settled in, the work begins to pile up, you must answer to your boss, your responsibilities increase, and maybe you've made a few mistakes.

Don't panic! Simply be aware that this happens to the best of us. For some it happens just months into the job, for others the first year works great, then they coast through the second year and meet up with the blahs in the third year.

Step 1: Make some bold changes, quickly. If you've slipped up, let your guard down, cut corners in organization, gotten sloppy with your appearance or started sneaking in a few minutes late and taking longer lunches—buck up! Change your evil ways. Reflect on reasons this job meant so much to you years ago. Recall how much you disliked job hunting. Now brainstorm. Write down all of the ways you can improve your performance at work. Pick one or two of the simplest things to do first and make the changes necessary to preserve your self respect and command the respect of your supervisors. People notice.

Step 2: Talk with your boss when you feel yourself slipping. He or she has likely already observed that you are slacking off. If you don't bring it up, your boss will, either very soon or at your annual evaluation. Approach the situation positively. Say something like, *"I feel like I need a small change to sharpen up my work."* Then, tell your boss what you plan to do to improve in the short term. Ask your boss what he or she can do to challenge you more. Do you want to be assigned to a new project? Do you want to give up an account that has you in the dumps? Can you be involved in an employee committee that helps improve the atmosphere of the office? Whatever the approach or possible solution, dedicate yourself to pull out of the slump or you may find yourself in the unemployment line, wishing you still had your "boring old" job back.

Step 3: Recognize if it's time to move on. You may have many legitimate reasons to quit a job: no opportunity for promotion or advancement, personality differences with bosses or co-workers, disagreements about policies and procedures, mistreatment, or intolerable boredom.

First, make the basic decision—will you quit the job you have now before you find another job, or will you start looking for another job while still employed? Your resources will undoubtedly have something to do with the decision. If you quit one job before you have another one secured, you will need a way to support yourself. You may qualify for unemployment benefits after a certain length of time, but often, if you leave a job voluntarily, unemployment benefits are not available. Do you have enough savings to pay all of your expenses until you've found another job?

It takes about one month for every $10,000 in salary to find a comparably paying job. In other words, if you were making $40,000 a year, count on a job search taking four months. Your final check will include pay for unused, accrued vacation days. If you have enough money to pay your bills, you won't have to panic and settle for the wrong job. Money's not the only issue, though. You need to consider your self-esteem. How will you feel about yourself out of work?

Dad says:
No matter how poorly things may be going at work, when it is time to move on, do not burn your bridges. Resist the urge to "get even" or tell everyone off before you walk out the door.

221

*D*ad says:
Avoid making any kind of permanent decision when you are emotionally upset. If something happens at work that upsets you, wait until you have calmed down before you make a decision to leave. Wait until you can make a clear, rational choice.

How will you feel if you stay at your present job? Will important people in your life look at you unfavorably if you don't have work? How much do you care what other people think? Will your family be supportive while you look for another job?

You should not have to put up with being mistreated or disrespected at work – you were looking for a job when you found this one. You can find another. If you end up leaving one job before you have another, don't let it reflect poorly on you. If a potential employer asks, simply say, *"I've always thought it was dishonest to look for employment on my company's time. I felt I owed it to the company to devote all my time and energy to my job as long as I was still on the payroll."*

Make a Smooth Exit

Step 1: Review your files and gather samples. Make a portfolio of non-confidential work that you can compile to show to other potential employers. Obviously, you should never take anything of a confidential nature or that would betray the company's standing.

Step 2: Go through your telephone file or phone book. Copy the names and phone numbers of any personal contacts you established while working for the company. Ethically, you should not take with you any contacts or clients that belong to the company.

Step 3: Give your boss at least two weeks written notice. This will give the company time to replace you. Offer to do whatever you can to ease the transition, including helping to train your replacement, if they will pay you for your time to do that, of course.

Step 4: Don't go over a list of grievances or gripes. When you announce your resignation, be brief and matter-of-fact. If your boss presses for details, be honest in your assessment of the situation but remain positive. You may want to simply state that it's time for you to move on and pursue some other interests. Remain professional.

Step 5: Ask your boss and colleagues for letters of recommendation. Even if you are leaving under difficult circumstances, your boss may agree to write a letter about some of your successes and contributions or about some areas where you did a good job. Also ask your boss and any department heads you have worked with if you can use their names as references. After you've left, drop a personal note to your boss and any influential colleagues or department heads you worked with. Thank them, comment on one or two positive things you learned or accomplished and wish them continued success.

Step 6: Do what you can to help the company as you leave. The people you leave will have better feelings for you, and you will have a greater chance of getting a positive recommendation, if you leave on good terms. You'll also feel better about yourself and maintain integrity and dignity. No matter how awkward it seems, attend farewell lunches or parties. You'll leave on a positive note and will be remembered with greater fondness. This helps when you need to use co-workers or bosses as references.

Do Almost Anything

Hold a Baby

While women have more of an opportunity and may feel more of a social obligation to hold a baby, this is also an essential skill for every man to learn. Both genders will be asked or expected to hold a baby at some point in time. You'll want to do this competently so that you don't look like an idiot and so that the child is safe. In the dating years, when sizing-up potential mates, a young man will want to know that his future wife can care for a child, while a young women will want to know that her future husband is, at the very least, not afraid of a baby.

Step 1: Hold the newborn firmly but gently. Use slow movements. If you are right-handed, place your left hand at the back of the baby's head so that your palm rests at the bottom of the head and the top of the neck. The muscles in a newborn's neck are not strong enough to hold up the head, so you must provide the support. Slide your other hand, palm open and up, under the bottom to the back, resting the child along your forearm. *(See Illustration A below.)* Now pull the baby gently in so that the right side of his or her body rests closely alongside your chest. Newborns like to hear your heartbeat and feel your warmth. This position also allows the baby to see your face as you look down. If it's more comfortable, once you have picked the baby up, move your left arm down under the baby, alongside your other arm, resting the child's head in your left elbow fold, making a cradle with your arms. *(See Illustration B below.)* If you are holding a newborn for the first time, it is best to try this cradle hold while sitting down in a sturdy chair or sofa, allowing the mother to place the child in your arms.

A.   B.

Step 2: Comfort and burp a baby. When an infant is crying, one of the best holding positions is chest-to-chest slightly over one shoulder. This is also the best position for burping a baby after mealtime. If you are right-handed, pick the baby up by placing your left hand at the back of the baby's head and neck, then slide your right hand and arm under the baby. Now, bring the infant's chest against your chest along the left side of your body so that the baby's head rests just above your shoulder. (*See Illustration A1 below.*) Now, slide your left hand and forearm down around to cradle the baby's bottom while your right hand and forearm rest against the baby's back. *(See Illustration B1 below.)* This way you can hold the baby upright against you, supporting his or her head, which allows you to pat the baby's back gently to get a burp. Place a burping cloth or towel over your left shoulder to catch spitup. Hey, spit happens.

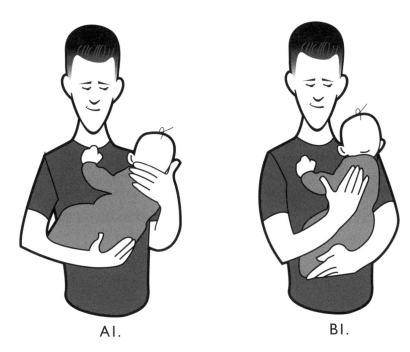

AI.   BI.

Step 3: Babies need a tender but firm touch. A newborn may bob his or her head, so always keep your open palm on or close to the back of the neck or head to manage such a movement. Anytime you hold a newborn away from your body, support the back of the neck and head with one hand while holding his or her body securely with the other hand and forearm. Don't make quick movements. You've probably seen men tossing a child into the air and catching him or her with outstretched arms to elicit squeals of laughter. Don't do this. *This is not appropriate for a newborn or infant. Never shake a baby. Shaking a small child can cause permanent brain damage, even death.*

Notes

6

Get Money Smart
Controlling Your Finances

When someone else is paying, like Mom or Dad, bills may appear to be nothing more than a monthly nuisance. You may not think about how paying the bills keeps a roof over your head, food in your belly, lights in your room and hot water in the shower—not to mention the television, computer, Internet and telephone. When you start living on your own, however, your name will be on all those bills and your money will be your own. How you save, spend and invest that money and how you pay bills, will determine your quality of life.

Dad's Top 5 Money Rules:
1. Set up a savings account. (Pay into savings each paycheck.)
2. Live within your means. (Do not buy on credit.)
3. Make do with what you have. (Reduce, reuse and recycle.)
4. Pay your bills first. (Pay for the necessities before the luxuries.).
5. Save for what you want. (And pay cash.)

First Things First

Step 1: Open a savings account. This will help build a good credit rating. However, don't start buying on credit even if all the credit card companies, furniture, clothing and appliance stores offer you a credit card. When you first get out on your own, make do with what you have. You don't need the best or newest of everything. Take pride in making ends meet on a tight budget. There is a big difference between what you need and what you want. You need an apartment, lights, heat, water and food. You want a vehicle, a telephone, a computer, the Internet, cable television, stylish clothes, movies and dinners out on the town.

Step 2: Pay for your needs first (including savings) then buy your wants. Decide the best price for a your wants whether it be for a stereo, computer, car, bicycle, television, bed or living room furniture. Calculate what you will need to save per paycheck. Put that money away. *Then pay for the item in cash.* You will save yourself interest fees and a potentially poor credit rating. Plus, you will learn financial discipline and actually value the merchandise more and take better care of it because it's yours outright.

Step 3: If you think a budget is an old-fashioned notion that doesn't really help at all, you're wrong. A budget is a necessity if you want to know where your money is going. A budget can help you pay for the essentials of life, take care of your financial obligations, build positive credit, plan for future purchases and save for investing. Without a budget, you'll find yourself spending all of your money until it's gone. You'll also be more likely to forget to pay the really important bills—such as rent, car payment and utilities—until those bills are past due. A budget will help you get the most value out of each dollar you earn.

Creating a Budget

Simply stated, a budget is the foundation for all of your financial planning. A good budget enables you to control your money. Once you have a well-designed budget, you can set priorities based on what's most important to you. Budgeting takes some time and maintenance but it's quite simple to understand. It's like maintaining your car—from time to time you may need a tune-up, but if you follow general maintenance guidelines it will run for many years. Establish a monthly budget, then maintain it every two weeks or so when you get paid. Stick to it and you'll be the master of your money.

Step 1: Find out how much money you earned during the previous 12 months and estimate what you will earn this year. If your income fluctuates, estimate month by month earnings then add them up for a year's total. Now, find out how you spent the money you earned. To do this, gather documents such as pay stubs, canceled checks, utility bill receipts, credit card bills, medical or dental bills, drugstore receipts, tax returns, mortgage or rent receipts and anything else having to do with the money you've earned and spent.

If you don't have all that stuff, estimate.

After your budget is initially designed, you can make additions or revisions without as much intensive labor. A budget or finance computer program, such as Quicken or Microsoft Money will help. If you prefer to manage your money the old-fashioned way, buy a budget book at any office supply store.

Step 2: Divide your expenses into categories. Divide your documents (bills, loan agreements, etc.) into separate files. Not everything you spend money on has equal importance in your life. Some spending, like a mortgage payment or rent, is clearly an essential, while other spending, such as going out to eat, is clearly non-essential. Add up how much money you've spent in each category over the past year. This

*D*ad says:
If you file financial papers when you first open them, fresh from the mail box, paying your bills and revising your budget will be a snap.

*D*ad says:
When money is tight, your budget is simple —pay for essentials. Cash or deposit your check and pay the bills. Don't splurge. Don't go out to eat or buy that blouse. You may even have to find ways to cut essential expenses such as utilities (turn off those lights) or groceries (cook from scratch) or gasoline (walk where you can).

exercise, though painful, will help you better prioritize your future spending. You might find you blow enough cash at restaurants each year to pay for your car insurance. You'll be surprised at how much of your paycheck is wasted on your wants, and that might explain why you are having trouble keeping up with your needs. Now, in your budget book or program record what you've spent and how much you plan to spend in each area per month.

Step 3: Assign each category of spending to one of four priorities: *Essentials,* those things you must have in order to maintain life; *necessities,* those things you consider necessary; *extras,* those things you enjoy, but could do without; and *one-time expenses,* those things that occur only once and wouldn't be listed on a monthly budget.

Remember that this is your budget, so you determine the priorities. You might want to have a general category of utilities, for example, or you might decide to break it down into the money you spend on natural gas, electricity, water, sewer, phone, cable television and Internet access. While each budget should be individually tailored, your breakdown of categories will probably look somewhat like this:

Essentials: mortgage or rent payments, utility bills, groceries, car payment, insurance premiums, gasoline and child care. (These are all the things you need to live and make a living.)

Necessities: savings for emergency, retirement programs, insurance deductible, debt repayment—including monthly credit card payments and medical and dental bills—medications, clothing, home maintenance, car maintenance, tuition, laundry, personal care and grooming items, spending money and donations to a church or synagogue. (Necessities are things that must be paid to maintain your particular lifestyle.)

Extras: special occasion gifts, art and music lessons, furniture, new appliances, meals at restaurants, entertainment such as movies and concerts, tickets to sporting events, tobacco and alcohol, candy and soft drinks, toys and games, DVDs, CDs, sports equipment, club memberships, books, newspapers and magazine subscriptions and vacations. (Extras are things that would improve upon your lifestyle but are negotiable.)

One-time expenses: reroofing the house, replacing the furnace, repairing the car or extraordinary one-time expenses. (A savings account is essential preparation for these often unforeseen expenses That's why it's listed under necessities.)

Step 4: Add up the totals. Time to dust off the adding machine or calculator. Add up what you spent in each category during the previous 12 months. List each category and its total on a sheet of paper. Now add up all of your income. Be sure to include every source of money, such as income tax refunds, interest form savings accounts, stock dividends and your salary, including any overtime. List each category and its total on a second sheet of paper. Now you need grand totals. Total up how much you spent and how much you earned. This will give you a clear picture of what happened during the previous 12 months. Next, you need to design an income for the next 12 months. To allow for inflation, add about 5 percent to each category. Your targeted savings goal should be 10 percent of your estimated income.

Most computer budgeting programs will have special features that help you better visualize your budget, such as colored pie charts or graphs. Pay attention to where your money is going in each category. If you are spending too much on extras, it's time to cutback.

Step 5: Balance your income against your expenses. How does your income compare with what you've spent? If you are able to cover all of your expenses, great. But if you are like many people living in the red (more expenses than income), you have several options.

Cutting Your Expenses

Step 1: Learn to cook and eat in. You would be surprised how much money you will waste by going out to eat or ordering in. Not only will you save money preparing your own meals, but you will also feel better and be able to maintain a healthier weight.

Step 2: Budget and save for what you want to buy. When you feel you need to buy new clothes, go out to a movie or attend a special event (any of those wants we talked about), budget for them. Write down everything you need to pay from your check then budget for one or two things you want. Put the rest in savings. Don't go on a spending spree every payday simply because you have extra cash in your pocket.

Step 3: Pay in cash or by money order. Don't get a credit card or even a checking account when you are first learning to deal with money. Design a budget for the month, then decide what items you will pay with your first paycheck and then with your second. Find a secure box for your money, get some envelopes, label each one according to the expense you must pay and place the cash for that expense in those envelopes.

Quick Cuts

• Reduce the amount you spend in some categories. You might decide to join a carpool instead of driving alone to work or you might buy only half the CDs and DVDs you bought last year. *Reduce in every other budget category that you can before you reduce the amount of money you are putting into savings.* Savings should only be cut as a last resort.

• Completely eliminate some categories from your budget. You might decide to quit smoking, drop your health club membership or stop taking music lessons. You might cut back on going out to eat from once a week to once a month.

• Figure out a way to produce more income. You might decide to get a part-time job or start making wooden toys to sell, for example, or create resumes on your computer.

When you run out of cash, you are done spending in that category. Right after you cash your check (the same day), purchase money orders to pay bills that must be mailed. Mail these essential expenses before you spend any cash.

Step 4: Buy your clothes at thrift stores. There are great second-hand stores now that sell $30 dresses for $3, a suit for $10 and slightly used jeans for $5. You can develop your own style and look great without spending a ton of money.

Step 5: Use coupons. There are coupons for everything: groceries, household items, personal hygiene items, clothes, books, large ticket merchandise, etc. Look around the Internet, check newspaper ads and pick up stores' in-house advertising brochures. Though you save just a bit on each item, the regular use of coupons can add up to big savings. The only caution is, don't buy a more expensive item or brand just because you have a coupon for it. Look for coupons on inexpensive items and brands that you regularly use. Buy in bulk when you can—the savings can be tremendous.

Write It Down

Once you've achieved a balance between what you earn and what you will spend, write it down. This is your budget. You can divide it any way you want to as long as it is easy to understand and track. It's usually easiest to divide up the year by monthly expenses, then by pay periods.

Step 1: Put your budget in writing. List essentials, necessities and extras with individual items under each one. Assign a budgeted amount to each item, such as: savings $50, rent $350, car payment $250, groceries $100, car insurance $80, phone $50, heat $40, lights $35, gas $20. Write down the amount of cash you received from your paycheck at the top right of the column. Every time you spend money within that period, write down on the line next to the appropriate category, subtract it, and come up with a new total representing the amount of money you have left. To make the process easier, you might want to prepare one master sheet that lists the divisions, categories and amounts. Then have the sheet photocopied and use a copy for each new pay period or monthly division. *(See Basic Budget Worksheet on page 248.)*

*D*id you know? *If you start to save just a dollar a day starting from age 18, you can invest those savings each year and be a millionaire by the time you retire. Just a dollar a day!*

Step 2: Adjust your budget often. Your budget will need to be adjusted periodically to reflect what's happening in your life. If you suddenly start spending more or less in a certain category because of circumstances beyond your control, such as increasing gasoline prices, you need to be able to adjust. Keep working on your budget—it will change frequently, reflecting your personal situation. But stick to it, and you can achieve financial goals you may have thought impossible.

Step 3: Write down everything you spend. Keep a daily record of every penny you spend. Jot it down on a piece of paper you keep in your wallet, day planner or purse. Just take a second at the time of purchase and record what you've spent, as you would if you were writing a check. If you carry cash with you, you will be surprised how fast you spend your money and how those expenses add up, especially for little things like bus fare, coffee, snacks and gas.

Figure out how much miscellaneous spending you actually do and what you absolutely need to do, then budget an amount from each check to take care of these items – they can add up fast. Your miscellaneous allowance might be $20 or $50 from each check. Otherwise, if you haven't budgeted for something, don't buy it. Whatever you spend, record the purchase.

To Pay or Not to Pay

No matter how carefully you have budgeted, the day may come when you encounter an unforeseen event that may take every penny of your paycheck. Hopefully, the emergency savings account you've been building will help you weather the financial storm. If it isn't sufficient, you're going to be faced with some tough choices. You don't have enough money to pay all of your bills and you have to decide which ones you will pay first. This is a temporary, emergency situation. You will need to pay all of your creditors as soon as possible, but for now you have to determine who will get paid now and who will have to wait. Communication is the key. *Let creditors know of your situation right away.*

Step 1: Pay essential creditors first or make arrangements with them. The basic rule of thumb is to pay your creditors according to how effectively they can collect from you. Pay first any creditor who can cut off an essential service, such as the landlord, who can evict you, and the utility companies, who can shut off your lights, heat, etc. Your car can be re-possessed, your car insurance can be cancelled and persons to whom you owe alimony or child support can garnish your wages by court order. For each creditor you need to know the due date, the grace period, the penalties for late payment and at what point they report to a credit reporting agency. Negative reports are usually made at 30 days past due, but sometimes creditors will wait until a payment is 90 days late before reporting it. If at all possible, you want to get through this rough patch without damaging your credit rating.

Step 2: Next, pay the creditors who take time collecting. Creditors who could repossess or foreclose, but who will take some time to do it, or creditors whose collection practices are not as effective as those in the first category are the ones to pay next. These may include banks and finance companies where you have secured or unsecured loans for anything other than a car. The IRS will take up to 10 months to begin collection procedures, but they are one of the few creditors who can also throw you in jail for non-payment. You don't want to get on their bad side. Credit card companies generally try to avoid canceling cards because it means they lose their leverage to get you to pay, but they may freeze your account until you are current.

Step 3: Finally, pay creditors who won't threaten court action. To be paid last are those creditors who will ignore your delinquency or whose collection methods are ineffective. These usually include hospitals, doctors, dentists and retailers. They

Dad says:
Learn to manage your cash first then get a checking account only after you can assure yourself that you will be responsible with your check writing. If you do not record your checks or balance your checkbook regularly, it can be very easy to write a bad check unintentionally.

BILL

*D*ad says:
Cut back on "nickel and diming" yourself into the poorhouse. What do you spend on coffee, soda pop, candy, restaurant lunches or cigarettes each day? Those dollars add up. Stop spending a quarter here and Dollar there every day and you will have more money at the end of the month.

will often work with you on an extended payment plan. Obviously, you never want to be caught in this situation. You can avoid it with some careful planning and an adequate savings account.

Finding Money to Save

What if you just can't seem to budget enough for savings? The answer is simple: get to work on some strategies that can help you trim expenses even from a tight budget. Consider these ideas:

Step 1: Pay off your credit card debts. Avoid using your cards for a while. You will save about 20 percent the amount you would pay in interest on your cards. Don't get a gold or platinum credit card. They do offer expanded services, but if you don't regularly use these services, such as free traveler's checks, they are not a bargain. In the meantime, you pay a higher annual fee for the privilege of holding the card. Consolidate your credit card debt into one or two low interest credit cards by transferring your balances from other high interest cards, then do not use them for purchases. Simply pay them off.

Step 2: Raise the deductible on your car insurance. You can save a significant amount on your monthly car insurance payments (called premiums) by changing your deductible from $250 to $500 or $1,000. The deductible is how much you will be required to pay on a claim before your insurance kicks in. How can you tell if the risk is safe? Generally speaking, your deductible can equal about one week's take home pay. Keep your deductible amount in your savings account, just in case.

Step 3: Avoid installment loans completely. If you wait until you have cash to pay for an item, you will get a real bargain, interest free. If you do need to borrow, shop around for the best possible interest rate. A difference in just a few percentage points can save you thousands of dollars over the life of a five-year loan.

Step 4: Cancel service contracts on appliances and new cars. You don't need them. Such merchandise is usually covered by warranty and you can keep the money instead. Don't buy a new car without a warranty.

Step 5: Take full advantage of your health insurance plan. Many people don't use services they are entitled to because they don't want to bother with filling out forms. Find out how much your plan covers and get reimbursement on everything you can, such as prescription drugs and eyeglasses.

Preparing for Emergencies

An emergency fund is not the same thing as a savings account. Your savings account should be just that—money you save, not money you dip into every time the furnace needs repair or the car needs new brakes. Your savings account is a way for you to accumulate enough money to eventually begin investing and realize tremendous returns. An emergency fund is a separate account where you stash enough money to see you through an emergency.

Step 1: Build an emergency fund equal to three months salary. At the very least, you should have the amount of your insurance deductible set aside for an emergency. It should be kept in a regular savings account that you can dip into on a day's notice. Never use a money savings plan (like a CD) for your emergency fund because there may be a substantial penalty for early withdrawal. You need immediate access to your emergency fund.

Step 2: Budget regular deposits into the fund. If you start from scratch, you need to budget regular deposits until your emergency fund is established. If you can't come up with any extra in your budget, consider taking on a part-time temporarily and devoting your entire take-home pay to your emergency fund. Having direct deposit of your paycheck into a checking account, savings account and emergency fund will help you stick to your goal of saving money.

Step 3: Know what constitutes an emergency. There's only one steadfast rule for an emergency fund: Withdraw money only in the event of an unforeseen event. Poor planning is not an emergency. A trip to Disneyland is not an emergency. A new wardrobe for autumn is not an emergency. The furnace breaking down at the end of January is an emergency. A serious medical problem not covered immediately by insurance is an emergency. If you break your eyeglasses and need a new pair to drive or work, that's an emergency. Transmission breakdown on the family's only car is an emergency. The family breadwinner losing his or her job is an emergency. A car accident that requires you to pay your $500 deductible is an emergency.

Tracking Your Bank Accounts

If you've dealt with a bank at all, you know the basic in and outs of savings and checking accounts, but you may not be familiar with the many different kinds of accounts available to anyone with a dollar to deposit.

Checking accounts. You deposit money and usually pay a monthly service charge for the privilege of writing out checks against your deposits. Some banks offer overdraft protection to depositors who are creditworthy. Some even offer free checking. Shop around. Be aware that most banks have a computer program that hooks them to other banks. If you have bounced checks repeatedly or owe fees at another institution after closing your account, other banks may not open a checking account or a savings account for you. The lesson here—deal honestly and responsibly with any bank where you have an account.

Passbook savings accounts. Passbook savings accounts have traditionally charged no fee and paid a lower interest rate, but they are a good, solid, no-frills account for someone who has less than $500 to save. Some banks no longer pay interest on passbook savings accounts because of the many other account types available. They simply keep your money in a safe place for you. If your bank does not pay interest on savings, consider moving your balance to another bank that will.

Interest-paying checking accounts. Depending on the amount of your minimum balance each month, you will be paid interest on the money in your checking account. Banks vary in the way they figure interest, in the fees they assess and in the minimum balance they require. Look at a number of banks before you choose one. Interest-paying checking accounts usually don't pay off if you habitually write your checking account to below $100 each month.

Money-market deposit accounts. Some banks allow depositors to open money-market deposit accounts for a small investment of a few hundred dollars. Put a small amount of money in this kind of account only if it pays interest and charges no fees.

Certificates of Deposit (CDs). If you have a large amount of money to deposit and you don't foresee needing a percentage of it in the near future, you should consider depositing part of it in a certificate of deposit. CDs pay significantly higher interest rates, but there are stiff penalties for early withdrawal depending on the bank. Be aware that your money will be tied up for six months to five years or longer while you earn interest.

Savings accounts. You've budgeted at least 10 percent of your income for savings. How do you go about making the most of your savings dollar? First of all, put your money only in a federally insured institution. If something goes wrong with the bank, the government will back up your deposits. Regardless of what you decide to invest in, tie your money up for as brief a period as possible. You need access to your savings account at a moment's notice. You don't want to find yourself in an emergency and learn that you can't withdraw your savings for 10 years.

Shopping for a Bank

With deregulation in the banking industry, banks are now in stiff competition with each other. Every financial institution competes to offer bigger and better services to their customers. As a result, you have more choices than ever before when it comes to banking.

You can have a checking account at one bank, a savings account at another bank and a certificate of deposit at a third bank—depending on where you can get the best deals on which services. Or, if you want to do all your banking in the same place, you can shop for a bank that offers what you need.

To find the best bank, consider several factors. Which banking services are most important to you? If you never travel, free traveler's checks won't really attract your business. If you don't want a safe-deposit box, it won't matter that a bank offers a free one to each depositor. Look for a bank with top-notch customer service, extended hours and no-fee automatic teller machines.

Step 1: Decide what you want most in a bank. Make a list of the services you need or want and the banks that offer them free of charge or at low cost. Some of the options commonly offered include:

- Low-fee or no-fee savings and checking accounts.
- High-yielding insured savings.
- Interest-bearing checking accounts.
- Overdraft protection on checking accounts.
- Free checks.
- Free traveler's checks.
- Quick credit for deposits.
- Numerous branches, with one near you.
- Extended evening and weekend hours.
- Drive-up windows.
- Automatic teller machines.

Step 2: Visit banks in person. Once you have your list in hand, go to the banks listed. Many banks offer Internet and computer banking, but it's still a good idea to visit in person. Determine whether they offer what you want. Find out the rates on savings and interest-bearing checking accounts. Compare all of the services. Most banks have a pre-printed list of services and rates—simply ask at the information desk.

Step 3: Meet the branch manager or assistant. If you're busy, it's a real temptation to use the drive-up window. But make it a point to get out and walk into the lobby on a regular basis to take care of your transactions. You will become a familiar face. If you ever have a problem or need help, you will be more than a name on a deposit slip.

Step 4: Make sure a good deal is really a good deal. A bank might significantly lower the monthly fees on a checking account in order to attract your business. Don't accept it at face value. The bank might sharply increase the fee for buying new checks or for using an automatic teller machine in order to cover its loss.

Step 5: Use more than one bank. If you can get some good deals at one bank but some of the services you want at another, split up your accounts between two or more banks. You should have your savings account at a bank that pays the highest interest and your checking account at the bank that charges the lowest fee and gives you the greatest banking convenience. Don't compromise on what you want and need just to stick with a single bank.

Step 6: Consider an out-of-town bank for investments. If you can't get the rates or service you want locally, investigate what's available elsewhere. Go to your library and read some financial newspapers. They regularly feature banks that pay the highest going rates. If you can double your interest and don't need daily access to your money, it's worth it to bank by mail. Check out banking on the Internet. Many banks offer bill paying and budgeting utilities online.

Step 7: Watch for better deals. Even after you've opened an account, stay on the lookout. Large banks are constantly expanding and chances are good that a new bank will open up eventually in your area. New banks usually offer incentives to attract new customers—and you should be one of the first in line ready to take advantage of the deal!

Establishing Good Credit

Like it or not, credit is important. Your ability to get a loan for a large purchase in the future—a home, a car, furniture, even a college education—will be based on your credit history. Whenever you apply for credit, the creditor will make a decision using a scoring system that is based on your ability and willingness to repay the loan, your income, the amount of debt you already have and your assets. Your willingness to repay is demonstrated by your payment history on past loans. Most companies who extend credit make reports to all of the major credit bureaus. That means that your payment history with existing creditors will be available to potential lenders at the touch of a button.

What if you've never used credit before and you want to establish a good rating now? The key is to start small and gradually build your credit-worthiness.

Step 1: Open a savings account immediately. You can begin building a good credit rating by getting and keeping a savings account as soon as possible. Dad or Mom may have already done this for you. If so, keep and deposit money in that account regularly. Longevity with a bank or credit union earns you advantages when you apply for a loan, a credit card or retail credit. Credit unions often offer great deals on savings accounts—this is a good place to apply for your first loan. They usually have fewer restrictions and requirements than banks.

Step 2: Open a checking account at a local bank. Handle the account responsibly. Try to keep a minimum balance in the account at all times. Don't bounce checks. If you can't handle a checking account responsibly, don't open one. Having no credit history is better than having bad credit.

Step 3: Pay your bills on time. If you have a credit card, pay the monthly payment on time and don't go over your limit. Pay all of your bills—rent, car payment, utilities—on time every month. If you run into trouble, call your creditor, bank, landlord or service company immediately and explain the situation. Most will set up a payment plan and not report the slow pay to the credit bureau. Some may even allow you to skip a payment, tacking the interest onto the end of the loan. If you procrastinate, ignore or just sit on bills because you can't pay them, your credit rating will be damaged. Don't bury your head in the sand.

Step 4: Apply for a small secured loan. The loan will be guaranteed with the money in your savings account. Repay the loan promptly and don't make any late payments. The more good pay loans on your credit report, the better.

Step 5: Apply to a local retailer for a credit card. Handle the card responsibly, never exceed your credit limit and make prompt payments. Establish credit slowly then apply for a credit card. After you have had the retail credit card for a year, apply for a national bank card, such a Visa, MasterCard, or American Express. Because of your good credit, your limit may be as high as $5,000 to $10,000. Having room on your credit card is not the same thing as having money, however. Be careful—use your credit card for convenience, not to buy a bunch of things you can't afford. Pay off the balance promptly each month.

Use Credit with Caution

Simply stated, credit is the practice of paying for goods in installments while you enjoy use of the items purchased. It has become a way of life in America, but many people have come to rely too heavily on credit.

Did you know? The credit scoring system varies slightly from one financial institution to another, but most look at factors like whether you own or rent your home, how long you have been employed at your job and how long you've lived at your current address. It's all designed to determine your stability.

Dad says:
One way to establish
good credit is to
borrow money that
you do not need.
Set the money that
you borrowed aside
in a savings account
and repay the loan
consistently until it is
paid in full.
This may cost you
a small amount in
interest, but it will
establish your
good credit.

Credit has definite advantages: you can pay for essentials over an extended period of time; you can have what you want when you want it and pay for it later; you don't have to carry large amounts of cash or go through the inconvenience of trying to write personal checks; and you get a detailed record of monthly purchases with each month's bill.

But credit has definite disadvantages, too: it costs money, because you pay a fee to use your card and you pay interest on your purchases; it makes you susceptible to theft; and worst of all, it is very easy to overspend, buy on impulse and sink too far into debt. Sometimes it's the type of debt that is difficult to pay off unless you win the lottery.

Step 1: Research what types of credit are available. The Internet is a good source. Knowing what kinds of credit are available and how to handle consumer credit can enable you to enjoy the advantages of credit without being zapped by the disadvantages.

There are two basic kinds of credit available:

Open-ended credit allows you to make purchases on credit repeatedly up to a pre-determined limit. Your limit may be $1,000, for example—as long as you make your payments on time, you can continue to charge and pay for purchases on the card as long as you don't exceed $1,000 at any one time.

Closed-end credit is given for a one-time purchase of a specific item, such as a car. You agree ahead of time to the amount of the payments, the number of payments and the length of the loan.

Step 2: Decide which offer is best. Credit cards are available from many different companies. You can get a bank credit card, such as a Visa or a MasterCard, a gasoline credit card, a retail credit card, which is good only at a specific store, or a specialized credit card available only to certain people, such as members of a specific club or organization.

Step 3: Know how much you will pay in interest and fees. Before you sign up for a credit card, look at how much it's going to cost you. Is there an annual fee? A sign up fee? When do interest calculations begin? Many cards offer a 25-day grace period before they start charging interest. How are the finance charges calculated? You should only pay on the adjusted balance, or the amount you still owe, instead of on a previous balance.

Step 4: Look carefully before you choose an installment loan. What's the interest rate? How are finance charges calculated? You should pay finance charges only on an adjusted balance, not on the original loan amount. What is the length of the loan? You don't want a 3-year loan on an item that will be worthless in two years. What collateral do you need to offer? Is there a penalty for early payment? Find out all the specifics.

*D*ad says:
In essence, take the time to find out what you're getting into before you accept credit of any kind. What you think is a great deal may prove to be a grave mistake.

Safeguarding Your Credit Cards

As mentioned previously, using credit cards opens you up to theft and fraud. Make sure you safeguard your cards, and your own identity, when you use them to make purchases.

Step 1: Minimize the chance of theft. Keep your credit cards in your wallet. Never leave them in a drawer, a jewelry box or a glove compartment. Carry with you only the credit cards you intend to use. Ideally, you should limit yourself to one credit card. You'll reduce the chance of losing other cards and you'll cut down on the temptation to spend impulsively.

Step 2: Know the laws. If your credit cards are lost or stolen, your liability is limited by federal law to $50 per card. Once you notify the company that the card is missing, you cannot be liable for any purchases made after your notification.

Step 3: Safeguard your credit card numbers. All someone needs is your number in order to make purchases and have them charged to you. Never give your credit card number out over the phone to someone who calls you and says he needs it for any

reason. Make a list of each credit card you hold, its number and the name and telephone number of the issuing company. Keep this list in a safe place so that you can notify card issuers immediately if your cards are lost or stolen.

Step 4: Scrutinize your monthly credit card bill. Open your statement the day it arrives, even if you won't be paying it for a few weeks. Keep all credit receipts clipped together until you receive the bill, then check each one against your bill. If you find charges for purchases you did not make, you need to contact the card issuer immediately to dispute the charges.

Step 5: Watch the clerk the entire time with your card. If he or she makes a mistake and voids a transaction, ask for the spoiled receipt so that you can tear it up. After you sign the receipt, make sure you have all the carbons (if you don't, ask the clerk for them). Take the carbons with you and dispose of them somewhere else.

Review Your Own Credit Report

A credit bureau is a central clearinghouse for information on consumer credit. Every time you apply for a loan, make a payment or fail to satisfy a debt, a report is made to the credit bureau. There may be several different bureaus in one city, and each retailer may report to different bureaus. You can find credit bureaus listed in the yellow pages of your local telephone directory.

Step 1: Take your credit report seriously. Your credit rating is critical. It shows a potential creditor that you do or do not pay your bills on time. Negative information stays on your credit report for a very long time; bankruptcies stay on your record for ten years, while other information, positive and negative, will stay on for seven years.

Step 2: Visit your local credit bureau. Ask for a copy of your file. You can also request one over the

Internet. Some companies offer the first report for free; for others there may be a minimal charge, but it's worth it. You should review your file carefully to make sure all the information on it is accurate. If it is not, you have the right to challenge the information and have it removed.

Keeping Financial Records

If you have many financial transactions, you could quickly be forced out of house and home by all the receipts and records piling up. On the other hand, you may be understandably nervous about throwing them away. How do you know what to keep and how long to keep it?

Step 1: If it involves the IRS, keep it. By law, the IRS has three years to challenge your tax return and you have three years to file an amended one. Just to be on the safe side, keep any documents that impact your tax returns or your standing with the IRS for six to seven years. Keep all tax filings indefinitely as proof of earnings in case you encounter trouble down the road collecting Social Security benefits.

Step 2: Keep important documents in a safe-deposit box. Some records are more critical than others, so they need to be guarded more carefully. These include, but are not limited to, mortgage deeds, car titles, property appraisals, most recent five years in tax returns, a household inventory, records of major expenditures on your property, records of paid-off debts, a list of debts owed to you with supporting evidence, stocks and bonds, birth certificates, marriage licenses, military discharge papers, passports, citizenship papers and a copy of your will.

Step 3: Keep some records at home in a fire-proof safe. These include copies of tax returns, current leases, credit card numbers, securities serial numbers, insurance policies, service contracts, warranties, medical records and wills.

Did you know? You can order your credit reports from the nation's three major credit bureaus over the Internet for a nominal fee. Do this and you won't be surprised the next time you apply for credit.

BASIC BUDGET WORKSHEET

Income	Budgeted Amount	Actually Spent	Difference + or -
Paid Wages			
Bonuses			
Interest Income			
Dividend Income			
Capital Gains Income			
Miscellaneous Income			
INCOME SUBTOTAL			
Expenses			
Mortgage/rent			
Gas			
Water			
Electric			
Garbage/Sewer			
Cable/Broadband			
Internet			
Telephone			
Charitable Donations			
Home Repairs			
Auto Payments			
Gasoline/Oil			
Auto Repairs			
Auto Insurance			

Do Almost Anything

Tip Like a Pro

A tip, sometimes called a gratuity, is something that you give voluntarily or beyond obligation to someone to show your appreciation for a service they provided to you. People who travel a lot know the benefits of generous tipping because, in most cases, you get better service, especially if you become a recognizable, repeat customer. For the rest of us, it's just common social courtesy to leave a tip in the proper amount.

Step 1: Know who does the tipping. Generally, the person picking up the bill is also responsible for the tip. So if your date is paying for dinner, let him or her decide what and whether to tip the server. If you are the driver of the car being parked by a valet, then you will do the tipping.

Step 2: Know who and what amount to tip. When you plan your budget for travel or recreation expenses, plan for tips. Use the following guidelines on how much to tip the most likely service people you will encounter on a trip or outing in the United States:

• *Barber:* Tip $2 to $3.

• *Bartender:* Tip15-20% of the bill. If you have drinks at the bar before a meal, settle up with the bartender before you go to your table.

• *Bellman:* Tip $1 to $2 per bag when he or she helps you get your bags to your room. If the bellman just carries the bags to the front desk and leaves, save the tip for the person who carries the bags to your room. Upon checkout, tip a bellman who helps with your bags.

• *Coat check:* Tip $1.

• *Cocktail Server:* Tip 15-20% of your total bar tab.

• *Doorman:* Tip $1 if the doorman hails you a cab. If he or she also carries your bags, tip $1 per bag.

• *Food Server:* Tip15-20% of total bill. For poor service, tip only 10% of the bill and talk to the manager. For good service, tip 15%. For excellent service, tip 20% of the total bill. Double time: If you spend enough time at a table that a server could have gotten two parties seated and served, then compensate by tipping twice.

• *Hair Stylist:* Tip 10-20% of the total bill.

• *Hotel Concierge:* Tip $5 to $10 for help with hard-to-get dinner reservations or theater tickets. Tipping is optional for just plain advice.

• *Maid Service:* Tip $1 to $3 per day. Tip daily because there might be a different maid. Leave the tip on your pillow. Tip on the last day also.

• *Manicure or Facial:* Tip 15% of total bill.

• *Massage therapist:* Tip 10-15%. Leave no tip if at a doctor's office.

• *Musician at table:* Tip $2 to $3 if you request a song. Tipping is optional if he just stops by and plays.

• *Open bar at receptions with bartender:* $1 each visit to the bar.

• *Pizza deliveries:* Tip 15% of total price, but no less than $2.

• *Restroom attendant:* Tip $1.

• *Room Service:* Ask the hotel desk if the gratuity is included in room service. If so, add nothing or $1. Otherwise, tip the server 15-20% of the total room service bill.

• *Restaurant Bill:* Examine the bill to see if the tip or gratuity has already been included, as it often is for large parties. You don't want to tip twice accidentally.

• *Self-service restaurant or buffet:* Tip 10% if the server delivers all or part of your meal or keeps your drinks refilled. Tip nothing if there is no table service.

• *Taxi, limo or van driver:* Tip 15% of the total fare but no less than $1.

• *Valet:* Tip $1 or $2 for parking or returning the car. It is not necessary to tip for parking, but always for returning the car.

• *Wine Steward:* Tip 10% of wine bill.

Step 3: Know how to calculate a tip. The easiest way to calculate a tip is to first round off the total bill. If dinner was $43.56, round that figure up to $44.00 total. Then get 10% of that figure by moving the decimal point one over to the left, that's $4.40 as a 10% tip. However, this is what you would tip if service was poor, and on most occasions you will want to be more generous. So, if you want to give them 15% for good service, divide $4.40 in half, which would be $2.20, then add that to the $4.40 to equal $6.60 as a 15% tip. If you want to tip 20% for excellent service, simply give them double the 10% which, in this case, would be $4.40 plus $4.40, equaling $8.80 as the total tip.

For instant calculations, check out the tip card provided on page 252. Just copy, cut, fold along the middle line and place in your wallet as a tipping guide.

---

*D*ad's Tip:

Going out to eat on a date is quite expensive these days. It is acceptable to offer to go "Dutch," or pay your way to the movies and split the dinner bill and tip. If your date pays for a night out one evening, offer to pay the next time and set a date. If someone takes you to a very nice restaurant and makes it clear that it is their treat, do not offer to pay the tip. The payer may not want you to know the total cost of the dinner and he or she should be allowed to determine the tip.

TIP CARD

$	15%	20%	$	15%	20%	$	15%	20%
1	.15	.20	17	2.55	3.40	33	4.95	6.60
2	.30	.40	18	2.70	3.60	34	5.10	6.80
3	.45	.60	19	2.85	3.80	35	5.25	7.00
4	.60	.80	20	3.00	4.00	36	5.40	7.20
5	.75	1.00	21	3.15	4.20	37	5.55	7.40
6	.90	1.20	22	3.30	4.40	38	5.70	6.60
7	1.05	1.40	23	3.45	4.60	39	5.85	7.80
8	1.20	1.60	24	3.60	4.80	40	6.00	8.00
9	1.35	1.90	25	3.75	5.00	41	6.15	8.20
10	1.50	2.00	26	3.90	5.20	42	6.30	8.40
11	1.65	2.20	27	4.05	5.40	43	6.45	8.60
12	1.80	2.40	28	4.20	5.60	44	6.60	8.80
13	1.95	2.60	29	4.35	5.80	45	6.75	9.00
14	2.10	2.80	30	4.50	6.00	46	6.90	9.20
15	2.25	3.00	31	4.65	6.20	47	7.05	9.40
16	2.40	3.20	32	4.80	6.40	48	7.20	9.60

$	15%	20%	$	15%	20%	$	15%	20%
49	7.35	9.80	66	9.90	13.20	83	12.45	16.60
50	7.50	10.00	67	10.05	13.40	84	12.60	16.80
51	6.75	10.20	68	10.20	13.60	85	12.75	17.00
52	7.80	10.40	69	10.35	13.80	86	12.90	17.20
53	7.95	10.60	70	10.50	14.00	87	13.05	17.40
54	8.10	10.80	71	10.65	14.20	88	13.20	17.60
55	8.25	11.00	72	10.80	14.40	89	13.35	17.80
56	8.40	11.20	73	10.95	14.60	90	13.50	18.00
57	8.55	11.40	74	11.10	14.80	91	13.65	18.20
58	8.70	11.60	75	11.25	15.00	92	13.80	18.40
59	8.85	11.80	76	11.40	15.20	93	13.95	18.60
60	9.00	12.00	77	11.55	15.40	94	14.10	18.80
61	9.15	12.20	78	11.70	15.60	95	14.25	19.00
62	9.30	12.40	79	11.85	15.80	96	14.40	19.20
63	9.45	12.60	80	12.00	16.00	97	14.55	19.40
64	9.60	12.80	81	12.15	16.20	98	14.70	19.60
65	9.75	13.00	82	12.30	16.40	99	14.85	19.80

Notes

Fix It Yourself
Home Maintenance & Repairs

Y ou will save money and gain personal satisfaction if you learn and practice simple home maintenance and make your own home repairs. However, as with anything in life, prevention is the key.

Before you move into a place, check to make sure everything works properly. Just because you may be renting and not buying, doesn't mean you should lower your standards on what you consider an acceptable dwelling. Check out the toilets, sinks, showers, faucets, drains, hot water heater, water pressure, heater and air conditioner or evaporative cooler, refrigerator, oven and stove, dishwasher and garbage disposal. If these items are in disrepair, ask the landlord to fix them before you lug all your stuff inside.

Of course, when you live in a place for awhile, some things will go wrong. Many home repair problems—like a running or stopped up toilet, leaky faucet, mildew in the bathroom, stained carpets, or a room that needs repainting—are rather easy to fix, if you know a few basics.

Preventing Problems

Good home maintenance and repair starts before you move in. If you want fewer repairs down the road, it's worth spending a little extra time inspecting your future home. Check the house for the following:

• Doors that open and close easily, without rubbing or sticking, and have good, strong locks.

• Unbroken windows that open and close easily and have good screens and locks.

• Fireplaces with dampers that open and shut freely, unobstructed flues and undamaged brickwork.

• Bathrooms with sinks and tubs that fill and drain quickly without gurgling.

• Bathroom fixtures free of rough spots, cracks, stains, chips, spots or other damage.

• Toilets that flush properly and do not run.

• Kitchen appliances in good working order.

• A chimney constructed of solid, undamaged brick and tight flashing. A good chimney should be two feet above the roof, unobstructed by trees, and equipped with a flue liner.

• Foundation walls free of large cracks.

• Windows with painted exterior frames that are square with sills free of termite and weather damage; a solid unbroken line of putty should surround the window panels.

• Snug-fitting outside doors of solid wood or metal with slightly raised sills and no cracks between siding and frame.

• Exterior siding free of damage and nail pops equipped with flashing where siding joins another exterior surface.

• Garage doors that open and close smoothly.

• Rain gutters with closed joints and spouts pointing away from the foundation.

• Plenty of exterior lighting with grounded electrical outlets.

• Exterior concrete sidewalks, driveways and patios slightly sloped to facilitate water drainage.

• A dry basement.

• Plenty of ventilation and insulation in crawl space and attic.

Red Flags

Inevitably, a few problems will crop up that are impossible to foresee, but some tell-tale signs will warn of most major problems and even a few minor ones. The following should serve as red flags, alerting you to the potential problems with a house:

Red Flag 1: Uneven floors. To check for an uneven floor, put a marble in the center of the room. If it rolls, the floor isn't level. Watch out for a floor that creaks, as well as worn, cracked, split or stained flooring and large or numerous cracks in the interior walls.

Red Flag 2: Water stains or sunlight coming through roof, ceiling or walls. Water stains on ceilings and walls usually indicate a leaky, sagging or leaning roof. If you see sunlight through the roof in the attic, the house may have worn, loose or missing roof shingles. Also, look out for discolored, chipped or broken shingles or asphalt shingles that shine.

Red Flag 3: Tell-tale signs of leaky pipes. Leaky faucets or drains and mold, mildew or standing water under sinks, usually indicate leaky pipes. Conspicuously new sections of copper, brass, iron, steel or plastic pipes may be a signal that more pipes will have to be replaced soon. Also be concerned about a noisy furnace.

Red Flag 4: Mildew or decay on the exterior of the home. The following are signs that this home may have problems with siding: mildew; obvious decay near joints or the lower edge of outdoor siding; sagging, rusting or splitting rain gutters and downspouts; large vertical wall cracks and bulging walls in the basement. On the foundation, look for wide or long cracks; a significant amount of missing or cracked mortar in exterior masonry; wood siding that has split, cracked or splintered, metal siding that is discolored, dented or worn; signs of termite, carpenter ant or carpenter bee infestation (look for white powder, sawdust or mud termite tubes on the foundation).

Red Flag 5: Windows that aren't square and large cracks in walls and floors. When the residence was first built, the windows were certainly square. If they aren't anymore, there may be a problem with the foundation. Make sure the floor beams and joists are not sagging or decayed. Be leery of large trees within 20 feet of the house whose roots can compromise the foundation and the pipes.

Choosing a Good Spot

The house you are considering buying or leasing may meet all of your maintenance standards, but how do you feel about the neighborhood? You've succeeded in finding a healthy house—now make sure it's situated in a healthy neighborhood, too.

Step 1: Choose a neighborhood that will increase in value. Ask a real estate agent what are the three most important things about a house and they will tell you the old adage—location, location, location. Where your house is situated will not necessarily impact repairs, but it can affect value. Make sure the neighborhood is zoned residential so that no one can set up a business or an industrial plant across the street. The homes surrounding you should be of comparable or better quality. Look for well-kept homes and yards.

Step 2: Look for a convenient location. Before you choose a neighborhood, consider how much time you want to spend commuting. You'll want a home close to good schools, shopping, churches, hospitals, dentists, parks and other community attractions. You may want easy access to public transportation and well-controlled flow of traffic to avoid bottlenecks and the noise and pollution that come along with them.

Step 3: Think noise level and attractiveness. You will probably want to steer clear of a house located near an airport, a railroad, a fire station, a major highway or an industrial park. Avoid neighborhoods with clear signs of deterioration, such as cluttered yards, rundown homes or broken vehicles. Be wary of neighborhoods with an excessive number of homes for sale.

Setting Up a Tool Box

You're living on your own. You have stocked the kitchen with pots and pans, the cupboards with spices and the medicine chest with first-aid supplies. Now you'll need some basic tools to take care of minor repairs, hang pictures and measure the wall for a new chest of drawers.

Hammer. Buy a solid 14- to 18-ounce claw hammer. You can use it to pound in nails as well as to remove them.

Screwdrivers. You will need two, one flat head and one Phillips head. You may want to get several different-sized heads to handle various jobs. You can even buy one screwdriver that has six interchangeable magnetic heads. A cordless electric screwdriver is helpful.

Pliers. Make sure they include a wire cutter. Channel-lock pliers can be adjusted and look more like a wrench than pliers. You should get ones with five or six adjustable widths. Needle-nose pliers cut wire and can be used to work in tight places, hold tiny screws and strip the insulation away from electrical wires. Check the quality by closing the blades—you shouldn't be able to see light between them.

Checklist
Tool Box Essentials
❒ Hammer
❒ Screwdrivers
❒ Pliers
❒ Saw
❒ Utility knife
❒ Putty knife
❒ Tape measure
❒ Staple gun
❒ Nails
❒ Screws
❒ C-clamps

Saw. Get a basic, all-purpose saw with medium teeth. You can purchase a shorter, more lightweight saw that is more convenient to keep in a tool box than a traditional full-length one. A hacksaw will saw through thin metal, unlike an all-purpose saw.

Utility knife. This knife should have a retractable blade that can be used to cut wallpaper, cardboard, picture mats, plastic floor tile and other things you can't cut with scissors.

Putty knife. Use a 1-inch putty knife to patch holes, scrape putty and remove peeling paint or wallpaper. The best quality putty knives have blades that flex easily and are firmly screwed into wooden handles.

Tape measure. Get a self-winding metal tape measure that measures at least ten feet and that locks at the right measurement.

Rubber toilet plunger. The most convenient kind has a removable wooden handle that screws into a rubber head.

Staple gun. Quality staple guns enable you to tack things with ease. They are available in different models and sizes. Make sure the staples fit the gun.

Nails. The most commonly used sizes are one and two inch nails. Keep some on hand for repairs.

Screws. Get a variety of sizes.

Four-inch C-clamps. These can be used to hold things together while glue is drying or to anchor items that you are sawing or nailing.

Toolbox. Get something to hold it all. Toolboxes are available in all price ranges. They can be very simple or extremely complex, featuring different levels and separate compartments for nails, screws, bolts, etc. You don't really need anything fancy. Choose one that is lightweight so that you can carry it around with you from repair to repair. It really only needs to keep your tools organized.

The Right Glue for the Job

Use the following glues for the following materials:
- Rubber cement—paper, leather, cardboard, fabric
- White glue—cardboard, leather, wood
- Yellow wood glue—wood
- Instant glue—glass, ceramics, hard plastics, metal
- Hot glue—cardboard, tile, ceramics, wood, craft projects
- Epoxy—glass, tile, metal, masonry
- Spray adhesive—paper, small cardboard, fabric

Clear heavy gel glue works great on almost anything as long as you follow instructions and let it dry. It's water-soluble in the first phases—you can wash it off with soap and water—but when it's dry it's permanent. Because it's a gel, it doesn't usually drip or run unless you've used too much. It's as strong as instant glue and can also serve as an insulated plug where needed to seal around windows or doors, much like weather stripping. You can find gel glue at most hardware stores, where it is labeled "Goop" Household Contact Adhesive and Sealant.

Toilet Trouble

Step 1: Buy a plunger *before* **you have a backed up toilet.** One of the most disgusting problems to deal with is a backed up toilet bowl that allows wastewater to overflow onto your bathroom floor. If you have a carpeted floor, this can turn into a huge cleanup project. Make sure you have a sturdy plunger right by the toilet. Do not wait to purchase a plunger until you have a problem, because you will need it at a moment's notice.

Step 2: Do not use your toilet bowl as a trash can. The toilet bowl is not a garbage disposal or a paper shredder. The only things going down the toilet should be human waste and toilet paper, *not* cotton swabs, rubber bands, hair balls from your hair brush, cardboard toilet tissue rolls, sanitary napkins, moldy food from a smelly fridge, torn up love notes or wadded up term papers. You may think one little thing won't matter much, but those little things get caught up on one another and can create huge clogs. To prevent clogs, flush after every use and turbo-clean your toilet regularly using either a toilet bowl product that dissolves clogs (make sure the product is sewer safe) or a cup of bleach poured into a drained toilet bowl before flushing. That will keep the toilet drain clear.

Step 3: Learn to clear a clog. When you use the plunger, make sure the rubber end is completely under water and that it fits tightly against the hole at the bottom of the bowl. Push down and the plunger will create a vacuum to force water down the outflow passage. Now pull the plunger back to break the seal. Repeat until the toilet flushes normally.

Step 4: If the humble plunger won't work, try a drain auger. This piece of equipment is also called a toilet snake. You may want to wait to purchase one until you absolutely need one (when a plunger won't do the job) because an auger costs much more. Some equipment rental stores also rent them. Push the toilet snake down into the outflow passage in the bowl, twisting and pushing through the pipes as far as possible. Rotate the snake to make it go through the pipes easier and remove clogs as it progresses. Once the snake goes as far as it will go, pull it out slowly again, rotating it as you do so.

Stopping a Running Toilet

The constant draining or leaking of a toilet can get on your nerves and increase your water bill. Take off the tank lid and examine how the toilet operates.

Step 1: Get to know how your toilet works. Water flows from the supply tube into the tank, filling it to within one or two inches of the top. A ball-shaped float shuts off the supply of incoming water when the tank is full. Connected by a metal rod to another valve, the float triggers the supply tube to stop filling the tank.

As the level of water rises in the tank, so does the float, lifting the rod with it, until it eventually causes the valve to close. If that doesn't work, an overflow tube sends the excess water down into the sewer instead of overflowing the tank. If your toilet runs and never shuts off after you flush, you lose fresh water to the sewer. If you pay for water, this can get expensive.

Step 2: Take care of your float. If the float stops the incoming water too soon, there may not be enough water to clean out the toilet bowl. Using a bowl or pitcher, add some water to the tank. If the float does not stop the water before it reaches the overflow tube, you will hear leaking. To fix these problems, gently bend the float rod up or down so that the water will run for a shorter or longer period of time until the float shuts off the valve. If the float develops a leak and fills with water, it will sink rather than float, in which case you will need to replace it. If the valve connected to the float becomes defective, you may have to replace the entire mechanism. You can find all sorts of toilet supplies at any hardware store.

Step 3: Pay attention to the rubber ball or flap. When you flush, the toilet handle lifts a rubber ball or flap at the bottom of the tank. This allows the water from the tank to drain into the bowl and push waste down into the sewer. When the tank empties, the rubber flap should fall down again, blocking the exit valve into the bowl. Fresh water should now run to fill the tank. A problem may exist if the flap falls back too soon, if it takes too long to fall back or doesn't fall back at all. Most of these problems can be corrected simply by adjusting the various parts that connect the flap to the flush handle. Made of rubber, flaps tend to deteriorate every few years. When this happens, you will hear the toilet leak. Buy a replacement flap from the hardware store and follow instructions to install. If your toilet continues to run or overflow, seek a professional's attention.

Plunge into Plumbing

Water drips, runs, splashes—and it's inside your house. If you have plumbing problems, start with shutting off the water. As soon as you see water leaking from a pipe, through a wall, from a ceiling or running across a floor, shut it off to keep damage to a minimum while you investigate the problem. Make sure you know where the main shut-off valve in your home is located—usually in the basement, utility room or crawl space—but be aware that sinks and toilets usually have individual shut-off valves attached to them.

Step 1: Shut off all the water in the house. If you can't identify which fixture the leak is coming from, you need to quickly shut off all the water to the house. The main shut-off is usually located on the outside wall where the main pipe enters the house or next to the water meter. Turn shut-off valves clockwise to turn them off.

Step 2: Unclog a stopped up drain. If water is sluggish or won't drain at all, use a rubber force cup similar to a toilet plunger. If that doesn't work to dislodge the clog, use a chemical drain opener, following label directions carefully.

If you still can't free up the drain, get under the sink. Put a bucket under the pipe, and open it. Fish a wire up the pipe and pull out any debris you can reach. Clogs are usually made up of accumulated hair and grease. Replace the trap and run scalding hot water through the pipes.

Step 3: Fix low water pressure. If you don't seem to have enough water pressure, it's time to do a simple test. You may have hard-water scale buildup in your pipes. To find out if you might have such a problem, turn the water on full force, making sure all valves are fully open. If water gushes out at first and then slows down to a small stream, your pipes are restricted. This isn't something you can solve on your own. A professional plumber will need to replace the pipes involved. If you can afford it, avoid galvanized steel pipes, which tend to encourage buildup.

Step 4: Stop a leaky pipe immediately. A leak in a wall pipe is usually caused when the pipe behind the wall becomes damaged. Turn off water immediately and call a professional plumber. In some cases, the pipe can be repaired or replaced without cutting the wall. The most common cause is a corroded or frozen pipe. If the pipe joints screw together like a lid on a bottle, you might be able to repair the leak yourself by tightening the joint. You might also be able to repair a burst pipe with a clamp-on pipe patch, available in home center or plumbing supply stores. If neither of these approaches works, call a professional plumber.

Step 5: Fix an overflowing dishwasher. A large piece of food, built-up grease or a dishrag may be clogging the screen around the drain. If so, simply remove the source of the clog. Other possible causes include a fault in the electric controls or damaged pipes. You should turn off the current to the dishwasher (unplug it if it is a portable model) and call a repair service.

Caring for Carpets

The carpet in your home represents a substantial investment. Unfortunately, the carpet can become a victim of the unusual wear and tear, damage and stains. Some preventative care on your part and prompt removal of stains can prolong the life of your carpet and preserve your investment in its beauty.

Step 1: Vacuum carpets thoroughly and regularly. Heavy traffic areas should be vacuumed every day and other areas should be vacuumed every four to seven

Did you know? One-half cup of bleach down your bathtub drain and your sink drains twice a month should eat up most clogging elements and keep water draining smoothly.

days. Regular vacuuming does not wear your carpets out more quickly. On the contrary, it removes particles that can cut the carpet fibers if they aren't removed.

Step 2: Vacuum carpeted stairs daily if they get daily wear. Use the brush attachment or upholstery nozzle on your vacuum cleaner. If your stairs get extremely heavy use, consider covering them with a vinyl or nylon runner for protection.

Step 3: Clean carpets regularly. Your carpets need a strong cleaning to get rid of the deeply embedded dirt that isn't removed by vacuuming. You should clean carpets three to four times a year (once every three months) or more if your family tracks heavy soil into the house. You can rent a carpet cleaning machine for $20 or $30 at most major drug stores, supermarkets and hardware stores. The place where you rent the machine will also sell you shampoo.

You can also clean your carpets yourself by spraying on a shampoo foam available in grocery stores and home centers, working it into the carpet with a damp sponge, allowing it to dry and vacuuming it out. You should hire a professional carpet cleaner once a year to thoroughly clean all residue from your carpets.

Step 4: Remove stains promptly. The longer they sit, the more stubborn stains become. Remove excess material by blotting it up with a light-colored clean towel or by scraping it with the dull edge of a knife. Clean the stains by rubbing in the solution recommended on the stain removal chart. Gently brush the pile to restore the original texture once the stained area has dried. Finish by vacuuming.

Carpet Stain Reference Guide

Asphalt . . . . Detergent and volatile solvent

Beer . . . . .1 tsp. liquid detergent and 1 tsp. white vinegar in 2 cups lukewarm water

Berry stain . . . . .1 tsp. liquid detergent and 1 tsp. Ammonia in 2 cups lukewarm water

Bleach . . . . Liquid detergent and lukewarm water

Blood (wet) . . . . . Liquid detergent and cool water

Blood (dry) . . . . .Warm detergent, ammonia and lukewarm water

Butter . . . . .Cleaning fluid and cornmeal (enough to make a paste), leave for two hours then vacuum

Gum . . . . Volatile solvent

Chocolate . . . . . . Liquid detergent, ammonia and water

Coffee . . . . .Liquid detergent, white vinegar, volatile solvent

Cola drinks . . . . . Liquid detergent

Crayon . . . . .Paint remover (buy washable crayons and markers)

Food dye . . . . Liquid detergent and water

Polish . . . . Paint remover and liquid detergent

Grape juice . . . . . Rub in salt, let sit and vacuum

Gravy . . . . Liquid detergent

Ink . . . . Paint remover, volatile solvent, detergent

Lipstick . . . . Paint remover

Mascara . . . . . . .Paint remover volatile solvent detergent water

Milk . . . . Liquid detergent

Nail polish . . . . . Volatile solvent

Oil paint . . . . Paint remover

Latex paint . . . . . Liquid detergent and water

Tea . . . . Liquid detergent

Urine . . . . Liquid detergent and white vinegar

Vomit . . . . Warm detergent, white vinegar and water

Wax . . . . .Volatile solvent, apply heated iron on clean rag

Wine . . . . .Liquid detergent, ammonia, white vinegar, water

Ask Mom

For comprehensive clothing stain removal guide, see *Where's Mom Now That I Need Her?*, pages 243 - 247 "Quick & Dirty Stain Removal."

Did you know?
If mildew grows on the grout between bathroom tiles, mix one-half cup liquid laundry bleach in two cups of warm water. Use an old toothbrush to scrub the solution into the mildew. Wait a few minutes, rinse with clear water and wipe the area dry.

Banishing Mildew

You don't have to live in a humid climate to have a mildew problem. Mildew thrives in all parts of the country. It's not limited to a single season, either, and if you don't spot it and get rid of it, it can literally rot whatever it's growing on. Mildew is often accompanied by mold, and both can cause serious allergies and sometimes, in the worst cases, environmental illnesses for those living in the household.

Step 1: Keep your home well ventilated. Mildew and mold thrive on moisture and heat in places with little or no ventilation. They are stubborn and spread rapidly, causing a characteristic musty odor which is extremely difficult to get rid of.

Step 2: Determine if the stain is mildew. Mildew causes a brownish stain that looks like dirt. Often it is black. To determine whether the stain is mildew, wet the corner of a rag with household laundry bleach and hold it against the stain for one minute without rubbing. If the stain looks the same when you pick up the rag, it's likely dirt. If the stain has disappeared or gotten a lot lighter, it's mildew.

Step 3: Make your home inhospitable to mildew. The key to getting rid of mildew is to kill the fungus. It's not enough to just wipe mildew away. You have to kill it—it is a living, growing organism—or it will come back, even if you can't see a trace after you have cleaned.

In The Bathroom: Use commercial mildew removers for use in the bathroom. You will find them in the same area of the grocery store with bathroom cleansers and toilet bowl cleaners. You should follow label directions carefully, but, in general, spray the mixture on, wait a few minutes, rub it in with a soft brush, rinse it off and wipe the area dry.

On Painted Surfaces: To get mildew off painted surfaces without damaging the surrounding paint, make a mix that contains one cup liquid laundry bleach, two tablespoons powdered cleanser containing trisodium phosphate (like Spic-n-Span) and two quarts water. Scrub the solution on the mildewed area, allow it to dry completely and rinse off with plenty of clear water. As soon as you can, repaint the area to discourage further mildew growth.

Step 4: Prevent mildew from growing in the first place. Keep outside walls free from foliage, such as shrubs and trees that keep the house shaded and damp. Trim shrubbery so that sun can reach the foundation, siding or brickwork. Check your lawn watering habits. Don't allow sprinklers to keep your siding or foundation wet all the time.

Keep damp areas in your house—such as bathrooms, closets, crawl spaces and the basement—well ventilated to discourage mildew growth. If there is a window in the bathroom, keep it open at least partway. If not, install a fan and run it periodically. After you have finished showering, extend the shower curtain and let it dry. Install vents to closet doors or replace them with louvered doors.

Step 5: Use mild heat in stuffy areas, such as closets. You can leave a 25-watt bulb on in a closet to provide enough heat to keep the closet dry. You can also buy electric heating cables that can be taped into the walls of closets and other closed off areas. Keep things dry to discourage mildew growth. Never leave damp or wet towels in a heap—hang them immediately after showering or bathing. Do not throw damp clothes into the hamper.

Step 6: If you can afford it, purchase a dehumidifier. If you live in a humid climate, do what you can to dehumidify. Vent your clothes dryer to the outside. Dehumidifying chemicals, available in sealed bags, can be hung in closets and other closed areas until they themselves become damp. Then you can dry them in a low-heat oven and reuse them.

Repaint to Brighten a Home

Repainting a room or two can make a house a home. If you rent, however, make sure it's okay with the landlord before you go to all the trouble of painting. If your landlord says no, think of other ways to brighten a room. Try wall hangings, posters, photographs, new curtains or even temporary, removable wall trimmings or designs (found in most wallpaper stores.) You may also be able to do some stenciling with washable paints. Just make sure all traces of the paint will wash off and don't do anything too intricate because you'll have to wash the walls before you move out.

Step 1: Choose the right color. You will find paints in different colors and finishes. Decide on a color first. Paint stores feature an array of color samples on small strips of cardstock called "chips." Take a few you like and look at them in the light of the room you plan to paint. The lighting at home may be quite different from the lighting in the paint store.

For best results, you need to invest a little front money. Buy the smallest amount of paint the store will sell you. Some stores will give you a sample or allow you to buy a small sample. Take it home, paint a little on the wall where it gets full light and let it dry overnight. Do you like what you see? If so, have the paint store mix a full batch for you. If not, go back to the store, explain what looks wrong and try again. Keep trying until you get what you want, but don't be too particular. It's best to choose a pre-mixed color that you like so that you can buy an extra can for touch-ups and not have trouble matching the color. If you do have your own unique color mixed, make sure you buy at least two extra cans for future touch-ups.

Step 2: Know how much paint you will need. Even though the paint store will use a precise formula to mix your color, no two batches mixed at different times will match exactly. You may run out of paint with half a wall left to go. Make sure you get enough paint to finish the job. To figure out how much paint you will need, measure the length and width of each wall (don't forget the ceiling, if you're painting that). Multiply the length by the width of each wall to get the number of square feet. Add the figures for all walls and ceilings to be painted to get the total number of square feet. Don't worry about subtracting square feet for doors and windows. You can use the extra paint for touch-ups.

Now divide the total number of square feet by 100. The resulting figure tells you how many quarts of paint you need for one coat. Divide that by four to get the number of gallons you need. Most painting jobs require two coats, so buy two times the number of gallons.

Step 3: Choose the right paint type. Paint comes in two general types—oil-based and latex or water-based. *Oil-based paint* must be thinned with turpentine or solvent, which means your brushes and other tools have to be cleaned with paint thinner. It has a stronger odor when wet and takes three or four times as long to dry. But you should take the time involved to use oil-based paint if the surface will get a lot of wear, if it will be exposed to dampness, such as in a bathroom, or if it has previously been covered by a lot of layers of paint. You should also use oil-based paint on metal surfaces, on objects that bear weight like chairs or on surfaces that bear heat like radiators.

Latex water-based paint works well on ceilings and walls that get a normal amount of wear and for furniture in good condition. Latex paint has little odor when wet and can be thinned with water. This means brushes and other painting tools can simply be rinsed with water for cleaning. In warm weather or in a heated room, latex paint will dry completely within a few hours.

Step 4: Choose the right finish. Paint finishes range from flat—with no sheen at all—to high-gloss which shines like lacquer. The finish you choose will depend on personal taste as well as where you will apply the paint.

Flat paint works best on ceilings because it will not reflect a lot of light or cause glare. You can also use flat paint on walls, but it picks up fingerprints much more readily and is difficult to clean.

Satin-finish paint is one step up from flat in shine. Use satin-finish in areas where you want a subtle luster or a light sheen. Many people prefer satin-finish paint for interior walls because it looks nice and cleans easily.

Semi-gloss paint is the most widely used for interior walls. It can also be used to accent. You could paint your walls with satin-finish and use semi-gloss on chair rails, moldings or woodwork. Semi-gloss works best on bookshelves and wood furniture.

High-gloss paint, with the greatest amount of shine, looks almost like lacquer. High-gloss, an oil-based paint, is recommended for metal surfaces and for surfaces that bear heat, such as radiators. High-gloss can also be used to paint furniture if you want it to have a lacquered appearance.

Prepare to Paint

Step 1: Clean the surface. Unfortunately, once you have selected color, type and finish, you can't dash right home from the paint store and start sloshing paint on your walls. If you want a professional-looking job, you need to take time to prepare the surfaces you will paint. Use a dry cloth or a vacuum to go over all walls and remove dust. Then get rid of any soil, grease or mildew on the walls. Use a no-rinse detergent to wipe down walls in the kitchen, which usually have a thin coating of grease on them from cooking residue. If there are mildew stains on the bathroom walls, wipe them off with liquid bleach. Remove all picture hangers, nails, switch plates, outlet cover plates, and other hardware, such as knobs or handles.

Step 2: Use a primer. If you start from scratch with unpainted wallboard, you will need to purchase a primer (a liquid that you paint on to help the regular paint adhere to the walls). If possible, the primer should be the same brand as your paint. Before you paint on the primer, sand all joints and pound in any protruding nails (nail heads should lie below the wall surface). If you choose a dark color to paint the room, you can make your job easier by stirring half a pint of paint into every quart of primer. By darkening your primer, you should be able to cover your walls with one coat of paint.

If you paint walls, ceilings and woodwork that have been painted before, you don't need primer, but you need to rough up the surface. You can rub it with steel wool or sandpaper. If you tackle an entire wall or a whole room, use liquid sandpaper that simply paints on with a brush.

Step 3: Fill in holes and cracks before you paint. Use spackle (a white, putty-like compound available at paint stores) and a spackle knife (a flat, broad tool that smoothes spackle) to fill in cracks and small nail holes. You will first need to make the crack big enough so you can fill it with spackle. Pull the point of a metal can opener down the length of the crack to open it. Slightly overfill cracks and holes with spackle, then smooth by wiping with the spackle knife. Allow to dry, then sand to a smooth finish. Clean up excess with a damp cloth.

If you have large holes in the wall, fill them with plaster. Someone at the paint store can help you choose an appropriate plaster. For best results, keep it moist enough to work with easily. Wet down the area you're filling with a damp cloth, fill with plaster, wet the surface of the plaster and smooth it. When dry, sand the patched area until smooth.

Dad says: Don't try to rush through a painting job. Clean your brushes and tools well after a good day's work, then start again the next day. Make sure you have adequate light in the room to paint. Natural light is especially helpful so that you don't miss any spots.

*D*ad says:
The best strategy is to start painting at a window or other source of light and work away from it. As you finish each section, check it against the light. Did you miss any spots? New paint will look wet and glare in the light, while the old paint beneath it will look dry.

If you paint metal, make sure you have removed rust and applied a rust inhibitor. Coat the entire surface of unpainted metal with a primer. If the metal surface has been previously painted, use the primer to cover any rust spots.

Painting a Room

Step 1: Get the right tools. For most jobs, you will need brushes of varying widths, an angled brush, a roller, a pan, flat sponge applicators for latex paint only, wide masking tape, a small ladder and razor blades. Wear old clothes, old shoes and a hat—some paint will splatter, no matter how carefully you paint.

Step 2: Tape carefully before you paint. Tape around windows, doors, cupboards, closets, baseboards, electrical fixtures. Using wide masking tape, run tape along inside of windows right next to molding, so you will paint on the tape instead of the glass. Tape along the carpet at the baseboard to avoid drips. Tape around door knobs, light switches and electrical outlets. Unscrew and take off plates. Move as much furniture out of the room as you can and cover anything that remains with old sheets or tarp. Also cover the carpet. Remove tape and covers only when entire job is done and paint is dry.

Step 3: Paint carefully and thoroughly. Paint in this order—ceilings, walls, doors, window frames, baseboards, and, finally, the trim. Get a few friends to help you, then turn up the music and make it fun.

Make sure you have enough paint on your brush. If you use a roller, dip it about halfway into the paint, roll it very gently on the pan grid to smooth it and press the edges against the pan to squeeze excess paint out. Not doing this will leave paint trails on the wall.

Never paint in uniform sections or stripes. Instead, work in 3-foot sections at a time and use large Ws and zigzags to fill in each section. Go over each section several times as you fill in, smoothing out excess paint or ridges. Overlap each section to keep the whole job looking smooth. You want to catch any missed spots while you are still painting. *Once latex paint has dried, you can touch up spots you missed, but if oil-based paint dries, and you find you've missed some spots, you will have to repaint the entire surface.*

Step 4: Know what technique works best on different surfaces. *Walls.* If you paint the walls with different paint than you used to paint the ceiling, you need to carefully paint a border around the top of the walls where they join the ceiling. Use a brush that's between two and three inches wide. Don't leave a straight edge—you don't want the brush line to show when you paint the rest of the wall. Work in three-foot sections of wall, using the W and zigzag methods to fill in each section. When you move to a new section, start three feet from where you left off and work toward the wet paint, not away from it.

Doors: Begin by painting the door frame, if you use a different color than you did on the walls, you should wait until the walls dry completely. Use a small brush. You can also use wide masking tape to mask off the wall adjacent to the door frame. After you have finished the door frame, paint the edges of the door. Finally, paint the door itself. When painting a door, start at the top and move down to avoid dribbling paint on a surface you have already finished.

Window frames: Use a small, angled brush to paint window frames. If you want to, you can use masking tape on the glass panes to keep paint off the glass. If you do get paint on the glass, use a razor blade to scrape it off after it has dried.

Baseboards and trim: Wait until the walls have dried completely before painting the baseboards and trim. Protect walls and the floor by using wide masking tape at the very edges of the baseboards to allow for slipups. When the paint has dried, carefully pull of the masking tape.

When to Ask for Help

Even a beginning fix-it person can do plenty of handy repairs around the house, but don't try doing everything on your own, especially if you know little or nothing about it. Some repair jobs might look simple on the surface but can lead to major problems that will be expensive and time-consuming to have fixed professionally later on.

Step 1: Never try to repair an appliance under warranty. If you have a current warranty or guarantee on the item, have the manufacturer or a licensed repair service repair or replace it. If you try to fix the problem and fail, you may make a bigger mess of it, will invalidate the warranty and end up having to pay for the service or replacement yourself.

Step 2: Check with a contractor before you demolish a wall. The wall could be a structural support and you could end up with a cracked or crumbled home and more of a fix-it job than you are prepared to deal with.

Step 3: Don't do your own roofing or roof repairs. You could ruin the roof and necessitate a full replacement. Even worse, you could fall and injure yourself, which is more common than you think.

Step 4: Don't do your own wiring. Never attempt to do internal wiring unless you are a licensed electrician. Faulty wiring repairs can cause home fires, sometimes invalidating your homeowner's insurance, if you don't electrocute yourself first.

Step 5: Don't open your home to the elements. Don't start any project that opens up part of your home to the outdoor elements unless you can complete the project the same day. You will face weakened security and possible inclement weather.

Step 6: Use common sense and intelligence. Think before you act. Don't try to fix an appliance until you've unplugged it. Don't unscrew a faucet handle until you've turned off the water.

Do Almost Anything

Shine Your Shoes

Wearing dress shoes and boots that gleam is not just an old-fashioned notion. People really do make assumptions about you, consciously or subconsciously, based upon the condition of your shoes. Everyone should know how to shine a good pair of shoes. You'll want to put your best foot forward when you step out to make a good impression. You can safely shine most leather shoes and boots with shoe polish. To spruce up suede shoes, however, you may want to purchase a special spray and brush from a shoe store.

Step 1: Get your supplies together. You will need saddle soap to clean leather shoes or boots, paste polish the same color as your shoes, a soft polishing cloth or brush, water and a soft clean buffing cloth.

Step 2: Spread polish over the shoe. If you are right-handed, hold the shoe in your left hand by placing your hand, palm down, inside the shoe. With your right hand and a polish cloth, spread a thick layer of paste polish over the leather of the shoe. Allow this polish to dry for five minutes.

Step 3: Start the shine. Wrap a soft, clean cloth around your index finger so that you have a smooth area on the end of your finger. Dip this in water so that it is thoroughly wet but not dripping. Using small circular motions, buff the dried polish with the wet cloth until the leather starts to shine.

Step 4: Build the shine. Still using the damp cloth on your finger, apply a fine layer of polish in a circular motion. Keep rubbing lightly until a hazy shine develops. Keeping the rag damp, build up the shine with thin layers of polish applied in circles with light pressure until a glossy shine develops. After the first heavy coat of polish, you need to use minimal amounts of polish to build up the shine. If you use too much, the solvent in the polish you are applying will dissolve the base you've already built up and you'll have to start again in that area.

Step 5: Buff the polished shoe. When sufficient shine has developed, use a clean, dry, soft cloth to give it a final buff and remove any haze.

Spit Shine Anyone?

The term "spit shine" comes from street shoe polishers who used to spit on their cloth (instead of using water) to build the shine on their customers' leather shoes. The proven theory is that polish will adhere to the leather instead of the cloth if the cloth is sufficiently wet. Keep building thin layers of polish until you have a completely smooth surface that gives off a glossy shine.

> ***D**ad's Tip:*
> *If you don't have shoe polish on hand, you can use petroleum jelly to
> shine your shoes. Make sure the shoe is clean and dry. Using your
> fingers, apply a thin coat of petroleum jelly in circular motions over the
> entire shoe. With a clean, soft, dry cloth, buff the shoes until they shine
> and no longer feel greasy to the touch.*

Do Almost Anything

Pack for a Trip

Take time to pack well for any trip, whether it's a weekend getaway or a two-week vacation. Don't just throw a pile of dirty clothes into your suitcase and hope for the best. You will be uncomfortable and disappointed with your trip if you aren't dressed for the occasion. You'll almost always use fewer clothes than you take with you, so pack light.

Step 1: Items you need quickly should be easily accessible. Pack things you might need at a moment's notice in a shoulder bag, sports bag or backpack. These might include medications, eyeglasses or contacts, sunglasses, driver's license, wallet or pocket book, traveler's checks and cash, credit cards, maps or directions, important phone numbers, notebook and pen plus, plane, train or bus tickets. This is where you would also keep special coupons you might use on the road, a reading book or magazine, a packet of wet cleaning cloths, sunscreen and small versions of a first-aid kit and a sewing kit.

Step 2: Pack cash and traveler's checks in different bags. If a bag or case is lost or stolen, you'll still have access to another stash of money. For example, put one-third of your cash and/or traveler's checks in a money belt or fanny pack that you wear, put another third in your wallet, backpack, purse or carry-on bag that you will keep with you at all times. Pack the last third in traveler's checks in your suitcase.

Step 3: Pack bathroom essentials in one case. Put all of your toiletries (toothbrush and toothpaste, soap, wash cloth, shampoo, conditioner, razor, lotion, hair gel or mousse, brush and comb, hair spray, hair dryer or curling iron, hand mirror and makeup, etc.) in one carrying case or bag. That way you can simply grab that case and a towel when you head for the bathroom. Choose travel sizes of essentials whenever possible. Pack anything that might leak or spill in zip-type plastic bags. Before you pack anything in a plastic bottle, loosen the lid, squeeze the bottle gently to force out some air and replace the lid tightly. This will create a vacuum to prevent leaks.

Step 4: Plan what to wear each day of your vacation. Bring only one outfit for each day and remember to mix and match, using some items more than once, such as jeans, t-shirts or jackets. Choose clothes appropriate to activities and weather. Don't forget your swimsuit if you plan to hit the pool or the beach. Pack nicer clothes if you want to go out on the town or take in a show. Pack clean underwear and stockings for each day you will be gone, then take two or three extra for unforeseen emergencies. Also take a large plastic garbage bag to store dirty laundry in. That will keep your dirty clothes from soiling the clean ones. Bring some modest pajamas and a robe, especially if you will be traveling with others and staying at the home of friends or family. Pack one pair of casual shoes and one pair of dress shoes, depending on what activities you have planned. Don't bring your entire shoe wardrobe. Wear some comfortable shoes while traveling. Pack shoes in medium-sized plastic bags (bread bags work well) to keep them from soiling your clothing.

Step 5: Take care of your clothes. If you plan to take clothes that need to be hung, purchase a hanging garment bag. If you do not have one, you can use a large, heavy-duty garbage bag; poke a hole in the bottom of the bag and pull the tops of your hangers through it, smoothing the bag over the clothing. Now, put an elastic band or garbage bag tie around the necks of your hangers to keep them together during travel. In a pinch, pack the clothes, hangers and a small empty spray bottle in your suitcase. Then hang and spray the clothes to loosen wrinkles as soon as you get to your destination. If you aren't using a garment bag, place tissue paper between the folds on clothing to keep wrinkling to a minimum. To keep sweaters and other knits from creasing or crumpling (and to save room in a cramped suitcase), roll them instead of folding them before you pack them.

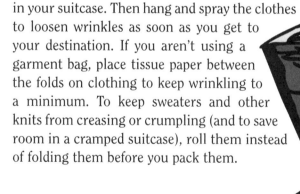

Notes

Notes

Clean Up Your Act
Housekeeping Basics

Housecleaning is a have-to, not a want-to. Don't put off the job until it becomes almost impossible. The real secret to keeping house is to do a little bit every day.

People who don't keep a clean home will tell you that it's next to impossible to keep a home clean, but don't believe them. If you take it in small doses, consistently, you will live a more comfortable, more sanitary, healthier, more serene and brighter existence. Really—a clean home can make a big difference in your ability to live a better life. You can find things easier, get ready quicker, fix meals faster and enjoy having visitors.

Keeping house doesn't mean you're a neat-freak who needs to control everything and impress people. It means you take pride in yourself, your belongings and your surroundings. "Keep" is the key word here. If you keep things up, you won't feel overwhelmed by this essential daily task.

Keeping Your House Clean

Step 1: Gather some cleaning essentials. You don't need any fancy tools or equipment, especially if you clean up small messes before they become big messes. You will need a liquid cleaner (dish detergent will even work), a clean cloth and towel for dishes, some rags, a scrub brush, a broom, a dustpan and an inexpensive vacuum. (Keep in mind that people in the olden days who didn't have vacuums swept their carpets everyday—a good, stiff broom will do in a pinch.)

Step 2: Have enough storage space. Housekeeping will be easier if you have a place and space for everything you own and use. Remember the adage: A place for everything, and everything in its place. If you have books, make sure you have a bookshelf. If you have videos, DVDs, CDs, etc., make sure you have a place to store them. Invest in a small, sturdy filing cabinet for important papers. Have enough closet and drawer space for your clothes. Use under bed storage boxes for occasionally used or seasonal items. If you do not use something on a consistent basis, give it away or throw it out. This goes for personal grooming items that you really do not use, poor-fitting clothes or shoes and appliances that gather dust.

Step 3: Do daily jobs daily. Housecleaning is not rocket science. You've got the living room, the kitchen, the bathroom, the bedroom(s) and, possibly, an office or den. Your daily tasks in these areas will include cooking, doing the dishes, sweeping, taking out the trash, wiping up spills and cleaning daily-used items, such as tables, sinks, shower and tubs. You'll also have to make beds and keep important papers in order and under control.

The kitchen and bathroom will take the most effort because you use them constantly throughout the day. Everyday, you eat, usually at least three times a day, so cooking, cleaning up the kitchen and doing dishes will be a daily task. *Accept it. Do it. Move on.*

Don't make it into something complex. It's when you let those dirty dishes stack up that it becomes a dreaded, time-consuming chore. Cop the attitude that breakfast, lunch and dinner will be finished only once you've cleaned, dried and put away the dishes, utensils, pots and pans.

Demand (or ask nicely) for the help of anyone in the home who placed a piece of food in his or her mouth for that meal. If they don't put in the work, they don't get the reward. The same goes for you. Whoever uses something should put it away. If you have children, roommates, a spouse or partner, the rule is – if you are big enough to take it out and use it, you are big enough to clean it up and put it back. Don't be anyone's maid and don't expect anyone to clean up after you.

Step 4: Set aside just one hour a day to do housework. C'mon, how much time do you spend chatting or surfing the Internet or watching a bad television show? One hour a day is nothing. You can even break it up into two half-hour increments. Get up a little earlier, go to bed a little later or skip one sitcom. In the first 30 minutes, do a quick run through the whole house or apartment. Pick up things out of place and put them in the right place. Then sweep floors and pick up any large dust bunnies on the carpets. Tie up the trash sacks and put them near the door to be taken out. Wipe up any spills on counters or tables. That shouldn't take more than half an hour.

Now, with your other 30 minutes, choose one big job to do for that day. These "big" jobs include dusting, vacuuming, scrubbing the floors and sinks, cleaning the toilet and tub, cleaning out the refrigerator, scrubbing the stove and oven and washing walls and windows.

That's seven big jobs—one for each day of the week. If you do these tasks once a week, each one (even that refrigerator) should not take any longer than 30 minutes. Then, Ta Da! You'll have a sparkling house everyday of the week (and nothing to be ashamed of when you get unexpected company).

Ask Mom

For information on homemade cleaning products, see *Where's Mom Now That I Need Her?*, pages 70 - 71 "Recipes for Things You Can't Eat."

Ask Mom

For more about housecleaning basics, see *Where's Mom Now That I Need Her?*, pages 61- 62 "Making Life Easier" and pages 65- 69 "Can't I Just Be a Slob?"

Step 5: Tackle big jobs one per each day of the week. Some people like to tackle big jobs by room. That's fine, but it might take more than a half hour to do everything that needs to be done in the kitchen, for instance, in one fell swoop. Then it becomes this huge chore that you will most likely put off for another day, giving all that dirt one more day to pile up.

It's smarter to divide the big jobs by task—one per day. When you do this consistently, you will be surprised how every room remains clean throughout the week. And if you do get backed up on something, it won't take an entire afternoon to accomplish.

Many of us grew up in families that set aside a few hours, or sometimes the whole day, on a Saturday or Sunday to do housework. How boring and sad. This is a big waste of a weekend when you could be out doing fun weekend stuff with family and friends. The only exception would be when it comes time for spring cleaning. But that's just one sacrificed weekend, not a whole year of them. And if you do spring cleaning right, the job can actually be fun.

So, let's see, Monday is for dusting, Tuesday for vacuuming, on Wednesday shine up all the sinks and mop the floors, Thursday you will get out the scrub brush and sanitizer for the toilet and bathtub, then on Friday, clean out the refrigerator just before dinnertime and have end-of-the-week leftovers. Now, the tougher jobs, like scrubbing the stove and oven, and washing the walls and windows, are left for Saturday and Sunday. But even those will take only 30 minutes or no more than an hour if you do them every week. All you need is a little discipline and routine.

Step 6: Look at your house like you do your body. Would you wait until the weekend to take a shower, comb your hair or brush your teeth? No, these are daily tasks. Your house needs daily hygiene as well. When you stick to a schedule every day, you will actually start to take pride in your work and wonder why everyone can't get their act together. Maybe after you've practiced for a while you can share your secret with others who struggle to keep house.

Cleaning Dad's Way

• Unplug the phone, turn off the TV and turn up the music.

• Set a timer for 30 minutes, or a specific amount of time to clean. Do as much as you can in that period of time. Stop when the bell rings. This helps you know that this cleaning business will not go on forever.

• Make a small cleaning checklist for every room and tape it to the inside of a cupboard door or drawer. Then check the task off when completed. This is the adult version of those job charts and stars you earned by doing chores as a child. It still works.

• Start at the top of the room and work your way down. Dust while you clean clutter on counters, desks and tables, then pick up things off the floor, and, finally, vacuum or mop.

• Keep decorative baskets in every room to hold keys, change, toiletries, odds and ends and various things that add clutter to a room. Putting these things in a basket gathers them all in one place and gives the illusion of a clean and tidy room.

• To keep your house smelling fresh, dust baking soda onto carpeting at night. The baking soda will absorb musty odors, and you can vacuum it up in the morning.

• Place a clothes hamper in every bathroom and bedroom. Don't toss clothes on the floor, bed, couch or chair. If it's clean, hang it up. If it's dirty, put it in the hamper. Don't put clean clothes in the hamper in an attempt to avoid hanging or folding them. You'll hate yourself on laundry day if you have to wash clean clothes because you didn't take the time to hang them up.

• Always pick up the family room or living room before going to bed. Also start the dishwasher. This way you'll have a nice home to wake up to and you can put the clean dishes away before you go to work or school.

Cleaning Shortcuts

The Blanket Toss: If you have a project that takes up a lot of space, or a child who uses a lot of room to play, spread things out on a blanket on the floor. Then, if you have unexpected company, you can just throw everything in the middle of the blanket, fold it up and take it into another room, or place it in the closet until you can take the time to put it all away properly.

Keeping Up Appearances: The best thing you can do to make your house "look" clean every day is to pick up clutter (even if you just put it all into one box or a clothes hamper with a lid until you have time to clean in earnest.) If you do this too often, however, you will soon have big jobs left in every corner of the house. Don't leave dishes in the sink—at least rinse them and

*D*ad says:
Don't Walk Around It.
If something is in
your path, such as
shoes, a piece of lint,
a box, a toy or a tack,
stop right then and
there, pick it up and
put it in its place or
throw it away.

put them in the drainer or dishwasher until you can wash them. Make the beds—even if you just toss a clean comforter and smooth it out over the top of a messy bed. Sweep the floors and vacuum. You may want to use a hand-held dust buster or a manual push broom.

Use Paper to Clean: Use disposable paper towels to clean up. This keeps you from having to launder dishcloths and towels quite as often. Paper towels also kill germs more effectively than cloth towels and sponges since they don't harbor germs to begin with. Use crumpled newspaper and rubbing alcohol or vinegar to clean windows for streak-free drying.

Use One Trash Bag: When you gather the trash from each room, don't make a dozen trips around the house picking up wastebaskets and taking them outside to the garbage. Instead, get a big plastic garbage bag and take it to the wastebaskets, emptying all of them into it on-site, then toss the big bag into the trash outside.

Line Waste Baskets: Use free plastic grocery bags or buy plastic garbage bags to line your waste baskets. This will save you from having to scrub the trash cans each time you dump them. If you want to be really organized about it, keep a few of the plastic trash liners folded up at the bottom of each wastebasket. When you throw away the garbage, a fresh bag is ready and waiting to be put into place.

Use an All-Purpose Cleaner: Buy something that works on stoves, sinks, tubs, mirrors, walls and floors. Don't buy a separate product for each task. You will save money and time because you won't be searching for and switching cleaners and tools with every task. Keep your rags, cleaner and scrub brush in a cleaning bucket. When it's time to do the job, you have everything in one place. Pick it up and go at it.

Do Laundry Once a Week: Make a date with the washer and dryer. Take a soda and sandwich. Have a picnic. Read a good book. Whatever you do, do not procrastinate doing your laundry. One, you will run out of space for dirty clothes. Two, they will start to smell up the house. Three, eventually you will be naked.

Use a Mesh Bag for Delicates: Put your stockings, underwear and delicate items into a small mesh bag (often sold as a "lingerie" bag) before you put them in the washing machine. You can do this to keep track of different family members' clothing items and eliminate sock widows forever. If losing one sock is a common problem, pin pairs together before throwing them into the washing machine.

Keep Bedding Together: For easy bed-making on laundry day, fold and wrap matching top and bottom sheets and one pillow case together, then place them in the second matching pillow case. Store the clean bundle in a drawer. Always try to have two sets of bedding. That way you can strip and re-make the bed, then clean the dirty sheets and pillowcases. Do this every other week or, at minimum, once a month.

Make Work Stations for Routine Tasks: You know you will need certain items for certain tasks, such as laundry, scrubbing floors, cleaning windows, cooking meals, baking treats, or even paying bills and writing letters. Put all necessary tools together neatly and within easy reach of where you usually perform the task.

Do It Now, Don't Wait: Make your bed as soon as you get out of it. Rinse out the pan, bowl or dish as soon as you empty it. Clean a spill or sweep up a mess as soon as it's made. Scrub your feet at the end of your shower or bath, then scrub down the shower and bath. Take a minute to do the task at hand instead of letting it wait and pile up with all the other tasks. This will save you time, extra work and frustration.

When to Deep Clean

For everything there is a season. Sometimes you need to make a fresh start, toss out the old and clean up what's left to look like new. Most of us know about the ritual of spring cleaning. Many of us dread the seemingly monumental task. So break the job up into manageable parts. Heavy-duty cleaning once every season (every three months) makes more sense than once a year.

Step 1: Reduce your possessions. Every week, sometimes every day, you accumulate new stuff, but your house doesn't get any bigger during the year—you need to get rid of the old to make room for the new. Get into those closets and drawers and decide what needs to go. Safely store warm winter clothes and take out those colorful spring shorts, shirts, dresses and shoes. Look through your books, toys, games, videos, CDs and appliances. Donate the items you don't need or use to your favorite charity or hold a yard sale.

Step 2: Get organized, then reorganize. Create efficient storage for sporting goods, camping equipment, recreational vehicles and gardening tools. Put up hanging boards for tools. Install a pre-fabricated cupboard or shelves above the washer and dryer for laundry supplies. Anything that hasn't been used for a year, give it away or throw it out. Make room for the car in the garage. If you're using your garage as a storage unit, get rid of that stuff. It's taking up valuable space.

Step 3: Schedule a weekend clean fling (every 3 or 4 months). Enlist the help of family and friends. Prepare cleaning buckets with supplies for each helper. List what needs to be done in each room. Set a time deadline. Since the clutter has already been removed, cleaning should go smoothly.

Focus on washing walls, doors, floorboards, and vents. Move furniture and vacuum under it. Dust or scrub blinds and clean drapes. Scrub floors and fixtures until they gleam. Get into crevices with a toothbrush. Use a deodorizing and disinfectant cleaner. Get serious about cleaning. Wash all windows inside and out. Finally, clean carpets using a professional carpet-cleaning machine. Then take the gang out to dinner at a pizza parlor while the carpets dry.

Spring Cleaning

In the olden days, spring cleaning was a necessity after a winter of coal heating left a sooty film throughout the home. Spring cleaning today is light by comparison and can be a fun way to welcome the change of seasons.

Step 1: Spring clean outside. Clean and repair outdoor furniture. These items should be stored indoors, in the garage or shed, during the winter. Let them air out in the sunshine when spring comes. Get yourself out there, too. Inspect the yard and area around your home. Look for winter damage, roof leaks, missing or broken tiles or shingles and loose steps on the deck or patio. Make necessary repairs.

Step 2: Wake up your yard! Clear away dead foliage and weeds from flowerbeds, vegetable garden and lawn so that new growth will not be damaged. Begin major spring landscaping projects, like planting new shrubs or trees, turning soil and feeding or treating the lawn. Look for carpenter ants, termites and other pests. Call an exterminator if you see signs of infestation. Check out nails, screws and tabs on decks, siding and trim. Will you need to do some painting or staining touch-ups? If so, order paint now to be ready for a cool spring weekend to do the job.

Step 3: Check out the cooling system. Do this yourself or arrange for an inspection of your home cooling system. If you use window-mount evaporative coolers or air-conditioners, haul them out of storage and hook them up. Clean or replace vents and filters. Bring out the fans and place them in the rooms where they will be used. Check the security of all screens and windows and make necessary repairs. Turn your thermostat down so that your air conditioner and furnace do not compete with one another. Do a quick inspection of your hot water heater and drain any sediment that has accumulated. Call a professional for any of these tasks that you are not absolutely sure you know how to do. It's better to spend money now to have things done properly than to spend more money later fixing things after you've invested time and energy in your first attempt.

Summer Cleaning

You want to have time for fun in the summer—that's why you did all that heavy-duty spring cleaning. Summer cleaning is really more about preventative maintenance.

Step 1: Wash down the outside of the house. On one of the first days of summer, say one of the weekend days when you wash your car, also wash down the outside of the house—the brick, siding, porches, decks, sidewalks and driveway. You'll be surprised how much better a good clean rinse can make a drab house look.

Step 2: Control garbage can odors. Flies and odors come with summer heat. Garbage goes bad faster. Keep a large, closed trash container just outside your garage and take it to the curb for pickup every week. Rinse the large garbage can and smaller trash containers outside with a garden hose, dump the water, then spray the trash cans with disinfectant. Turn them upside down, leaning against the curb or steps, and let them dry. You should also hose gutters to clean out leafy debris. Summer thunderstorms won't cause chaos if your gutters work right.

Step 3: Tackle patio and sliding door tracks. Summer is open-door season, so be sure your doors open smoothly. Get a bottle of degreasing cleaner, a screwdriver and cleaning rags. Spray the tracks generously and let sit for a few minutes to loosen dirt. Wrap the screwdriver with a rag and make several careful passes along the track to get out the gunk. While you're at it, take an oil spray (like WD-40) and lube the hinges of home and car doors to stop squeaks.

Step 4: Check outdoor play equipment for safety. Sand down bumps and rough spots. Tighten screws and hammer in loose nails. Tighten loose bolts and cover with plastic protectors if possible to ensure children won't hurt themselves. Protectors also keep bolts from rusting with summer water play.

Step 5: Restock the medicine chest and make a first aid kit. Summer time is the time for scrapes, cuts, bumps, bruises and other assorted emergencies. In the bathroom, sort through outdated medication. Discard what is not being used. The first aid kit should be stocked with adhesive bandages for scrapes, calamine lotion for insect bites, and hot/cold packs for strains or sprains.

Step 6: Make an emergency list for babysitters and children. Post an emergency list of numbers by each household telephone. If you use only cell phones, make sure there's an extra one to leave at home with the children. Include numbers for parents at work, a family contact in case of an emergency and the number of nearby neighbors. Don't forget numbers for the fire department, police department, poison control center and ambulance. Make sure your children and their babysitters know how and when to call 911.

Fall Cleaning

Step 1: Take advantage of professional cleaning discounts. Late summer and early fall are slow times for home maintenance and cleaning companies. Look for end-of-summer discounts for carpet cleaning, gutter installation and window washing.

Step 2: Check your furnace or boiler. If you have not had your furnace or boiler serviced and tuned-up in the past year, call a serviceperson to make an appointment. Annual servicing can improve efficiency and save money. Also make sure fluepipe and chimney operate smoothly before the nip gets in the air. If your family uses space heaters, have the heaters checked for safety. Carbon monoxide (CO) is a major hazard of fuel-fired space heaters. Adequate ventilation and a good CO detector are vitally important.

Step 3: Check all carbon monoxide and smoke detectors. Replace batteries if needed. Exhaust gases contain carbon monoxide, an odorless gas that can kill. Carbon monoxide (CO) can be produced when almost any fuel

Ask Mom
For a comprehensive list of First Aid supplies, see *Where's Mom Now That I Need Her?*, page 267 "First Aid Essentials Checklist."

293

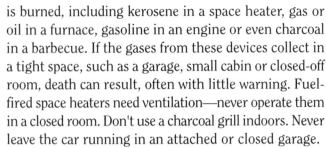

is burned, including kerosene in a space heater, gas or oil in a furnace, gasoline in an engine or even charcoal in a barbecue. If the gases from these devices collect in a tight space, such as a garage, small cabin or closed-off room, death can result, often with little warning. Fuel-fired space heaters need ventilation—never operate them in a closed room. Don't use a charcoal grill indoors. Never leave the car running in an attached or closed garage.

Garages can be very dangerous if a car is running, especially if the door is closed. CO can accumulate to lethal levels. Also, CO can be drawn into the house, sometimes through pathways that may not be recognized. Tell every driver in your household never to leave a car engine running in an attached or closed garage. If you need to warm up a car, do it outside the garage. Turn it on with an extra key and lock the car door before leaving to let it warm it up.

Fireplaces typically force large amounts of air up the chimney. However, if the damper is closed when the fire is finished, smoldering embers will produce abundant amounts of CO that can enter the living space. Gas-fueled kitchen ranges and stovetops can produce CO and other noxious gases. Use a vent fan, and never use a gas oven or stove to heat the home.

Winter Cleaning

Step 1: Check around the outside of the house. Clean and store patio furniture, umbrellas and children's summer toys. Touch up paint on trim, railings and decks. Use a wire brush to remove flaking paint. Prime bare wood before you paint it. Check caulk around windows and doors. Follow manufacturer's recommendations to re-caulk if needed. Inspect external doors and garage doors. Do they close tightly? Install weather-stripping and door thresholds if needed. Wash exterior windows. Drain and store garden hoses. Install insulating covers on exterior spigots. In hard-freeze areas, blow sprinkler systems free of water. Check gutters and downspouts. Clear debris if necessary.

Step 2: Deep clean inside before the snow falls. Focus on the public or shared rooms, including the living room, family room, entryway and guest bath. Vacuum drapes and window treatments. Clean window sills and window wells. Vacuum baseboards and corners. Vacuum upholstered furniture, or have it professionally cleaned if needed. Move furniture and vacuum beneath and behind it. Wash interior windows.

Step 3: Prepare warm and cozy winter beds. Turn mattresses front-to-back and end-to-end to equalize wear. Launder or clean all bedding including mattress pads, pillows, duvets, blankets and comforters. Store summer and spring bedding and bring out winter blankets.

Step 4: Prepare the kitchen for holiday cooking. Clean and organize kitchen cabinets, paying particular attention to baking supplies, pans and equipment. Clear counters of all appliances not used within the last week. Pull refrigerator away from the wall and vacuum the condenser coils. For bottom-mounted coils, use a long, narrow brush to clean coils of dust and debris. Wash light fixtures.

Step 5: Inspect all major appliances. Stock up on softener salt now, and avoid staggering over icy sidewalks with heavy bags. Check and empty the central vacuum's collection area. Clean electronic air cleaner elements monthly for most efficient operation. Wash them in an empty dishwasher. Clean or replace humidifier elements before the heating season begins. Inspect washer hoses for bulges, cracks or splits. Replace them every other year. Check dryer exhaust tube and vent for built-up lint, debris or birds' nests! Make sure the exterior vent door closes tightly when not in use. Buy a winter's supply of furnace filters. Change filters monthly for maximum energy savings and indoor comfort. Drain sediment from hot water heaters.

Step 6: Be prepared for snow or rain on walks and driveways. Make sure you have a good snow shovel, a de-icing compound, waterproof floor mats, gloves, boots and an ice scraper. Rock salt does melt ice, but it will also eat away at concrete.

Ask Mom
For a detailed listing of supplies for winter traveling, see *Where's Mom Now That I Need Her?*, page 303 "Checklist for Emergency Road Kit."

Dad says:
"*Be honest. Work hard, keep your wits about you and make time to enjoy life's simple pleasures. Live well, laugh often and love big.*"

Step 7: Gather household emergency supplies. These should include enough food, water and supplies to last four days without power or help. Choose food that doesn't require heating or refrigeration, such as canned meats, soups and stews, cereal, and energy bars. Make sure you have a manual can opener; paper plates, cups and plastic utensils. You'll want to store one gallon of water per person per day for four days. Stock up on flashlights and batteries, a battery-powered radio, a battery-powered clock, a cellular phone, first aid kit, four-day supply of all prescription medicines, blankets and cold-weather clothing for each family member, pet food and additional water for household pets. Keep your car's tank full of gas in the winter as a possible refuge.

Step 8: Be prepared for winter traveling. Winter transportation can mean ice, snow and hazardous roads. Before traveling, give every car a winter preparedness inspection: Check antifreeze; check and replace older batteries; keep the gas tank near full to avoid freezing water in the fuel line; check tires and spare tire for proper inflation. Pack emergency supplies in a backpack in case you need to abandon your car. An emergency backpack should include a jacket, hat, gloves and sturdy, snow-proof boots for each traveler; nonperishable food; cellular phone; money or credit card.

Where's Mom Now That I Need Her?

Not all necessary tips on how to survive away from home come from Dad. Mom also has some secrets to share. That's why we first published *Where's Mom Now That I Need Her? Surviving Away From Home*," which offers essential tips on health and nutrition, shopping and cooking, an extensive laundry and stain removal guide, a complete first-aid section, symptoms of common illnesses and home remedies, a guide to let you know when to see a doctor, quick car and bicycle maintenance and important personal safety tips.

Of course, *Where's Mom?* is a must-have cookbook as well. Mom shares all of her quickest, easiest, tastiest and most nutritious recipes that even a cooking novice can whip up in no time. Together, these two books provide all you need to know to live happily and successfully on your own. They teach you not only how to survive, but also how to thrive, away from home.

Do Almost Anything

Tie a Tie

When finished tying a tie, the tip of the tie should just touch the top of your belt buckle, and the narrow end of your tie (in the back) should not hang lower than the wide end (in the front).

Step 1: Begin with the correct lengths. Button the top button of your shirt and push the collar up. When you start to tie your tie, the wide end of the tie should be on the side of your dominant hand (for this example, that will be your right hand). Pull the tie around your neck. The narrow end of the tie should be in your left hand and should stop at the fourth button down on your shirt. This should allow the wide end of the tie, in your right hand, to hang down twice as long as the narrow end.

Step 2: Cross right over left. Bring the wide side of the tie over the narrow side. *(See Illustration A below.)* Then wrap it around and under the narrow side. *(See Illustration B below.)* Wrap the wide side over the narrow side again. *(See Illustration C on page 298.)* Bring the wide side under, up and through the open "V" shape at your neck just below your collar. *(See Illustration D on page 298.)* This will make a loop in front.

Step 3: Tie the knot. Now bring the wide side down through the loop you just made. *(See Illustration E on page 298.)* Tighten this knot, adjusting it by pulling on the narrow side (in back) with your left hand and the wide side (in front) with your right hand. Now, holding the wide end of the tie in your left hand and the knot of the tie in your right, draw the knot up comfortably around your neck. *(See Illustration F on page 298.)*

A.

This is a mirror image.

B.

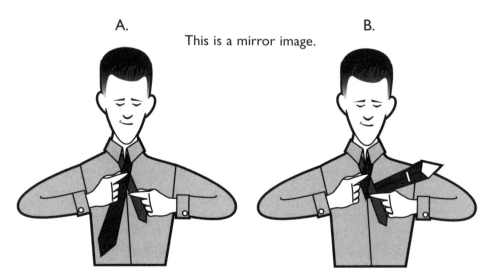

C.

D.

E.

F.

---

*D*ad's Tip:
If you are tying a tie on someone else, pull the tie around the other person's neck with the wide side of the tie in your right hand (which would be their left side) and follow the above steps.

Tie a Bowtie

On a few special occasions, you may need to know how to tie a bow tie. Be ready for those memorable moments in your life when you will tie your own bow tie or be asked to tie one for someone else who doesn't know how.

Step 1: Begin with the correct lengths. Button the top button of your collar. Pull the tie around your neck so that the end in your right hand falls one inch below the end in your left hand. *(See Illustration A1 below.)*

Step 2: Cross right over left. Cross the longer end over the shorter end, then pass it back and up through the open "V" shape at your neck just below your collar. *(See Illustration B1 below.)* Tighten this to fit snugly but comfortably around your neck.

Step 3: Start the bow. Now, double the short end of the tie over itself to form the front loop of the tie. *(See Illustration C1)*. The fold should be to the left and the free end facing right. Bring the long end of the tie over the center of the loop you just formed. *(See Illustration D1 on page 300.)*

Step 4: Finish the bow. Double the long end back onto itself. *(See Illustration E1 on page 300.)* Making the second loop with the fold facing right and the free end facing left. Push this loop through the opening behind the tie. *(See Illustration F1 on page 300.)* Pull the loops to adjust so that the bow tie is even. *(See Illustration G1 on page 300.)*

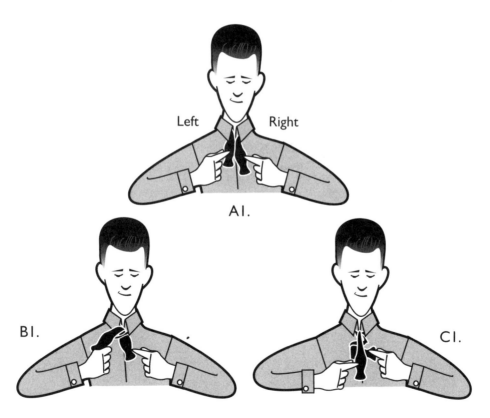

Left   Right

A I.

B I.   C I.

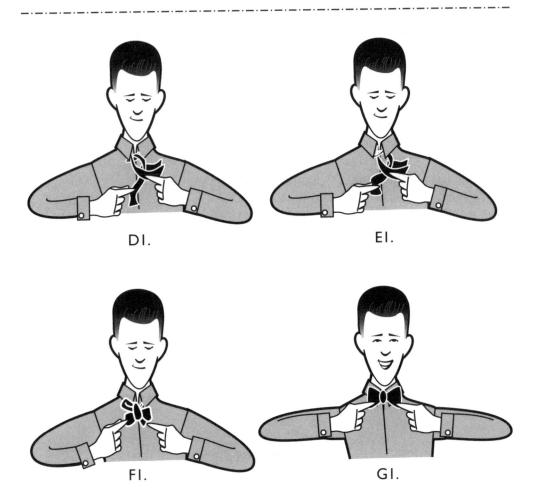

DI.

EI.

FI.

GI.

Dad's Best Advice

Index

314

A Survival Guide with Good Taste

When you leave home for the fist time and venture on your own into the world, take clean socks and this book. *Where's Dad Now That I Need Him? Surviving Away From Home* is your guide to making it in the world. Here you'll find the secrets and know-how that Dad practiced daily to put a roof over your head, keep the family car running, make a living, pay the bills on time and save money for some fun and recreation.

Now it's your turn to do all those necessary tasks for yourself. And just in case you weren't taking notes, we've compiled the most essential tips. You'll find information on renting and furnishing your first apartment, buying and maintaining a vehicle, finding work you enjoy, managing your money, being a savvy consumer, making simple home repairs and housecleaning short cuts.

But this isn't just a worldly survival guide. *Where's Dad?* is also a fantastic cookbook! Dad offers his tastiest recipes for tailgating parties, outdoor grilling, Dutch oven cooking, chili favorites, super sandwiches, specialty drinks and old-fashioned homemade ice-cream. The recipes all have one thing in common: They are easy to make even for a beginner.

Because you will be missing Dad, we've also included blank pages at the end of each recipe section where you, or your father, can pen in "Dad's Specialties," those hot new recipes he picked up from his buddies as well as the time-honored recipes that have been passed down by fathers for generations.

Keep this book handy, along with its companion guide *Where's Mom Now That I Need Her?,* to use as a reference for meeting your current challenges and future goals as you survive away from home. You'll be surprised how easy it is to make it on your own—with a little help from Dad.

For more information on retail, premium sales or quantity discounts, please contact ASPEN WEST at 801-565-1370 or info@aspenwest.com.

About the Author

Kent P. Frandsen was born and raised in Utah. When he was very young, his parents purchased a mountain ranch to raise cattle. There, horse-back riding and fixing fences, Kent acquired an appreciation for the great outdoors and learned the value of a hard day's work. Kent's father passed on his talent as a handy-man with a do-it-yourself mentality. One of four sons, Kent helped his parents build a family home and a vacation cabin while he was still in high school. It was then too, that he inherited his first classic car that he drove through college—a 1955 Chevrolet Bel Air. Now he drives a restored 1964 Thunderbird Convertible that he insisted be painted fire engine red.

Outdoor cooking is Kent's passion. One of his favorite moments, caught in a photograph, shows Kent in his swimming suit preparing a feast on the barbecue grill during a hot tub party—in the middle of winter!

Kent first collaborated with his mother, Betty Rae Frandsen, in writing *Where's Mom Now That I Need Her? Surviving Away From Home*, which launched a successful family business. He continues to "survive on his own" in Salt Lake City, where he is president of Aspen West Publishing and Distribution.

With the printing of this new, updated version of *Where's Dad?*, as well as the release of a newly revised *Where's Mom?*, here's solid proof that if Kent can do it, you can survive on your own, too!